WITHDRAWN

Qualitative Methodology and Sociology

In loving memory of
Alfred Silverman

Qualitative Methodology and Sociology

Describing The Social World

DAVID SILVERMAN

Ashgate

Aldershot • Brookfield USA • Singapore • Sydney

Published by
Ashgate Publishing Limited
Gower House
Croft Road
Aldershot, Hants
GU11 3HR
England

Ashgate Publishing Company
Old Post Road
Brookfield
Vermont 05036
USA

Reprinted 1986, 1989, 1998

British Library Cataloguing in Publication Data

Silverman, David.
   Qualitative methodology and sociology: describing the social world.
   1. Social sciences—Methodology
   I. Title
   300'.72   H61

Library of Congress Cataloging in Publication Data

Silverman, David.
   Qualitative methodology and sociology
   Bibliography: p.
   Includes index.
   1. Sociology—research   2. Ethnology—methodology
   I. Title.
   HM 48.S533   1985   301'.01'8   84-29054
   ISBN 0-566-00884-X   ISBN 0-566-00887-4

ISBN 0 566 00884 X Hardback
ISBN 0 566 00887 4 Paperback

Printed and bound in Great Britain by
Biddles Ltd, Guildford and King's Lynn

Contents

Introduction

I imagine that two initial questions may be asked about a book with this title: why *qualitative* research? why this *additional* text on qualitative research?

I think that the answer to the first question is straightforward. It is worth discussing strategies for qualitative research because so much sociological research is now qualitative. As late as the 1960s, the picture was very different. In that decade, around 90 per cent of the papers published in the two leading American sociology journals were based on quantitative survey research (Brenner (ed.) 1981). Although there are no comparable figures for the UK, I suspect that until the late 1960s, survey research was just as dominant here. Today, however, the picture is very different. Encouraged by theoretical critiques of positivism, qualitative methods now occupy a central position in both teaching and research.

However, if we examine this critique of positivism, we discover that much of it is curiously negative. Critics were much clearer about which practices they wanted to avoid than about those they recommended. Shorn of some rhetoric, I think the following three assumptions were central to this critique:

1. Analytically, we cannot put our commonsense knowledge of social structures on one side in the misplaced hope of achieving an objective viewpoint. In an inter-subjective world, both observer and observed use the same resources to identify 'meanings'.
2. Methodologically, it should be recognised that a statistical logic and an experimental method are not always appropriate for the study of this inter-subjective world. Random sampling methods and the use of control groups derive from a logic which is not necessarily applicable to a post-positivist universe.
3. Practically, because we are dealing with an inter-subjective world, policy interventions based on a stimulus-response model of change are neither analytically nor politically acceptable. We can no longer, therefore, accept a picture of objective 'experts' manipulating 'variables' to produce 'better' outcomes as tolerable for research practice.

Even this minimalist reading of the critique of positivism emphasises its negative nature. No clear alternative modes of analysis were provided for the student, while the intending researcher was left without even basic guidelines. True, a number of helpful methodology texts were produced from the late 1960s onwards. However, these did not altogether satisfy the diverse needs of the student and the researcher. For the student, most of these texts tended to be too narrow. Accounts of particular techniques, like participant observation or the interview, gave more detail than the student needed, while providing an insufficient understanding of the research process as a whole. Collected case-studies of how research is done offered a useful debunking of appeals to strict procedure but could leave the student convinced that 'anything goes'. Finally, general texts like Cicourel (1964), Glaser and Strauss (1967), Denzin (1970) and Schwartz and Jacobs (1979), provided important critical reviews of the literature, but suffered a little from using relatively narrow analytic viewpoints — interactionist or ethnomethodological.

The qualitative researcher has, if anything, been in a worse plight than the student. Buffeted by the new waves of theoretical fashions, first coming from Chicago, then from California, and finally from Paris, (s)he can hardly be expected to feel secure. Each text suggests a reassessment of accepted analytic paradigms; each tends to establish a new polarity (meaning versus structure, ethnomethodology versus constructive sociology, critical sociology versus (presumably) non-critical sociology) and invites the choice of one pole. In such a climate, a critical choice of elements from different paradigms comes to look like a dangerous eclecticism rather than a refusal to follow fashion.

Again, despite the theoretical rejection of positivism which all these 'schools' affirm, the beginning researcher is able to find little guidance about what might be an acceptable non-positivist methodology. It is small wonder, then, that the better young researchers are haunted by the fear of anecdotalism — using favoured examples to support their analyses. I recall vividly the concern expressed to me recently by a Ph D student that he could be utterly undone at his oral examination by the charge that his case-study was unrepresentative. The existing literature, it seemed, had failed to give him much confidence in any form of non-statistical logic.

This book tries to meet some of the needs of such researchers, while offering an accessible reference source appropriate to the requirements of undergraduate students taking courses in research methods. For the student, I have aimed to produce a readable text which is clearly structured and is based on a large number of examples from published research. For the beginning researcher, I have sought to deploy an argument which tries to overcome some of the inadequacies and inconsistencies of the existing literature.

Three themes hold together this argument:

1. There is little analytic merit in choosing between many of the polarities current in theory and methodology. In a study to which I return at several points in this book, Mary Douglas (1975) argues that a commitment to one side of a polarity is likely to reflect bad experiences of social contacts with other groups (i.e. across categories). Put in this way, it is hardly surprising that many sociologists should share with the Ancient Israelites a fear of mediating entities which cut across categories. Conversely, this book argues that mediating entities are often to be welcomed. So we need not be either interpretivists or positivists, micro or macro analysts, or even qualitative or quantitative researchers. Equally, structuralist, neo-Marxist and Foucaultian perspectives may *sometimes* be fruitfully added to interactionist and ethnomethodological themes. As Saussure taught us at the beginning of the century, no meaning ever resides in a single term; everything depends upon how the constituent elements are articulated.

2. Contrary to the impression that such eclecticism may create, in qualitative research 'anything' does *not* 'go'. The title of this book seeks to emphasise the analytic issues involved for post-positivists in the apparently simple task of description. If we reject a purely external account of social reality, to what extent can we, in Moerman's (1974) phrase, 'trust the native'? As I try to show, particularly in Chapters 2 and 5, sociological description cannot conclude by reproducing participants' categories. However, I do not infer from this that either description or explanation can appeal to a uniform, context-free reality perceived by the observer. In this complex movement between lay and analytic understandings, we may feel more confidence in the observer's account when it attends to the situated character of action, while producing explanations which include 'deviant' cases and depend on rather more than a few fragments of favourable data extracts.

3. The issue of the practical applicability of research has only arisen for some more theoretically-oriented researchers as a result of competition for scarce research funds. In this book, I argue for taking much more seriously such issues. Following Foucault, I criticise forms of intervention which end up by imposing social 'experts' on the population, or by 're-educating' the public. Instead of such élitist solutions, I discuss practical interventions which open organisational spaces for people to use in their own way. Rather than being a legislator for change, I see the researcher as someone who facilitates changes which mobilise the innovatory capacity of ordinary people.

Having said what this book tries to do, I ought to point out what it does not do. First, it is not a 'cookbook': it does not discuss in detail many of the practical issues involved in the research process (e.g. how to obtain access, how to present oneself to research subjects). Some of these issues, I believe, can only be settled by practical experience. Others involve concealed analytic issues (e.g. about the character of observation) which are discussed in this book.

Second, I do not attempt an exhaustive description of every qualitative technique. For instance, there is no discussion of the life-history method -- although Chapter 8 on interview data raises issues which, I would suggest, are applicable to this method. Again, I do not have a chapter on the analysis of documents or texts, although Chapter 3 and the last part of Chapter 7 discuss highly relevant examples. Overall, to use military metaphors, the book is rather more concerned with strategy than with tactics.

The text is organised in three interrelated parts. Part One consists of a single chapter on the research process. It is intended to give a sense of how the analytic and practical aspects of research invariably involve departures from what might be defined in any rules of sociological method. It also serves to provide a sketch of some of the key issues discussed in the rest of the book.

Part Two attempts to establish my argument that central polarities in sociological theory are often of little use in research. In Chapter 2, I illustrate the point via a comparison of Durkheim's emphasis on the factual character of social structures and Weber's concern with 'interpretive understanding'. Using contemporary studies, I suggest points of contact between both positions. Chapter 3 develops Saussure's 'relational' method. Via examples of recent studies of political and literary texts, I show how the issue of 'articulation' is central to a variety of forms of sociological analysis. This allows me, in Chapter 4, to offer an account of the interweaving of macro and micro structures based, in part, on the work of Michel Foucault.

Part Three is concerned in more detail with the practice of qualitative research. It consists of chapter-length, critical examinations of ethnography, conversational analysis, the role of quantitative methods in largely qualitative research, and of the place of interview data. The book concludes with a discussion of practical interventions based on qualitative work.

I owe a special debt of gratitude to Robert Dingwall of the Centre for Socio-Legal Studies, Oxford. He has given me extensive, helpful and sensitive comments on the whole of this manuscript, often at very short notice. Although I have been unable to incorporate all of his points, his comments have allowed the writing of this book to proceed dialogically rather than monologically. I also thank my colleagues at Goldsmiths' (Chris Jenks and Gerry Stimson) as well as Paul Acourt, Geoffrey Baruch, Stewart Clegg (University of New England), Sue Fisher (University of Tennessee), Barry Glassner (University of Syracuse) and Christian Heath (University of Surrey) for their comments on parts of the text. I am also grateful to Danielle Silverman for discussion which encouraged me to write Chapter 9.

Sarah Montgomery and Olive Till have laboured to interpret my awful long-hand and to type the manuscript. I am most grateful for their help.

D.S.
London, 1984

PART ONE: THE RESEARCH PROCESS

1 The research process

In some academic disciplines there is an approved way of presenting your research findings. In this approved version, called the 'scientific paper', the account works through the following stages:

1. A statement of a hypothesis to be tested.
2. An account of the sample studied and the methods used.
3. A description of the results.
4. A discussion of the meaning and implications of these results.

Conceived as a model of the logic of sociological research, the scientific paper format presents a number of difficulties. As Glaser and Strauss (1967) have pointed out, it assumes that a logic of hypothesis-testing is the primary basis of scientific enquiry. While this *may* be appropriate to the kind of data processed by the natural sciences, sociologists have to bear in mind that social variables are intrinsically more difficult to isolate and test. As Weber (1949) and Schutz (1964) have observed, there is a sense in which social reality is pre-defined and pre-constituted by its participants. Consequently, a researcher's *prior* definitions of concepts and hypotheses *may* impose a meaning on social relations which fails to pay proper attention to participants' meanings. Moreover, at the final stage of the analysis ((4) above), the researcher is forced to make *ex post facto* interpretations of unexpected findings which have an unknown relation to how participants themselves define the situation.

Now this is not to say that reporting participants' meanings is the sole end of sociological research. If that were so, then sociologists would be quite incapable of explaining why things don't always turn out as participants expect (except by reference to lay understandings of 'luck', 'plots', etc.). Nor is it to deny that hypothesis-testing may be entirely proper, particularly where the area has been very well explored. I only want to observe that an exclusive concentration on hypothesis-testing is inappropriate as a description of what most sociological research does, and as a prescription of what it ought to do. Since hypothesis-testing research is usually, although not exclusively, quantitative in nature and most sociological research is qualitative, it fails, at the simplest possible level, to capture 'where (much of) the action is' in current sociological work.

However, even in the natural sciences where the scientific paper format is standard, the chronology it represents is widely recognised as mythical. Philosophers of science who differ as much as Popper (1972) and Kuhn (1970) are none the less broadly agreed that the published version of research reflects a reconstructed logic with a problematic relation to how the research was carried out and, more certainly, to how it was conceived — jumping out of the bath and shouting 'Eureka' is not, after all, something to be emphasised in a sober scientific journal; nor would scientists want to publicise the murkier motives that make them cling to one scientific theory and to reject plausible evidence that it doesn't work.

If the scientific paper is, in some sense, a myth, then it is appropriate to consider the various ways in which sociological research *actually* unfolds — as opposed to how it is sometimes described. I shall consider sequentially five related aspects of the research process:

1. beginning research,
2. reviewing the literature,
3. specifying the research problem,
4. conducting the study,
5. looking at the implications.

It may be worth stressing that these areas are not intended to describe features that arise in the same way in all sociological research, nor to prescribe a sequence of stages that matches the required chronological order of 'proper' research. It is more concerned with variety than doctrinal purity — the variety of problems that arise and the varied responses that have been offered.

BEGINNING RESEARCH

I suspect that the earliest stages of research depart most from the logic and chronology implied by the format of the scientific paper. Most research is generated by a series of chance circumstances relating to the particular investigator and to the economic, social and political context in which (s)he works.

Sociology, like society, has its own division of labour. Researchers build up an expertise in sub-areas of their discipline. They familiarise themselves with the field, learning the varied substantive and methodological literature appropriate to it. When they publish their own work, they become known as specialists in that area. By the time they come to contemplate further research, they are labelled in certain ways and would find it awkward, in intellectual and career terms, to branch off in a different direction. Appointments committees, when new academic posts still existed, tended to favour evidence of 'sound' (i.e. integrated) research and to look askance at people who had dipped into a number of fields ('dilettantes').

Being a specialist has the additional advantage that one becomes familiar with the institutional arrangements in the field and develops contacts with participants who might offer access. Sometimes, this will generate a request from such a person to research a topic that (s)he defines as a significant organisational 'problem'. Sometimes, the investigator may make a direct approach. In both cases, a balance has to be maintained between the social (or, more likely, managerial) problems raised by participants and the sociological problem that will concern the researcher. This is not to imply that sociologists are not often concerned about social problems themselves. However, they are unlikely to feel committed to a piece of research unless both their professional expertise is appropriate and social problems are defined in the broadest possible terms (i.e. not simply managerially or administratively).

If the host organisation offers funding, then the process of defining the research problem is likely to be particularly delicate. Even where funding is sought from independent bodies, like Research Councils, the presentation of the research, and perhaps even its direction, is likely to be influenced by the fashions and crises of the moment. Alert researchers will not fail to notice the current 'in' subjects which often relate to the state of the economy and the policies of current governments (for instance, the policy of de-institutionalising old people and mental patients which fits nicely with the perennial obsession with cost-cutting).

More respectable academic concerns are, however, usually also involved in the generation of research. Although there are a wide range of such concerns, I shall select three different ways of beginning research:

1. large-scale theoretical concerns,
2. a puzzling datum,
3. a methodological problem.

Each concern groups together a range of possible substantive and theoretical approaches. The three are distinguished from one another only in the way they start to conceive a research problem.

1 Large-scale theoretical concerns
Sociological grand theory has occupied and retreated from the centre of the stage in a series of cycles. The nineteenth century was the apogee of grand theory. As the discipline was established, early writers sought to develop large-scale theories able to account for the vast economic and social changes that had taken place in Western Europe and to define a delimited area of knowledge that was specifically sociological. Consequently,

the rationale for research of the time was usually in terms of these large-scale concerns. So Durkheim, in erecting a stable analytic territory for sociology (social facts), also established a theoretical problem (social order) and a research topic (social integration). His research on the division of labour, suicide and religion consistently explores these themes.

Equally, Weber worked in relation to a research topic (the rationalisation process) that fitted the grid of his own research dynamic (forms of rationality) and preferred analytic frame (*cultural* facts). No less than Durkheim, his work on religion and bureaucracy was a response to these large-scale theoretical concerns.

With the development of empirical sociology in the United States between 1920 and 1950, through both survey research and participant observation studies, grand theory lost its prominence. It was to be reborn during the next 25 years in relation to the social theories of Talcott Parsons and to a rediscovery, first by American humanists, then by French structuralists, of Karl Marx. So for much of this period, particularly 1960–1975, sociology largely consisted of arguments about conflict and consensus and about functionality and historicity, until, in the final few years of the period, the quantum leap proposed by ethnomethodology shifted some of the parameters of the debate.

Unfortunately, unlike the earlier period of the ascent of grand theory, few of the participants felt obliged to engage in research to demonstrate their claims, being content to deny that, as action theorists, Marxists or structuralists, they were positivists. Partly as a backlash to this theoretical jamboree and perhaps in the context of the less optimistic and economically problematic years following the oil crisis of 1973, a more cautious tone had begun to prevail by the late 1970s.

2 A puzzling datum

As empirical research once again became more acceptable, so investigators returned to finding topics within the material thrown up by their observations. With the respectability of the discipline more or less established in the nineteenth century, research no longer had to have the function on every occasion of re-asserting the viability of the subject nor of sustaining a particular grand theory of society. Like researchers in other disciplines, we could pursue puzzles and problems encountered in delimited areas. Some examples may clarify this way of generating a research problem.

The case of Down's Syndrome children (Silverman)

A few years ago, I was conducting research on the social organisation of consultations in a paediatric cardiology clinic. The primary focus was on how doctors presented clinical options to parents, and how parents responded and intervened. It became clear that parental intervention was related to three sets of factors — their experience of clinic routines, the character of their child's condition, and the treatment that the doctor suggested. In particular, in the early stages of the child's career at the clinic, doctors tended to make decisions for parents and the parents themselves were content to have their child defined in largely clinical terms (e.g. as a child 'with a heart murmur requiring cardiac catheterisation' rather than as, say, a 'happy baby').

However, a number of consultations did not follow this pattern. Here, both parents and doctors concentrated on the *social* formulations of the child. So, for instance, the child's 'enjoyment of life' was used by both sides as a good reason not to engage in what were here defined as 'meddlesome' operations. Moreover, instead of the decision about catheterisation being made by the doctor, parents were asked to decide whether such clinical intervention was appropriate. It transpired that these 'deviant' consultations usually involved handicapped Down's Syndrome children. Careful investigation revealed the ways in which, at each stage of the consultation, the doctor spoke to the parents in special terms (Silverman 1981). It was concluded that the 'social construction of the child' served as a way of implementing a clinic policy of non-intervention on such children. In this way, a puzzling datum served as a stimulus to research.

Why defendants plead guilty (Sudnow)
While observing procedures in a Public Defender's Office in California, David Sudnow noticed that a great deal of time was spent in negotiations between Public Defenders and the District Attorney's Office (Sudnow 1968). These negotiations usually assumed the guilt of the suspect and were simply concerned with determining the charge which should ultimately be laid against him. The prosecution were prepared to reduce a charge in order to get the defendant to plead guilty. Guilty pleas satisfied organisational pressures by allowing for rapid settlements of cases, so making more time available in crowded court schedules.

Sudnow showed how the familiar technique of 'plea-bargaining' was dependent on commonsense assumptions about what constituted a 'normal' crime and what would motivate a guilty plea, while ensuring that the accused received a 'proper' punishment. His study explained a puzzling datum that Sudnow had noticed earlier: a large majority of defendants in criminal cases in the state of California plead guilty.

Undemocratic radical political parties (Michels)
Many years earlier, Robert Michels (1962) had been puzzled about the internal structure of the German Social Democratic Party (the SPD). Although its aims were democratic and egalitarian, its internal structure

was authoritarian and gave very little role to rank-and-file members.

Michels explained this contradiction between theory and practice by suggesting that the demands of the political battle encouraged parties to develop teams of experts and full-time officials who increasingly became out of touch with the orientations of ordinary members. Moreover, he argued that, particularly in left-wing parties like the SPD, people had psychological predispositions which encouraged firm leadership. These forces combined to generate what Michels called an 'iron law of oligarchy'.

Although further research and recent experience (e.g. the British Labour Party in opposition 1979–83) has suggested that Michels' iron law may not be so 'iron', his work again demonstrates how a puzzling datum or unexpected observation may provide an incentive for worthwhile research.

3 Methodological issues

We have seen how grand theories and puzzling facts may provide an incentive for research. However, as sociology has matured, it has increasingly generated research at an intermediate level which is based on issues which are neither so abstract as grand theory nor so concrete as a puzzling datum.

Some time ago, Robert Merton (1957) argued for such an avoidance of extremes of abstraction and concreteness. However, his 'middle range theories' were tied to a logic of verification based on hypothesis-testing. As Glaser and Strauss (1967) pointed out, this overlooked how research might *generate* theory and was inappropriate to most qualitative work.

A more promising middle way is found in research which arises out of a critical response to the methodological and policy limits of particular research styles. A good example of what I have in mind is offered by Mehan's (1979) work in the sociology of education. He notes that the nature and sources of the link between schooling and achievement are relevant both to the theory of social stratification and to the very practical political and policy issues. However, although large-scale quantitative studies have been useful in studying gross differences *between* schools: 'they are not helpful in revealing the social processes of education that take place *within* particular schools . . . [and] very few practical policies have been produced' (Mehan 1979:6 6; my emphasis). Mehan suggests three primarily *methodological* problems with these large-scale correlational studies which try to link schooling and performance.

1. These studies have attempted to use an 'input–output' model of schooling. However, indices of input, such as the number of books in the school library or the opinions of teachers, do little to explain variations in output (i.e. educational performance).

2. There is no way of knowing where the presumably missing input variables are to be found. This leads to considerable disagreements of what the missing factors are likely to be (e.g. ability grouping or classroom arrangements).

3. 'Correlational studies seldom provide similar findings on the same topic . . . [and] even produce contradictory interpretations of the same data' (Mehan 1979: 7).

Mehan concludes that these problems have arisen because of the concentration of research on macro correlational studies which has excluded sufficient *direct* study of the process of education as it actually occurs inside schools:

> While schooling is recognized as an intervening process between background social context and later economic and academic attainment, the school has been treated as a *'black box'* in between input and output factors . . . what actually happens inside schools, in classrooms, in educational testing situations, at recess, in lunchrooms, in teachers' lounges, on a practical everyday basis has not been examined by the researchers who debate the influence of schools. (ibid.:4–5; my emphasis)

Mehan's own research has tried to overcome these kinds of methodological problems by paying close attention to the social organisation of teaching and classroom knowledge in actual teaching situations.

The discovery of analytic 'black boxes' has proved an incentive to his research and to a range of other work outside the territory of the sociology of education. For instance, sociological accounts may well depend upon narrative forms similar to those used in ordinary story-telling. To pursue the matter further, Sacks (1974) developed an elegant research apparatus for coping with the problem of how we derive adequate, everyday descriptions of phenomena — a 'black box' for any descriptive enterprise like sociology.* Again, Birdwhistell (1970) and Heath (1983) have offered ways of overcoming the absence of adequate methodology for treating the non-verbal aspects of human communication — a previously unresearched topic.

REVIEWING THE LITERATURE

Once an incentive for beginning research has been provided, the investigator's first task is to review the literature. This serves both a negative and a positive function. On the negative side, a literature review can ensure that new research avoids the errors of poor earlier work or merely reiterating the findings of some good previous study. More positively, it can provide a rigorous basis for new work by suggesting what I would call 'a typology with empty boxes'. Let us examine this positive function first.

*For a fuller account of Sacks' work on description, see Chapter 6, pp. 134–37.

1 Incomplete typologies

Grand theory bequeathed to sociology conceptual schemes which for generations ordered how sociologists looked at reality. For instance, Weber's distinction between three bases for claiming legitimate authority and Durkheim and Marx's contrasting concepts of 'anomie' and 'alienation' served as invaluable grids for interpreting various forms of social interaction.

However, as Weber himself emphasised, it is in the nature of concepts that, while they help to order our thought, they also deflect attention from those areas which they fail to label. So any related group of concepts, or typology, by excluding certain areas from its ambit, either unintentionally or by design, necessarily creates a set of ignored or undefined areas.

This is what I mean by 'a typology with empty boxes'. By identifying such vacua in conceptual schemes, a literature review can provide a sound analytic basis for further research. Two examples will illustrate the point: Gouldner's (1954) study of the forms of bureaucracy and Lipset *et al.*'s (1962) research on a surprisingly democratic American labour union.

The forms of bureaucracy (Gouldner)

Gouldner notes how Weber's 'ideal-type' of bureaucracy was partly based on studies of governmental bureaucracies. This meant that the concept had two limitations: first, many bureaucratic organisations exist outside government (i.e. in business and industry); second, in non-governmental bureaucracies, the issue of consent is more problematic. For civil services in democratic countries, the source of laws and rules arises in popular consent based on freely elected parliaments. However, no such processes arise in most industrial corporations. Consequently, consent cannot always be assumed — people do not obey a rule just because it has come from the corporate bureaucracy: sometimes they ignore it, sometimes they strike.

Gouldner concluded that, in such cases, the source of consent (or conflict) has to lie outside the formal rule-making structure of the organisation. Instead, the degree of consent is likely to derive from the perceived *source* of the rule and whose interests it is perceived to serve. In particular, where a rule is seen to be imposed by one vested interest upon another, then consent will be problematic and, in certain circumstances, for instance where economic rewards are insufficient to tolerate it, the rule will be openly challenged. Conversely, a rule that is perceived to serve everybody's interest will be freely followed without resistance. Gouldner calls the first kind of rule 'punishment-centred' and the second kind 'representative'.

Gouldner's own research on a gypsum mine develops Weber's theory of bureaucracy by extending his typology into areas which had remained blank on Weber's original conceptual scheme. In doing so, it adds a useful area to our conceptual apparatus while instructing future students of bureaucracy to be conscious of the issues generated by consent. For instance, Gouldner neatly demonstrates the nuances that arise as a consequence of how a rule is perceived: deviance from a 'punishment-centred' rule is typically treated as wilful disobedience and punished. Conversely, someone who deviates from a 'representative' rule is assumed to be merely misinformed and is educated rather than punished.

A democratic union (Lipset et al.)
Lipset's work began from Michels' 'iron law of oligarchy', which I discussed earlier. Lipset noted that Michels had based his explanation of the prevalence of non-democratic forms on the questionable assumption that all large-scale organisations are indeed undemocratic. If you could locate a 'democratic' organisation, Michels' iron law would fall. It would then be necessary to develop a typology of the *range* of 'democratic' and non-democratic forms, and an explanation able to account for this variance. (I have put 'scare-quotes' round the word 'democratic' to imply that there is an awkward problem, which Lipset does not really resolve, about how 'democracy' is to be defined.)

A printer's union provides Lipset with an example of internal democracy. His study then shows how a lively unofficial group structure served to provide independent bases of support in the union and to overcome apathy about union elections.

Lipset's research exhibits the value of using a literature review to develop or extend a typology. As a consequence, his case-study took an example whose very *deviant* character proved to be a way of extending the *general* theory about the relation between organisational structures and democratic control.

2 Finding failures
I turn now to the negative function of a review of the literature: recognising and avoiding the errors of earlier work. Once again, Mehan's (1979) study of schooling provides a useful example of a sensitive appreciation of the dynamics of research.

We last encountered Mehan criticising macro-correlational studies in the sociology of education. He was aware, however, that the most favoured alternative — small-scale participant observation or field-studies — also had problems. While such studies at least offer analysis of the 'black box' of what happens in the classroom, some of their findings are dangerously impressionistic. What they gain in depth, they thus lose in rigour.

It is worth quoting Mehan at length about three weaknesses of field-studies:

First, conventional field reports tend to have an anecdotal quality. Research reports include a few exemplary instances of the behaviour that the researcher has culled from field notes. Second, these researchers seldom provide their criteria or grounds for including certain instances and not others. As a result, it is difficult to determine the typicality and representativeness of instances and findings generated from them. Third, research reports presented in tabular or summary form do not preserve the materials upon which the analysis was conducted. As the researcher abstracts data from raw materials to produce summarised findings, the original form of the materials is lost. Therefore, it is impossible to entertain alternative interpretations of the same materials. (Mehan 1979: 15)

Mehan's pointed remarks about the limits of conventional participant observation research go to the heart of the problem of sociological descriptions with which this book is concerned. In a more limited sense, it emphasises that a critical literature review can avoid over-hasty leaps from the frying-pan of macro-correlational research, with its questionable generalisations, into the fire of less than rigorous field-studies. Mehan's alternative favoured method — 'constitutive ethnography' — will be encountered in the next section of this chapter.

SPECIFYING THE RESEARCH PROBLEM

A common misconception about research is that there is a direct relationship between the breadth of the questions addressed and the value of the answers produced. This assumption explains the incredibly ambitious research proposals that are often submitted by people beginning PhDs, and even by students preparing an undergraduate research project.

If anything, however, the narrower the question you ask, the more likely will you be to produce a satisfactory answer. This should, of course, not be taken to extremes — asking nothing at all clearly provides no problems but is also pointless. None the less, there is no doubt about the incentive to rigorous thinking offered by the process of narrowing down one's research concerns into an elegant, manageable and relevant problem. Consequently, a great deal of time has to be spent with would-be researchers encouraging them to forgo the temptation to shoot off in every direction at once and to specify a well-defined and workable proposal. Such specification is best achieved not by the arbitrary lopping off of whole areas, but by asking oneself a number of interrelated questions. These include:

1. What is the theoretical issue?
2. What is the relevance of a macro or micro perspective?
3. How appropriate is it to use naturally-occurring data?
4. What mix of qualitative and quantitative methods is called for?

1 Issues of theory

Difficulties tend to arise here because investigators misconceive the place of theory in research. At one extreme, they may assume that 'theory' means the schools of sociology wearily served up in undergraduate courses. Hence the researcher need only specify at the outset his faith in, say, action theory, Marxism or ethnomethodology and all 'theoretical' problems will be immediately clarified. At the other extreme, it is maintained that the research task is primarily descriptive or exploratory and/or is mainly oriented towards a social problem. Consequently, theoretical considerations are not significant.

The first approach implies that all the researcher needs is a badge of affiliation to a theoretical school. According to the second approach, a sound method is quite sufficient. Both approaches are mistaken.

Now it is true that a commitment to a particular sociological school gives a useful prior orientation to social reality. However, a school is not a single unit: it generates collections of theories from which the would-be researcher must choose. At the other extreme of description and social-problem orientation, it must be recognised that the social world does not speak for itself. So, while aiming to stay close to the facts is laudable, in practice it means imposing by fiat a particular theoretical scheme upon reality.

Between both extremes are the theoretical or, better, analytical issues that are at the heart of research. We shall consider two illustrations of how such analytical issues can be specified: Mary Douglas's anthropological work on an African tribe, and Silverman and Jones' study of decision-making processes in a large bureaucracy.

Explaining anomaly (Douglas)

Douglas (1975) set out to describe the cultural universe of a Central African tribe, the Lele. Following a common anthropological approach, her ethnography concentrated on how the Lele interpreted the natural world, incorporating it into a system of cultural symbols.

She discovered that the Lele revered a scaly anteater (the pangolin). The pangolin cult was central to many aspects of the Lele's cultural order. Curiously, however, when that order was examined in detail, it was found that the pangolin *cut across* many of its categories. For instance, it does not fit entirely into the animal category: it only gives birth to one offspring at a time and unlike other animals that are hunted, it does not try to escape the hunter. Again, although it is a land animal, the Lele describe it as having the body and the tail of a fish.

The Lele's celebration of the anomalous pangolin enabled Douglas to specify her analytic problem. She notes that Levi-Strauss has suggested a natural propensity of mythical thought to postulate entities which mediate between the polarities established by cognitive categories. The anomalous pangolin seemed like just such a mediating entity.

Now, therefore, Douglas had her research problem. What symbolic function did the pangolin cult play in Lele culture? Furthermore, does comparative work suggest that anomalous beings are always celebrated in all cultures? And if not, why not? I shall return to some of Douglas's answers to these questions in a moment.

Explaining decisions (Silverman and Jones)
As part of a study based on senior management's concern about high turnover among young graduate administrators, Silverman and Jones (1975) obtained access to the selection and promotion procedures of a large local government organisation.

Their initial interest was in explaining why certain candidates were successful. Selectors discussed them in terms of notions of 'acceptability' and 'abrasiveness'. It seemed that factors like these, deeply rooted in middle-class English culture, were a good predictor of committee decisions.

However, this belief was shaken by the odd occasions when high marks would be given to a candidate who appeared, in the researchers' eyes, to have given a highly abrasive performance. More troubling, when audio-tapes of selection interviews were replayed to the chairman of the selection panel several months later, he frequently guessed 'wrong' about the panel's actual decision.

Silverman and Jones rejected the tempting possibility that these 'errors' were the result of chance factors or the lack of full data (for instance, the fact that the chairman was not able to *see* the candidates the second time around). Instead, they concluded that the acceptability-abrasiveness formula served primarily not as the *cause* of decisions but as a *rhetoric* with which to justify *any* decision. This conclusion served to specify the theoretical problem: the task was to analyse the formal practices through which history was rewritten for the purposes of assembling 'sensible' dossiers and files. The earlier work of Cicourel (1968) on juvenile justice and Zimmerman (1974) on social security agencies could now be mobilised and developed.

2 Macro/micro
In a concrete sense, this is a problem which is usually easily resolved. Most independent researchers lack the resources to carry out large-scale macro research and so, unless they can use convenient indices of apparently macro processes, like official statistics, they tend to concentrate on micro studies of small-scale processes.

However, it should not be assumed that micro work necessarily lacks a macro or societal dimension. First, any investigator who fails to understand the broader social context in which face-to-face interactions occur is not worth his salt. For instance, the 'problem' of staff turnover with which Silverman and Jones' management was concerned only arose in the context of the expanding job market of the expansionary days prior to 1973. Similarly, cuts in the British National Health Service and the fiscal crisis of American cities like New York provide the essential backdrop to many current micro studies of health care in Britain and the United States.

The second relation between macro and micro levels can arise in research that is sensitive to the analytic articulation of face-to-face interaction and cultural systems. Douglas (1975) offers an elegant example of this concern and so we shall briefly return to her work.

It appears that there are a range of responses to anomalous entities in different cultures. At one extreme stands the Old Testament with its injunctions against contact with anything anomalous — whether a pig (neither totally clean nor unclean) or a half-breed spouse — neither in your tribe nor fully out of it. At the other extreme are the Lele with their celebration of the anomalous pangolin as a cult animal.

Douglas suggests that the contrast between human and not-human (nature), symbolised in the Lele's response to the pangolin 'provides an analogy for the contrast between the member of the human community and the outsider' (Douglas 1975: 289). Where useful exchanges arise between *human* communities, then moving across categories (or mediation) will be celebrated in the *animal* world. In short,

> If the institutions allow for some much more generous and rewarding exchange with more than normally distant partners, then we have the conditions for a positive mediator [e.g. the Lele]. If all exchanges are suspect and every outsider is a threat, then some parts of nature are due to be singled out to represent the abominable intruder who breaches boundaries that should be kept intact [e.g. the Ancient Israelites]. (ibid.)

Douglas's classic study reveals how a small-scale ethnography can raise the broadest macro issues. Sometimes, fortunately, making links between micro and macro levels is less dependent on resources than on intellectual clarity.

3 Naturally-occurring data?

With the fall in popularity of survey research after about 1965, there has been a great expansion of work focusing upon naturally-occurring situations — the encounters that people have in the normal course of events. In this way, it is hoped to produce descriptions and explanations appropriate to the way in which people actually behave. Conversely, questionnaire and interview responses are seen to provide 'idealised' accounts of attitudes and behaviour which, because they are rationalisations, have an uncertain relation to actual situations.

Initially, following the success of the Chicago School in the 1930s, a great deal of work consisted of participant observation studies, usually in the symbolic interactionist tradition. More recently, the rigour of such work has come under critical scrutiny. One such critical response (to what Mehan calls 'field-studies') was discussed earlier.

As a result of these criticisms, two procedures for treating naturally-occurring data have come to the fore. Conversational analysis (c.a.) based on audio (and sometimes video) recordings of interactions has been concerned with the sequencing rules through which turn-taking and the like is accomplished (e.g. Sacks *et al.* 1974). The direction of this work is oriented towards the discovery of supposedly cross-cultural universals of interactional organisation. Consequently, until recently, the work has not been particularly concerned with the social context in which interactions occur (but see Atkinson 1982).

An alternative procedure which is concerned with context has been variously labelled 'ethnomethodological ethnography' (Dingwall 1981) and 'constitutive ethnography' (Mehan 1979). Like c.a., it is concerned with how members assemble the social world. Unlike most c.a., it is concerned less with universal procedures and more with the contexted practices through which particular institutional structures are reproduced. As Mehan puts it, using the sociology of education as an example,

> The central recommendation of constitutive studies of the school is that 'objective social facts' like students' intelligence, academic achievement, or career paths and 'routine patterns of behaviour' . . . are accomplished in the interactions between teachers and students, testers and students, principals and teachers, and so on. (Mehan 1979: 18)

In later chapters, I shall be centrally concerned with the practice of such ethnography and its attempt to develop adequate descriptions of social phenomena. However, it would be wrong to imply at this stage that the observation of naturally-occurring data is the *only* proper research method. Subsequently, I shall consider the value of the kind of 'contrived' data generated in interview accounts. As Voysey (1975) and Baruch (1982) have persuasively argued, research interviews offer access to a set of 'moral' realities firmly located in the cultural world. Once we rid ourselves of the palpably false assumption that interview statements can stand in any simple correspondence to the real world, we can begin fruitful analysis of the real forms of representation through which they are structured. In short, I recommend an approach to interview data of the same order as that adopted by Douglas and Lévi-Strauss to natives' accounts.

4 Qualitative/quantitative methods

Felicitously, when considering each of the polar oppositions that arise in specifying a research problem, I have, like Douglas, discovered a mediating entity (e.g. small-scale theories, micro studies with macro implications, or interview data with relevance for naturally-occurring realities). Not surprisingly, I shall make the same discovery when discussing this final polarity.

The popularity of quantitative methods started to decline in sociology in parallel to the decline in survey research after 1965. While other professionals, like psychologists, economists, clinicians and administrators, were inclined to discount any research not based on counting, sociologists after this date tended to feel rather awkward about being seen, for instance, carrying out a statistical test of significance.

Once again, Mehan's book on classrooms will serve as an instance of what I have in mind. Tabulating behaviour into discrete categories, he suggests, can obscure 'the contingent nature of interaction'. Moreover:

> because [such tabulations] focus almost exclusively on the teacher, they minimise the contributions of students to the organisation of classroom events. The classroom is socially organised. Teachers and students work in concert to create this organisation. (Mehan 1979: 10)

However, Mehan's critique of quantification in classroom settings is subsequently lessened by his use of some simple quantified measures to count units of interaction (relating to students as well as teachers). It is also limited by his justified criticism of the anecdotal character of certain field-studies.

Herein lies the potential value of simple counting procedures in mainly qualitative research. Such counting helps to avoid the temptation to use merely supportive gobbets of information to support the researcher's interpretation. It gives a picture of the whole sample in summary form, highlighting deviant cases and encouraging further qualitative analysis of regularities.

So quantitative methods *can* be a useful tool even in constitutive ethnography. As we have seen elsewhere, it is not simply a choice between polar opposites that faces us, but a decision about balance and intellectual breadth and rigour. Where used intelligently and appropriately, there is no reason why quantification has to be totally shunned in the 1980s, any more than it had to be central to respectability in the 1950s.

CONDUCTING THE STUDY

Given the huge range of possible research topics, no hard-and-fast rules for conducting research can be provided. What I offer here, then, is less a set of prescriptions and more a number of cautions and encouragements.

All relate to issues that may be overlooked by the inexperienced researchers. They are as follows:

1. chronology,
2. the problem of the 'underdog',
3. disconfirming evidence,
4. the problem of 'ironies',
5. deviant cases,
6. maintaining flexibility,
7. maintaining contact.

Chronology

In many research areas analysing data over time gives an invaluable, additional perspective. Attitudes and behaviour are revealed in process in relation to status passages rather than fixed to a particular role. Over time, we can seek to understand the *dynamics* of social relations.

In qualitative research, the work of the Chicago School pioneered the study of such dynamics. In particular, Howard Becker *et al.* (1961) showed how much behaviour was related to 'career contingencies', movements between statuses with different rights and obligations.

This process is most readily illustrated by referring to the usual experience of students. During each year of their course, they are likely to take on different assumptions about what is expected of them and how they can cope. As graduation approaches, they may redefine their identity and recast their perceptions of how they felt when they began their studies.

Like other status passages, student careers have both an objective and a subjective dimension. There are the formal requirements of a status and the kind of things that will happen to its incumbent (e.g. examinations, particular kinds of teaching). There are also the subjective identities that go with these objective happenings. To 'understand' someone, you must grasp where they stand in such status passages.

Geoffrey Baruch (1981) has illustrated the importance of time-series data in a less formal setting. In his work on parents with sick or handicapped children, he noticed how frequently he was told 'atrocity' stories. Such stories sought to identify some health care professional (a doctor at a school medical examination, a health visitor, the parent's GP) who had been tardy in determining the nature of the illness or thoughtless in dealing with the child.

Baruch had no way of knowing whether these stories were accurate but clearly they had to be taken seriously as they were told with such regularity. Curiously, however, he noticed that they were told far less frequently at second or third interviews with parents, held several months apart.

It appeared that what was happening was that parents were conscious of the guilt and responsibility that may accrue to the parent of a sick child. By identifying an external 'guilty party', they shift the area of 'blame', while establishing themselves as responsible people on the look-out for the best possible treatment for their child. At later stages of treatment, however, they feel less helpless about their situation and are able to display their moral worth through accounts of their helpful actions rather than through attributions of blame. Time was thus the key to understand the 'moral career' or such parents.

The problem of the 'underdog'

The Chicago School is known not only for the concept of 'career' but also for its detailed account of the 'underside' of society. It has produced studies of 'underdogs' like the hobo and the petty criminal, as well as of the day-to-day life of people in low status occupations (waitresses, dance-hall musicians). Such work is rightly acclaimed for its ethnographic detail and perceptive observation. It has founded a continuing tradition which aims to 'tell it like it is' from the point of view of down-trodden members of society.

Such reportage is valuable in itself. Unkindly, one might also say that it is satisfying to middle-class sociologists with social consciences. However, as its originators would agree, such studies of the underdog are necessarily *partial*.

This partiality arises from certain methodological problems inherent in taking the underdog perspective. First, do you trust what people tell you? This need not imply that people will lie, but merely that their accounts necessarily reflect their own situation and perception of problems at hand. In a classic study of power and status relations in industry, Dalton (1959) showed how the 'best' informants were often those without any stable position in the factory's clique structure. Consequently, unless you are very careful, you emerge with an outsider's view of an outsider's account of what is going on.

This leads on to a second problem. Can observation of underdog life be fully informative about the social and economic structures that keep them where they are? Don't you need to gather additional knowledge about such factors as the state of the labour market or the character of social mobility rates which are not directly available to observation in the field?

Finally, isn't some balance needed elsewhere to all the sociological studies of underdogs? Why is there so much work on the 'bottom dogs' and so little work on 'top dogs'? Obviously the issue of access is important. It may be part of underdogs' general vulnerability that they are more available than others for observation and social research. None the less, it is a curiously unbalanced sociological enterprise that can produce seemingly endless studies of the unemployed and of single parents but very little work on the middle and upper ranks of society. We know a great deal about the culture of low pay or even of 'affluent' workers. How much do we know about the culture and practices of the lawyer or the City of London?

Disconfirming evidence

Much of the textbook debate about the scientific status of sociology is somewhat fatuous. Nobody would now dispute that the cultural world has different properties from the natural world and that this implies that some different methods of investigation are appropriate. However, it is also an increasingly accepted view of science that work becomes scientific by adopting methods of study *appropriate* to the data at hand. Sociology is scientific to the extent that it uses appropriate methods and seeks to be rigorous and critical in its investigations.

One way of being critical is, as Popper (1972) has suggested, to seek to refute assumed relations between phenomena. This means overcoming the temptation to jump to easy conclusions just because there is some evidence that leads in an interesting direction. It also means trying to avoid what statisticians call 'spurious' correlations. For instance, just because X seems always to be followed by Y, does not necessarily mean that X *causes* Y. There might be a third factor, Z, which produces both X and Y or, alternatively, is produced by X and then influences Y.

Sometimes, it is possible to use quantitative means to guard against spurious correlations. Lipset *et al.* (1962), for instance, were aware that their suggested link between membership of a printers' social club and participation in union politics might be spurious — perhaps people who joined such clubs were more interested in union politics and so predisposed to participate more in elections? Consequently, they compared the participation rates of non-members and members who had the *same* prior interest in union politics. When they still found a difference in participation, they were more confident that they could take it seriously.

Lipset's attempt to control for spurious correlations was possible because of the quantitative style of the research. This had the disadvantage of being dependent upon survey methods with all their attendant difficulties. However, there is no reason why qualitative researchers should not feel obliged to work by the same standards of internal criticism when seeking to depict relations. As we saw in the previous sections, observation over time, involving respondents with a range of statuses, is itself a control on hasty conclusions.

The problem of 'ironies'

The first use of the term 'irony' in this context was by Garfinkel (1967).

He intended it to mean that investigators should avoid the temptation to treat behaviour and talk in one setting as undercutting what appears to happen in another setting. Garfinkel demonstrates that action makes sense *in context*. We should understand how that sense is accomplished rather than appeal to our other knowledge to discount it.

The implication of Garfinkel's position is that we have to be careful about inferring a master 'reality' in terms of which all accounts and actions are to be judged. This casts great doubt on the argument that multiple research methods should be employed in a variety of settings in order to gain a 'total' picture of some phenomenon (e.g. Denzin 1970). Putting the picture together is more problematic than such proponents of 'triangulation' would imply. What goes on in one setting is not a simple corrective to what happens elsewhere — each must be understood in its own terms.

An illustration may help. Baruch's (1981) work on parents' accounts was associated with Silverman's (1981) study of clinic routines. Now it would have been tempting to treat what parents said in their homes as an ironic counterpoint to what happened in the clinic — as perhaps the 'low-down' on the official front of doctor–parent encounters. However, this would have failed to recognise that clinic encounters and home interviews arise on different territory, with different participants and with different practical purposes. Each has to be understood in context.

This did *not* mean that comparison of what happened in the two settings was impossible. For instance, it seemed to us that processes whereby moral and clinical realities were articulated were enacted in both settings. However, it did mean that simple ironies were to be avoided as the stuff of theatre but not of critical inquiry.

Deviant cases

Another way in which research can be critical is to seek constantly to identify and to account for deviant cases. One way of identifying such cases is to code or classify all data. As Mehan points out, coding is one means of coming to grips with the complex character of reality:

> We code our materials into discrete categories because we do not want to be overwhelmed by the very flux that we are trying to comprehend. Interaction is too massive to be addressed in its entirety all at once. (Mehan 1979: 29)

Where material does not readily fit into the coding scheme, the scheme is modified until all the data are accounted for. In this way, the identification of deviant cases can serve to increase the reliability and inclusiveness of analytic schemes.

Two examples from my studies of clinics illustrate this point. In the first study of Down's syndrome children (Silverman 1981) discussed earlier, the deviant character of doctors' appeal to social factors high-lighted the more normal clinical emphasis in most other consultations. The explanation was found to lie in a usually shared doctor–parent pre-disposition not to contemplate cardiac surgery for such children.

In a study of hare lip/cleft-palate clinics, unusually children themselves were given the final say in decision-making (Silverman 1983). The combi-nation of adolescent patients and decisions about appearance turned out to constrain adults to take seriously the decision-making rights of patients. However, this did not serve to undercut the dominant position of medical staff. Many children were predictably rendered speechless when asked how they 'felt' about their 'appearance'. Moreover, when a child responded confidently, this could be used to cast doubt about whether he was really troubled about his appearance. Here, as elsewhere, the identifi-cation of a deviant form enabled the analytic scheme to be modified and extended.

Maintaining flexibility

I discussed earlier the limits of hypothesis-testing research of the kind recommended by Merton (1957). Inevitably, in much mainly qualitative research, the research problem will undergo several respecifications during the period of study.

The investigator must be open to at least two possible sources of change in direction. First, during research access to certain areas may cease, while access to others may open. For instance, while conducting research on the social organisation of cancer clinics in the British National Health Ser-vice, Silverman (1984) had an unexpected opportunity to observe consul-tations at a private oncology clinic. This allowed a unique and fascinating glimpse at an under-researched area and the possibility of comparative work across the public/private health divide.

A second source of change can arise as a result of increasing dissatisfac-tion with the research questions being posed. I have already shown how Silverman and Jones (1975) felt that it would not be worthwhile to pursue their original question about the reasons behind particular selection deci-sions. This led to a shift of focus towards the rhetoric of decision-making and the normal practices through which this rhetoric is mobilised.

Maintaining contact

In much research, the investigator will be dependent on the people who have granted him access. He will also be dependent on the goodwill of the people being studied. Success with one need not mean success with the other. For instance, a senior person may give access only for this to be 'sabotaged' by his subordinates. This is, of course, a potential source of research data, as well as a threat.

People will also rightly expect some feedback on the results of your research. Two kinds of response are usually made to such demands. Some researchers will steer away from feeding back their data for fear of influencing the future behaviour of the people they are observing. Others, however, will feel that such people's responses to findings are an important way of validating research. (See Bloor's (1983) discussion of 'member validation' discussed in Chapter 2, pp. 43–5.)

When a study has been concluded, however, there is usually little justification in fobbing off people interested in information. Indeed, such contacts can serve as a useful basis for clarifying the analysis and thinking through its practical implications.

LOOKING AT THE IMPLICATIONS

I conclude by looking briefly at some issues relating to the practical and theoretical implications of sociological research.

Practical issues

Mehan (1979) rightly rejects the 'authority' claimed by experts who present findings to laymen:

> I have trouble with this conception of the uses of research for a number of reasons: (1) it treats research as static information, a 'thing' to be transferred between people like a package; (2) it separates researchers from the larger community by treating the community as a passive audience, whose role is to accept the findings of research; (3) the researcher assumes a privileged position *vis-à-vis* the larger community because of the presumed superiority of knowledge gathered by scientific methods. (ibid.: 204)

Instead, he calls for a continuing dialogue 'to provide participants with ways of looking critically at social circumstances, so that they, themselves, can take action to make changes' (ibid.: 205).

I share Mehan's view of the practical implications of research. For instance, Silverman (1981) called for a programme to provide more information and discussion for Down's syndrome families so that they would be in a better position to make decisions where cardiac surgery was a possibility.

However, not all people are in an equal position to make changes in the organisation of social institutions. In the same study of paediatric cardiology consultations, it was discovered that first consultations, which parents perceived to involve life and death issues, were particularly stressful. None the less, they served an important function in allowing an initial diagnosis and treatment programme to be established by an experienced physician. Here, parents clearly had no power to change the situation which, in any event, served their children's interests.

Through discussion with the medical staff, an additional clinic was created some weeks later. Here the child was not examined and parents, who by now had usually come to terms with their feelings of shock, were able to talk things over with a doctor on the ward. Although this new clinic was 'imposed' on parents, it was not structured by researchers or senior medical staff. The junior doctors who ran it were not instructed about how they should behave, nor were parents told in advance what they might or might not ask or do. As a consequence, we found that both sides used the encounter in ways we had not foreseen — for instance, parents would often bring their children with them and get them used to the ward and to the playroom. This kind of non-authoritarian intervention, then, can encourage innovation at the ground level.

Theoretical issues

If the initial stages of a study are concerned with narrowing down the research problem, the concluding stage is a good time to broaden out once again. This is particularly true of theoretical and conceptual issues.

The model I recommend derives from Glaser and Strauss's (1967) discussion of theory grounded in data. They remark that research aims to produce a systematic account of the relationship between a limited number of variables, often confined to a particular setting. They call this 'substantive' theory and give an example of their own work which attempted to relate the information given to dying patients to what they called 'awareness contexts'.

However, analytic courage is then required to relate such substantive theories to more general concerns. Formal theory emerges when one seeks to explain a process that may arise in a *range* of settings. 'Awareness contexts', they note, are a central part of the process of status passage, wherever it occurs.

The leap suggested by Glaser and Strauss is not peculiar to particular kinds of study. What C. Wright Mills (1953) called 'the sociological imagination' demands that we always should be looking for relationships between the particular and the general.

FURTHER READING

For an account of the research process as conceived within the quantitative survey research tradition, see Selltiz *et al.* (1964) and Moser (1958). For an account that is closer to the concerns of this chapter, see Glaser and Strauss (1967). Becker and Geer (1960) also offer a very useful, chapter-length account of how qualitative data can be rigorously analysed.

Dingwall and Murray (1983) provide a recent empirical study which is consistent with many of my arguments about how theory and research can be critically integrated. Finally, a whole issue of the journal *Sociological*

Review (November 1979) is devoted to a number of useful articles on qualitative research.

Many of the issues discussed here are taken up later in this book. Chapter 3 pursues the problem of the relation between macro and micro levels of analysis. The problems of participant observation research and the use of 'triangulation' are discussed in Chapter 5. Chapter 6 examines conversational analysis critically. In Chapter 7, I consider the uses of simple methods of counting in qualitative research, while the potential value of interview data, relative to naturally-occurring data, is examined in Chapter 8. Finally, Chapter 9 looks at some of the practical and moral issues involved in applying social research.

PART TWO: OVERCOMING CONCEPTUAL POLARITIES

2 Society and the individual: structures and meanings

Until a few years ago, post-war sociology had been obsessed by battles between rival theoretical schemes. On the one side stood a loose and warring group of Parsonians, structuralists, functionalists and Marxists. They were agreed on only one thing — that social processes could *not* be fully explained by an appeal to individuals or to the meanings attached to situations. Instead, they argued for a varied list of structural factors that included 'society', 'system', 'functional prerequisites' and 'mode of production'.

On the other side of this theoretical divide, were ranged a rather more closely allied group of interactionalists, phenomenologists, methodological individualists and ethnomethodologists. They were agreed that social processes could *not* be fully explained by an appeal to social structures. For them, the concept of 'social structure' mystified or reified social processes that could only occur at a face-to-face level. Instead, they appealed to a set of situational and interpersonal factors that included 'symbolic interaction', the 'everyday world', the 'individual' and 'accounting practices'.

Fortunately, the impasse suggested by this divide was quietly overcome in three ways. First, while the guns of the theoretical war chattered above their heads, empirical sociologists were happy to continue their researches. These added to our knowledge of the social world, while often happily mixing concepts drawn from apparently competing theoretical schemes. Second, a new generation of theorists, grown weary with old battles, began to outline a useful way of resolving the rival claims of each side. Their realist perspective (Bhaskar 1975, 1979; Keat and Urry 1975) recognised the role of 'meaning' in social life without accepting that this dissolved the constraining power of social structures. It also offered, in Bhaskar's (1975) elegant formulations, a defence of scientific practice in sociology which replaced sloganising about positivism by a reasoned response to Popper and Kuhn's post-empiricist philosophies of science. Finally, a more careful reading of the sociological tradition revealed that past scholars were not so opposed to each other's ideas as had been suggested by the simplified versions presented in undergraduate courses. In particular, Durkheim (the supposed founder of the school of society) was mainly arguing against forms of psychological reductionism and calling for a balance between the claims of the individual and society. Weber (the 'meaning' man) would have had no trouble in agreeing with these arguments. Nor, in practice if not in precept, did Durkheim demur from Weber's call for a balance between causal analysis and interpretive understanding.

In this chapter, then, as elsewhere in this book, I want to reject a division of sociological practice into polar oppositions. However, any attempt to keep a discussion of such important concepts as 'society', 'structure', 'meaning' and the 'individual' within the confines of just one chapter presents clear difficulties. I would beg the reader's indulgence for the inevitable simplifications that follow. My concern throughout is not to give a faithful, still less complete, reading of the history of ideas but to take up some of the implications of different sociological theories for the research process.

It may help at this point if I give a brief overview of the order of topics that follows. The chapter is organised in two sections, with a brief excursion into the sociology of knowledge at the end. The first section is concerned with Durkheim's work and its aftermath. I briefly consider Durkheim's appeal to 'society' and look at continuities in his approach from unexpected sources. Bhaskar's 'realism' is shown to offer a way of analysing social structures which is freed of Durkheim's analytic rejection of meaning. This section concludes with a discussion of some of the research implications of treating society as prior to the individual.

In the second section, I examine the seemingly opposed Weberian tradition, emphasising that his primary unit of analysis is not the individual but culture. Once again via Bhaskar, I argue that social science may be interpretive while still recognising the power of social structures. Finally, three research problems associated with understanding meanings are briefly considered: the problematic status of members' validation of research findings, the limits of members' understandings and the organising power of categorisation devices.

The chapter concludes by raising the issue of the social roots of sociology's fascination with the polarity between a world of meanings and of structures. Via Marx and Foucault, it is suggested that rival conceptualisations of the subjective and objective character of the social world are primarily grounded not in abstract theories but in real social practices of individualisation and surveillance.

DURKHEIM AND 'SOCIETY'

In his essay 'Individual and Collective Representations' (1974),

Durkheim uses a discussion of the basis of psychology to develop an argument about the proper field of sociology. He shows that psychology is concerned with states of consciousness that he calls 'individual representations'. It is clear to him that such representations are related to physiological facts. In particular, neural processes affect consciousness and may even sometimes cause it. However, this does not mean that consciousness is *reducible* to physiology:

> A representation is not simply an aspect of the condition of a neural element at the particular moment that it takes place, since it persists after that condition has passed, and since the relations of the representations are different in nature from those of the underlying neural elements. It is something quite new which certain characteristics of the cells certainly help to produce but do not suffice to constitute, since it survives them and manifests different properties. (1974:24)

In the same way as the psychological whole is more than the sum of its (physiological) parts, so the social whole ('social facts', 'society') is independent of individuals:

> If there is nothing extraordinary in the fact that individual representations, produced by the action and reaction between neural elements are not inherent in these elements, there is nothing surprising in the fact that collective representations, produced by the action and reaction between individual minds that form the society, do not derive directly from the latter and consequently surpass them. (ibid.: 24-5)

Here, Durkheim is making the reasonable claim that analysts who insist that entities must always be reduced to their constituent parts are guilty of an absurd logical error. In the case of sociology, this position could not even stop at the level of individuals. After all, as Durkheim points out, individuals are composed of chemical elements. So the reductivist fantasy should logically conclude by explaining society in terms of chemistry.

Moreover, Durkheim avoids the tempting alternative to reductivism. He explicitly states (ibid.: 29) that the part *cannot* be derived from the whole, no more than the whole is explicable by the part. The attempt to explain *everything* from just one site is what is mistaken. Instead, Durkheim proposes no more than that sociology should seek for explanations at the *appropriate* level: 'We must . . . explain phenomena that are the product of the whole by the characteristic properties of the whole, the complex by the complex, social facts by society' (ibid.: 29) — as is well known, for Durkheim 'social facts' are the appropriate level for sociological investigation. They are to be recognised objectively by the constraint they exercise and subjectively by the sense of obligation they tend to create. However, in a footnote (ibid.: 25), Durkheim makes it clear that his definition of such facts was intended as a guide to research not as a metaphysical statement about the 'essence' of society. He is simply saying that if the researcher wants to identify the workings of society, then a proper place to begin is with regularities in action and belief.

This minimalist reading of Durkheim does not deal with such problems as Durkheim's quite arbitrary definition of certain social phenomena (like suicide) and his well-known tendency, despite his methodological prescriptions, to switch between social regularities and attributions of states of consciousness. Nor can it cope with those purple passages where he celebrates society as a god-like moral power (ibid.: 25, 54).

Durkheim can be excused from these errors by showing that sometimes his theory is better than his practice (in the case of definitions of phenomena) and sometimes his practice is better than his theory (the former recognises a need for balance between the forces of individualism and society which is sometimes absent from his theoretical worship of society). More important for our present purposes, however, is Durkheim's insistence on explanation at the appropriate level of analysis and his rejection of reductivism. Curiously, as we shall shortly see, this aspect of Durkheim's methodology is consistently supported by one of Durkheim's most effective critics.

The case of suicide

In the contemporary discussion about Durkheim's classic *Suicide*, it seemed for a while as if the debate was polarised between Durkheim's appeal to social facts as the cause of the rates of suicide and Douglas's (1967) insistence on understanding the 'social meanings' of suicide and his consequent suspicion about suicide statistics. So, while Durkheim had sought to correlate suicide rates with states of social integration, Douglas tried to identify the meanings of sudden deaths to the participants via an investigation of suicide notes, family reaction, and so on.

Viewed in the light of Durkheim's methodological arguments, it now looks as if he would have had an entirely adequate answer to Douglas's criticisms. It might run as follows:

1. Sociology is concerned with social facts.
2. Suicide involves a whole series of psychological, legal, economic and social facts none of which is reducible to the others.
3. Any attempt to explain suicide in terms of the individual's own definitions and other people's responses is entirely acceptable.
4. However it is only acceptable at its own level, i.e. as an account of interactions between states of mind — as social psychology.
5. The problem of producing a sociological explanation of suicide remains.

Only subsequently, in Atkinson's (1978) study, did an adequate sociological alternative to Durkheim's explanation of suicide become established.

Atkinson argued that the *social* construction of suicide arose not in presumed states of social integration but in observable practices found in coroners' courts. The key to understanding suicide, suggested Atkinson, was in the way coroners assembled and evaluated evidence. Unlike Douglas, however, Atkinson is not at all concerned with social psychology but with routinised practices that are recurrent and socially organised.

The implication is that there are shared points of agreement between Atkinson and Durkheim. This is, indeed, the case in at least two senses. First, the two agree that suicide is properly explicable in sociological terms as a social fact. For Durkheim, this social fact is produced by social integration, while Atkinson looks for socially organised practices (like collecting evidence in coroners' courts) which produce it. For both, however, sociologists should not treat suicide as a psychological fact. Families' and coroners' tendencies to treat it in this way are, none the less, not to be dismissed. Instead, such psychological versions of suicide are *data* which, for Atkinson, reveal the raw material through which the events are socially constituted.

The second point of agreement arises over the response to official statistics. For very different reasons, neither Durkheim nor Atkinson will call these into question. Durkheim is happy to accept such statistics because he treats them as reasonably accurate. Atkinson will not question the accuracy of suicide statistics because that would imply that it is possible to offer a more accurate count of the suicide rate.

Atkinson would reject this option for two reasons. First, from his point of view, the suicide rate for any society can only be a socially-produced phenomenon, dependent on the organised practices of investigators. To imply that you have access to greater accuracy is to suggest that suicide somehow speaks for itself, which it never does. Second, the rates that we do have are 'real' in the sense that people take them seriously and act upon them. To substitute other statistics might fail to recognise the social role of data which are officially recognised as factual.

I have illustrated these alternative positions in Table 2.1. It will be seen that, despite their tacit agreement about the fundamental character of sociological inquiry, Durkheim and Atkinson do carve out different areas of research. Bearing in mind Durkheim's preparedness to recognise the legitimacy of approaches at different levels of analysis, we should have no trouble in accepting research on social integration and the practices of coroners as non-competitive. They illustrate the wide range of perspectives which, none the less, through their attention to social organisation, remain distinctively sociological.

Bhaskar's 'realist' synthesis
The measure of tacit agreement between Atkinson and Durkheim shows

that sociological analysis need not deviate from its focus on social organisation. Even at the opposite pole to Durkheim's positivism, Atkinson's ethnomethodology will still refuse to explain social process in terms of the individual.

Table 2.1: Suicide as a social phenomenon

| | **Perspective** | | |
	Sociology (Durkheim)	Social Psychology (Douglas)	Sociology (Atkinson)
Character of suicide	Social fact, defined by society.	Psychological, defined by individuals.	Social fact, defined by social practices.
Nature of official statistics	Social fact, because accurate.	Inaccurate.	Social fact, not questionable through 'more accurate' information.
Area of research	Correlations between rates and states of social integration.	Meaning of events to participants.	Construction of suicide in coroners' proceedings.

In Roy Bhaskar's (1975, 1979) terms, this is because sociology operates with a 'realist' view of the nature of reality. Realism suggests that social structures are 'real' in the sense that they are partially independent of individuals and their perceptions. He quotes approvingly Marx's statement in the *Grundrisse* to the effect that: 'Society does not consist of individuals but expresses the sum of the relations within which individuals stand' (Bhaskar 1979:32). Bhaskar adds that it is equally mistaken to reduce society to groups. The *relations* within which both individuals and groups stand are primary to sociological analysis (as both Durkheim and Atkinson would agree). This 'relational' conception of the subject-matter of sociology implies, in terms that will be fully explored in Chapter 3, that explanation is never fundamentally concerned with particular elements or units but with the articulation of the relation between elements.

Bhaskar provides for a version of sociological explanation as a movement from people's experiences to the social relations and processes which necessitate them (ibid.: 32). Once again, it is worth emphasising the variation in what is treated as the central form of social relations (from mode of production in Marx, to mode of social integration in Durkheim, to interpretive procedures and the social organisation of face-to-face behaviour in ethnomethodology). The distinctiveness of the sociological perspective is that, despite the programmatic fervour of some of the more extreme statements by Durkheim and some ethnomethodologists, it recognises the reality of social relations while understanding that they could not exist independently of human activity.

Bhaskar puts this realist position succinctly:

(1) people do not create society: for it always pre-exists them and is a necessary condition for their activity.

(2) Rather, society must be regarded as an ensemble of structures, practices and conventions which individuals reproduce or transform but which would not exist unless they did so.

(3) Society does not exist independently of human activity (the error of reification) but it is not the product of it (the error of voluntarism). (1979:45–6; numbering added)

Bhaskar's realism has an important political message. Contrary to libertarians and crude anti-Durkheimians, to escape from alienation is *not* to escape from constraint into pure free will. Instead, it requires a transformation of the social conditions of existence 'so as to maximise the possibilities for the development and spontaneous exercise of [mankind's] natural [species] powers' (1979: 47).*

Researching structures of constraint
One of the social conditions of existence which is as constraining as any other is a system of human communication. Largely ignored by Durkheim, on the mistaken assumption that such a system could only be described psychologically, it has been studied in depth by ethnomethodologists like Atkinson. I shall discuss their account of invariant communication forms in Chapter 6. It is worth noting, however, that they appeal to structures of conversational sequencing that are equally as constraining and non-voluntaristic as any of Durkheim's 'social facts'. This is not to deny that individuals are free to ignore them. But, if they do so, they face the consequences of confusion, anomie or sanction.

For the moment, however, I want to describe an alternative account of the constraining forms of communication. By linking it to theories of the 'subject', I shall prepare the way for a brief further presentation of Silverman's (1983) research on a cleft-palate clinic, already discussed in Chapter 1. The aim will be to show how individuals are not pre-given starting-points for social analysis (the voluntarist fantasy) but are constructed as specific social subjects within particular communication structures.

*But see the critique of Bhaskar's romanticism p. 39.

The German critical theorist Jurgen Habermas is known (and properly criticised) for producing vast, abstract theoretical schemes with little apparent empirical direction. His most suggestive work has arisen in his discussion of communication structures (1972) and, more specifically, of what he calls 'systematically distorted communication'.

To understand how communication can be distorted in Habermas's terms, we must briefly look at his account of an 'ideal speech situation'. In summary, such a situation provides for the interchangeability between speakers of conversational rights (e.g. beginning topics, ordering, promising) and of subject positions (e.g. 'I', 'you', 'we'). It also implies a certain minimum of truthfulness and sincerity in what speakers say.

At first glance, an ideal speech situation looks like a libertarian or idealist argument against (communication) structures in favour of free will. If this were the case, it would fail to satisfy Bhaskar's insistence on the real and, hence, universal nature of social constraints. However, Habermas saves himself from idealism by suggesting that an ideal speech situation is *built into* the social conditions of existence. Human communication presupposes the interchangeability of rights and positions; it generally assumes that people mean what they say. Communication is systematically distorted from two directions: conscious strategic behaviour, in which people manipulate communication forms in order to achieve undisclosed ends, and 'naturalised' codes of communication which, often behind the speakers' own backs, determine intelligibility according to pre-given structural and linguistic forms.

One way of analysing such forms which pays particular attention to the positioning of the subject has been provided by Althusser (1971). Shorn of Althusser's debate with other Marxists about the character of ideology, his account of the subject starts from an analogy with the baptism service. Here, of course, Christians receive their name. But their constitution as subjects (with names) is achieved by linking their subjecthood to a transcendent or ruling subject (God). This, says Althusser, is a model which sets the pattern for the later identities that subjects will acquire. In all such cases, the person will be constituted as a small subject (s) facing a big subject (S). This 's–S' relation is the thread that connects the relation between child and God, pupil and teacher, worker and employer.

For Althusser, then, in becoming subjects we are firmly put in our place. Indeed the very concept of the 'subject' is ambiguous, encapsulating both free *subjectivity* and *subjection* to a higher authority.

It will be seen, even in this caricature, that Althusser offers a powerful way to theorise the role of individuals in communication structures which recognises that, far from being the origin of communication, they are constituted as subjects by such structures. Put more directly, in what the speakers say there arises not uniform psychological entities but constructed subjects.

Here Althusser is at one with French semiotic accounts of the subject which equally deny that the subject-voices we use ('I', 'you', 'me') refer to or picture psychic or physical entities. As Benveniste puts it: 'the instances of the use of I do not constitute a class of reference since there is no "object" definable as "I" to which these instances can refer in identical fashion' (1971:218). Benveniste goes on to ask: to what reality does 'I' (or other pronomial voices) refer? His answer is that 'I' is solely a 'reality of discourse', intelligible only in its differences from other voices and its relations to them.

This suggests an important modification of Althusser's argument. Although his emphasis on the constitution of the subject is underlined, there is no reason to assume that the *only* way in which subjects are constituted (even in capitalist societies) is along the lines of small and big subjects (s–S). There are multiple possibilities in a range of discursive forms which construct differences and relations between voices. This calls for empirical study of the workings of such discourses in a range of institutional settings.

Researching the 'subject'

In order to give a taste of what such research may involve, there follows a brief discussion of the start of a consultation in a cleft-palate clinic (drawn from Silverman 1983). The first few utterances are given below.

(Transcript 29:7; C. = consultant surgeon, D. = boy aged 12, O. = orthodontist. D. has just entered with his mother.)*

1 C. Hello (1.0) You're *twelve* now, aren't you Barry?
2 D. Yeah.
3 C. And it's two years since we saw you. (1.0) How are things going?
4 D. All right.
5 C. All right? Jolly good.
6 O. (   )
7 C. Mm. Jolly good. Let's have a look. (C. examines.)
8 C. Now then. This has got rather an *ugly* scar line hasn't it? It's rather (1.0) rather a lot of stitch marks. (1.0) Isn't terribly handsome, is it? What do you think about your looks, Barry?
9 D. (3.0) I don't know.
10 C. You (laughs). Doesn't worry you a lot. You don't lie awake at night/ worrying about it or anything?
11 D.   /No.
12 C. No, no. It *could* be improved, er, because I think the scar line isn't

*Symbols (1.0)   indicates pause in seconds
          (   )   indicates untranscribeable utterance
          ugly   indicates stressed word
          /   indicates overlapping utterances

brilliant (1.0) but it's, you're the customer, if you're happy with things the way they are then/that's
13 D.   /Well I hope to have it done.
14 C. Oh you would, oh. All right, well, (0.5) we'll see about that shortly. Now what about this nose of yours, you've got a bit of a . . .

Like other such consultations with adolescents at the clinic, the topic discussed here involves the prospect of further cosmetic surgery, usually on lips or nostrils. As will be seen, the surgeon initially assumes that Barry does not want an operation but Barry's interruption (at utterance 13) suggests that his previous apparent indifference to his looks still can mean that he hopes to have corrective surgery.

Medical consultations like this follow an interview format, where sequencing occurs through a 'chaining' of question–answer–further question which gives the questioner control over topic maintenance and change. The fact that the doctor asks the questions (e.g. 1 and 3) and controls the agenda (e.g. 7 and 14) shows how the *linguistic* code of the interview is here tied to a *structural* code embedded in the authority and information format of doctor–patient consultations. Overall, I shall try to show three things:

1. that the doctor's 'misunderstanding' at 14 is largely the result of the *unintended* consequences of the operation of such linguistic and structural forms;
2. that conscious strategic behaviour (in Habermas's terms) is difficult to identify; and
3. that, in the context of these linguistic and structural forms, a particular discourse is constructed here which constitute Barry as what I call a 'marginalised' subject.

Utterances 3–5 reveal what later turn out to be the unintended consequences of a 'greeting' sequence. The linguistic code of greeting involves the provision of purely formal responses to questions like 'How are you?' or, in this case, 'How are things going?' We assume that the questioner is not really interested in how we feel and offer formal replies like 'fine' or 'all right'. Given that the doctor's question at 3 can be heard as 'doing greeting', Barry is provided with no voice with which to speak — other than as a competent member who knows how to return greetings.

Barry's next chance to speak comes after utterance 8. Once more, however, what the doctor says tends to silence him. First, enquiries about the character of a 'scar line' and of 'stitch marks' may be heard to fall within clinical discourse. If so, Barry, who has had no opportunity to learn that code nor to apply it to a range of cases, can have no basis for replying. Even if other readings of what the doctor is saying are available to him (as perhaps is also the case at 3), the availability of the reading I am suggesting serves to create uncertainty about the 'voice' with which he could answer.

The second way in which the doctor's questions tend to silence Barry is by their appeal to the topic of his 'thoughts' about his looks. Now, in English culture, in most circumstances, subjects, especially male subjects, are not supposed to voice thoughts about their looks. The doctor is thus asking Barry to enter into a discourse with a very problematic grammar. Barry's non-committal utterance, after a pause at 9, is, therefore, the response of a subject placed at the margins of a clinical discourse and with an uncertain relationship to a discourse of looks. What Barry says at 9 is properly seen not as a reflection of Barry's state of mind, but as the predictable minimal response of a marginalised subject.

However, the doctor at 10 and 12 insists on treating Barry's response as an indication of the (contented) state of mind of a rational consumer ('the customer' of utterance 12). There is little evidence that this is strategic behaviour designed to guard against surgery — after all, the doctor throughout (especially at 8) indicates that he is quite prepared to contemplate a cosmetic operation. Instead, the misunderstanding seems firmly rooted in the way in which clinical or consumerist discourse can silence or marginalise the subjects at which they are directed. It is noticeable that, at 13, Barry makes his first positive statement by breaking into the doctor's summary of the situation and then refusing to respond in terms of the vocabulary of 'scar lines', 'stitch marks' or 'looks'.

By way of conclusion, it is worth emphasising three points that take us back to the theme of the reality of social organisation that I have been addressing in this section. First, what Bhaskar calls 'a necessary condition' for this consultation are the structural and linguistic codes I have been describing. Equally, these need to be reproduced and can be transformed in such face-to-face interactions. Second, it would be romantic to assume that if only such codes were swept away, then we would enter an era of free will. There is no 'real' Barry waiting to emerge. Barry can only be a socially constituted subject, defined in a process which, as Althusser points out, began at his christening. But third, against Bhaskar, it is just as romantic to assume that new or revolutionary codes in themselves can initiate an era of freedom. This is the revolutionary delusion which has been effectively undercut by post-revolutionary 'terror' and/or by coercion under new names ('people's courts' and so on). As Foucault's analysis of sexuality implies, change — and with it the prospect of a measure of freedom — does not arise in new or virgin codes but in a re-articulation of the codes in which real subjects are constituted. This is an argument developed at length in Chapter 3. For the moment, I turn to another presumed theorist of 'subjectivity' — Max Weber.

WEBER AND 'CULTURE'

One of the great *canards* of sociology is the statement that, while Durkheim was concerned with 'society', Weber's unit of analysis was the 'individual'. The evidence for this statement appears to be fourfold:

1. Weber is concerned with meaning, and the meaning of situations is defined by individuals.
2. Weber's hypothetical types of action seem to refer to rational and non-rational forms of individual action in ways similar to political economy.
3. His most acclaimed work, *The Protestant Ethic and The Spirit of Capitalism*, discusses the writings of individuals, like Luther and Calvin.
4. Weber implies that, while the conduct of research should be governed by 'scientific' standards, the choice of research topics and a view of their implications is left to individuals.

Each of these statements is seriously *misleading*. There is no necessary analytic or logical link between meaning and the individual. While it is true that psychologists find it useful to make such a link, sociologists are inclined to see the source of meaning in social structures — what Durkheim calls 'collective representations' and what Weber calls 'culture'. Second, Weber produces hypothetical types of *social* action. This is because he is always concerned not with an individualistic account to motives but with understanding action defined by cultural forms and based on the actor's taking account of others. Third, like Marx and Althusser, Weber refuses to take the point of view of the individual. In *The Protestant Ethic . . .* he is concerned, like them, with the economic and social construction of modern ideas of the individual. Finally, Weber implies that, in choosing research topics and assessing their implications, the social scientist is governed by the cultural ethos in which he lives. It is not insignificant that *The Protestant Ethic* begins by attributing a concern with this problem to Weber as 'a *product* of European civilisation'. So while Weber himself undoubtedly had an individualistic or 'decisionistic' (Marcuse) ethic (another way of putting this is to say that he was an old-fashioned liberal), this only encouraged him to stress the kind of *cultural* analysis which alone could reveal the modern fate of the individual.

Weber encourages a variety of sociological analysis which is primarily concerned with cultural forms. Like Durkheim, he seeks an identification of causes and an establishment of regularities. He differs from Durkheim's confident positivism only in his commitment to a pessimistic, German, neo-Kantian and part Nietzschean tradition which relativises the claims of science, adopts ideal-type concepts on a purely pragmatic basis, and is predisposed to cultural despair rather than

Durkheim's social engineering.

Using Weber's 1904 essay on ' "Objectivity" in Social Science and Social Policy' (Weber 1949), let us briefly establish four central elements of Weber's method.

The identification of 'meaning' and 'culture'

Weber wants initially to distinguish the social or cultural sciences from the natural sciences. First, there is the question of the understanding of meaning:

> in the social sciences we are concerned with psychological and intellectual phenomena the empathic understanding of which is naturally a problem of a specifically different type from those which the schemes of the exact natural sciences can or seek to solve. (Weber 1949:74)

Second, meaning and other factors combine to constitute 'a cultural phenomenon'. Finally, such a cultural 'configuration' is identified through its cultural and historical significance to 'us' as members of a culture

Meaning and cause

Analysis of meaning in no way precludes causal analysis. As Weber shows, each goes hand in hand:

> We wish to understand on the one hand the relationships and the *cultural* significance of individual events in their contemporary manifestations and on the other the *causes* of their being historically so and not otherwise. (ibid.: 72; my emphasis)

Weber gives an example of what he means by looking at the explanation of a 'money economy':

> The *cultural significance* of a phenomenon, e.g. the significance of exchange in a money economy, can be the fact that it exists on a mass scale as a fundamental component of modern culture. But the historical fact that it plays this role must be causally explained in order to render its cultural significance understandable. (ibid.: 77)

The search for regularities

Despite his initial distinction between the natural and cultural sciences, Weber emphasises also their points of contact. Apart from pure mechanics, he suggests that the exact natural sciences use qualitative as well as purely quantitative categories (ibid.: 74). Again, although social science is not concerned with 'laws' in the narrow natural science sense, it is concerned with establishing 'rules' and 'regularities' not as ends in themselves but as a way of establishing knowledge (ibid.: 80). The only way in which we can perceive social science as non-scientific is if we fail to understand the real character of scientific procedure in the natural sciences or fail to recognise the constraints (and advantages) created by the special kind of data with which the social scientist is concerned:

> In the cultural sciences, the knowledge of the universal or general is never valuable in itself. . . . An 'objective' analysis of cultural events, which proceeds according to the thesis that the ideal of science is the reduction of empirical reality [to] 'laws' is meaningless. It is not meaningless, as is often maintained, because cultural or psychic events for instance are 'objectively' less governed by laws. It is meaningless for a number of other reasons. Firstly, because the knowledge of social laws is not knowledge of social reality but is rather one of the various aids used by our minds for attaining this end; secondly, because knowledge of *cultural* events is inconceivable except on a basis of the *significance* which the concrete constellations of reality have for us. (ibid.: 80)

The use of ideal-type constructs

In order to understand cultural reality, Weber recommends the deployment of concepts based on the synthesis of many concrete individual cases and their accentuation into a unified analytical construct. This ideal-type construct, Weber adds, should logically fit together and pay proper attention to the meanings attached by actors in the situations represented. Ideal-types, like money economy or bureaucracy, have no moral connotation. They are research instruments which offer a horizon with which to analyse or 'confront' (ibid.: 110) empirical reality. Unlike Durkheim's 'conclusive definitions', they are working models, drawing attention to both structural and cultural regularities.

I now take up some contemporary judgements about the relevance of a Weberian emphasis on culture for research strategies in sociology.

Hermeneutics and realism

We have already encountered Bhaskar's appropriation of Durkheim's position to what he calls realism. In some way and, in my view, equally successfully, Bhaskar appropriates a sociology of meaning (in his terms hermeneutics, or the analysis of interpretations).

Bhaskar (1979) at once acknowledges three points of agreement with Weber's position. First, sociology deals with a reality which is already pre-interpreted by its members. Second, this defines how it is to grasp that reality. Sociology needs to interpret the meanings of social phenomena. This is because the sociologist exists in a subject–subject relation with what (s)he studies (unlike the subject–object relation of the natural scientist). Finally, interpretive sociologists, in Bhaskar's view, are wholly right to criticise positivist doctrines which imply that there is a single logic for all sciences whatever their subject-matter.

However, before any further implications can be drawn, Bhaskar reminds us of four relevant considerations:

(i) The natural sciences are *not* positivistic. They recognise that observation is theory-impregnated (Popper) and that knowledge is socially organised (Kuhn). They tend not to be deterministic — they deal with structures which set limits but do not determine what happens.

(ii) There is no need to limit explanations to actors' own understandings. Just because laws are inappropriate to the social world, does not mean that we have to be completely voluntarist:

> In given circumstances and considered in relation to their peculiar mode or operation, social structures can be just as 'coercive' as natural laws. . . . Conversely just as rules can be broken, so natural tendencies may fail to be realised. (Bhaskar 1979: 26)

(iii) Social structures (and their coercive effects) may be opaque to actors themselves.

(iv) To argue that social structures should always be reducible to the motives of individuals is a nonsense. Social contexts always give meaning to action and provide some of its consequences. Such contexts are not reducible to the perceptions of actors.

Apart from this fourth point, Weber would be fully in accord with Bhaskar's reasoning. He would also have agreed with Bhaskar's conclusion that: 'Human sciences can be *sciences* in exactly the same sense, though not in exactly the same way as the natural ones' (ibid.: 203). Not in the same way, because there *is* a difference from the natural sciences over what is to be explained (meanings as well as purely external regularities) and over the procedures to be used to establish explanations (interpretation as well as causal analysis). None the less, the *principles* governing the production of these explanations are substantially the same: 'because social objects are irreducible to natural objects and so possess qualitatively different features from them, they cannot be studied in the same way as them . . . they can still be studied 'scientifically' (ibid.: 26).

The problematic status of members' validation
Even though social structures may be opaque to the actors (or collectivity members), the value of an interpretivist perspective is that it draws attention to members' own understandings as a first-order topic for sociological investigation. This does offer a clear departure from the Durkheimian problematic. However, as we shall see in the next two sections, this can generate problems as well as insights. The first problem arises over validation of a sociological account.

Bloor (1983) has pointed out that a method of validation in the natural sciences is replication of an initial experiment by a second investigator. Since such experimental settings are rare in social science, a common claim made by sociologists of an interpretivist bent is that an analysis can be validated by the very members described, i.e. by demonstrating 'a correspondence . . . between the investigator's description and the descriptions of members of the collectivity that is being investigated' (Bloor 1983: 156).

Bloor points out that researchers' and members' accounts cannot be directly juxtaposed. Following Schutz, second-order sociological accounts will have an analytic purpose that may be irrelevant to members' first-order concerns. Instead of relying on direct comparison of these two accounts, the aim is to discover whether members understand and accept the researcher's account. Four techniques of such member validation are noted by Bloor:

(i) The attempted prediction of members' descriptions in actual field settings (e.g. how they would diagnose disease in a particular case).

(ii) The attempted prediction of members' reactions to hypothetical cases constructed by the observer.

(iii) The attempt by the researcher to 'pass' as a member in a particular setting or situation.

(iv) Seeing whether 'collectivity members recognise and endorse the sociologist's account of their social world' (ibid.: 157).

This last technique is explained further by Bloor:

> In effect, the member is asked to judge whether or not he or she recognises the sociologist's account as a legitimate elaboration and systematisation of the member's accounts. The member judges whether or not the sociologist's account seems familiar in that it refers to, and originates in, elements similar to those in the member's stock of commonsense knowledge. (ibid.: 157)

Using his own research experience, Bloor shows that this kind of member validation exercise involves many problems. These include: members' understandable lack of interest in a sociologist's research topic, their unwillingness to voice disagreements and their preference for consensus, the artificial character of interviews with members on such topics, and, finally 'the occasioned and temporally bounded nature of the validation exercise . . . [when members' views are not] invariant [but are] provisional, contingent and subject to change over time' (ibid.: 164). Bloor concludes that members' responses to research findings, however generated, are 'not immaculately produced but rather are shaped and constrained by the circumstances of their production' (ibid.: 171). Two things follow:

(i) 'Members' pronouncements on findings cannot be treated as a test of validity.'

(ii) None the less, 'a member validation exercise can generate material that is highly pertinent to the researcher's analysis' (ibid.: 172). This is achieved by treating the additional material 'not as a test [but] as data' (ibid.).

Bloor's discussion is a helpful rebuttal to over-eager proponents of the interpretive method. It reaffirms Bhaskar's point that, while lay understandings are crucial to sociological analysis, they cannot define its character or establish its validity.

The problematic status of members' beliefs

Treating members' accounts as data is Bloor's neat solution to the problem of the status of members' validation of research findings. However, it glosses over another, more important, question. What kind of data are members' accounts? How do such accounts stand relative to sociological accounts? What does it mean to say that members' accounts form the basis of sociological analysis?

Not surprisingly, the majority of such queries have been raised by Durkheimian or structuralist sociologists who could not be expected to be sympathetic to an interpretive sociology. A more interesting critique of the appeal to members' accounts has, however, come from the 'inside'. As a cognitive anthropologist, Michael Moerman was interested in learning the categorisation systems employed by natives in a particular culture. However, in studying a South-East Asian tribe, the Lue, he was troubled about what sense to read in natives' accounts. First, his questions related to many issues which were, from the natives' points of view, obvious, or non-existent. This suggests a problem of generalisation: 'To the extent that answering an ethnographer's question is an unusual situation for natives, one cannot reason from a native's answer to his *normal* categories or ascriptions' (Moerman 1974:66; my emphasis). Second, even when the ethnographer is silent and merely observes, his presence indicates to natives that matters relevant to culture should be highlighted. Consequently, people pay particular attention to what both he and they take to be relevant categorisation schemes — like ethnic or kinship labels. In this way, he may have 'altered the local priorities among the native category sets which it is his task to describe' (ibid.: 67).

However, there is more than a question of bias in presenting natives' accounts at work here. Even if the ethnographer 'correctly' grasps the native categorisation systems, can (s)he stop short at a description of it? Many ethnographers would answer in the negative and appeal to the conceptual apparatus which they use to fashion their second-order accounts. However, Moerman points out that anthropological theories and concepts are, in a certain sense, the very stuff of native conversation. Take the concept of culture change by 'cultural diffusion'. Moerman found that the Lue discussed this issue between themselves; it was, as he puts it, 'an old [Lue] wives' tale' (ibid.: 60–1). Equally, the ethnographer's favourite dichotomies between hill and lowland and civilised and primitive peoples are a South-East Asian commonplace. Consequently, his second-order analysis is merely a first-order analysis dressed up:

> Folk beliefs have honorable status but they are not the same intellectual object as a scientific analysis. The tribal–civilized or hill–plains dichotomy in South-East Asia is not an analysis or explanation of behavior. It is a native notion, for us anthropologists to analyse and not merely repeat as if it were our own discovery. The dichotomy is not an answer to the complexities of South-East Asian ethnology, but a problematic cultural phenomenon for us to investigate. (ibid.: 55)

The reader may be interested to learn that when the first sentence of this quotation was used recently in an undergraduate examination, the students almost entirely identified its author as a Durkheimian. Yet Moerman writes as an ethnomethodologist. Once again, we see parallels between the two positions that the earlier discussion of suicide research implied. None the less, Moerman, like Atkinson, is unwilling to go the whole way with the Durkheimian tradition and to ask questions, for instance, about the 'functions' of ethnic identification devices for social integration.

What research issues *does* Moerman establish? A clue is given by the initially opaque sub-headings of his article: 'Who are the Lue? Why are the Lue? When are the Lue?' To ask who are the Lue is fundamentally mistaken for three reasons. First, it would generate an inventory of traits. Like all lists it could be endless. The anthropologist could always, therefore, be accused of having left something out. Second, lists are retrospective. Once we have decided that the Lue are a tribe, then we have no difficulty in 'discovering' a list of traits to support our case. Finally, to identify the Lue is dependent, in part, on their successful presentation of themselves as a tribe. This, rather than 'Who are the Lue?' is, Moerman suggests, the proper topic for investigation. As he puts it: 'The question in not "Who are the Lue?" but rather when and how and why the identification "Lue" is preferred' (ibid.: 62). He adds that this does *not* mean that the Lue are not really a tribe or that they fooled him into thinking they were one. Rather their identity arises in the fact that people in the area use ethnic identification labels when they talk about other people.

Moerman's critique of anthropology provides him with his own research topic:

> 'Anthropology [has an] apparent inability to distinguish between warm . . . human bodies and one kind of identification device which some of those bodies sometimes use. Ethnic identification devices — with their important potential of making each ethnic set of living persons a joint enterprise with countless

generations of unexamined history — seem to be universal. Social scientists should therefore describe and analyse the ways in which they are used, and not merely — as natives do — use them as explanations. (ibid.: 67–8)

Moerman's research topic — the universal forms of social interaction — represents the current direction in which ethnomethodology, via conversational analysis, is currently heading. It has important links with contemporary theories like structuralism and Chomskyian linguistics. Although clearly not the only direction in which interpretive sociology can head, Moerman's critique emphasises that Weber's path of 'understanding meanings' (*verstehen*) should not terminate in empty reportage dressed up in professional language. The social world is no more reducible to members' meanings that it is reducible to purely objective structures.

SOCIOLOGY AND THE SUBJECT/OBJECT DISTINCTION

How was it that sociology over the last half-century became so obsessed with the opposition between meaningful subjects and the objective power of social structures? By introducing Foucault's work, I can sketch out an answer to this question, while, in accord with the purpose of this text, suggesting research issues which it, in turn, generates.

The first point to clarify is that before there could be a distinction between subject and object, the 'subject' would have to emerge on the historical stage. Today, we are so immersed in a vocabulary of the subject that we may forget the vast social and economic changes in Western Europe that ushered in the age of what Marx calls 'the isolated and free individual'. In the *Grundrisse*, written during the winter of 1857–58, Marx shows how such a notion arose with the dissolution of feudalism and the emergence of new forces and relations of production. This was associated with new theories of political economy at the end of the eighteenth century. By proposing a society of 'free competition', these appeared to detach people from their social bonds. Marx comments on the irony of this emphasis on the individual in a society dependent upon social production:

> Only in the eighteenth century, in 'civil society' do the various forms of social connectedness confront the individual as mere means towards his private purposes, as external necessity. But the epoch which produces this standpoint, that of the isolated *individual,* is also precisely that of the hitherto most developed *social* . . . relations. (Marx 1973:84; my emphasis)

At this time, the subject was emerging within philosophy as well as political economy. At the end of the seventeenth century, Locke's theory of the social contract had replaced feudal political obligations with a contract between free individuals able to accumulate and dispose of their

48

property (including their own labour). However, as Locke himself recognised, these new theories challenged the secure status of knowledge as well as of existing political structures. If 'subjects' stood between nature and truth, then we could no longer be sure about the standing of philosophical or scientific truths. There thus arose a crisis of representation. As Dreyfus and Rabinow (1982) point out, this theme is emphasised in Foucault's early work. In *The Order of Things* (1970), Foucault analyses an eighteenth-century painting of an artist looking at his canvas in order to reveal the newly problematic theme of a world mediated by practices of representation located in human subjects.

Dreyfus and Rabinow go on to show how, in Foucault's later work, the polarity between subject and object is no longer simply related to aesthetic or philosophical discourses but is firmly rooted in the social practices through which subjects are positioned. His *History of Sexuality* (1979) reveals how we are constructed as self-conscious sexual *subjects*. In *Discipline and Punish* (1977), we become *objects* of surveillance by ostensibly benevolent legal and penal institutions. The figure of the confessional (redefined as the psychiatrist's couch) expresses this subjectivity; the picture of Bentham's 'panopticon' (the humanised prison where everything was open to view) expresses objectivity.

Foucault's achievement is to reveal how the supposedly liberating social sciences have been hand-maidens in this exercise. At one and the same time, as Dreyfus and Rabinow put it, the human object, disciplined by surveillance, has been systematised by structuralism. Similarly, the human subject, constructed by sexual (and other) discourses, has been explicated by interpretive approaches. There is no hint of conspiracy here or elsewhere in Foucault's work. There is just the establishment of links and the exchange of resources at multiple, dispersed sites across the academic/political divide.

Foucault rids us of the illusion that our theoretical battles are carried on apart from society. He reminds us that whichever side of such polarities we choose, we remain on the side of the forces of power/knowledge. Even if it is illusory to suppose that knowledge stands in any one-to-one relation to freedom, Foucault's work at least encourages us to move away from the polarities of sterile academic debates and towards the world in which such polarities are routinely, and seemingly inexorably, deployed.

FURTHER READING
The realist position adopted in the early part is clearly presented by Bhaskar (1979). Durkheim's essays, published as *Sociology and Philosophy* (1974), provide a valuable opportunity to see him responding to his contemporary critics. For a further discussion of contemporary sociological accounts of suicide see Cuff and Payne (eds) (1979). The construction of

subjects as 'voices' in communication is examined in Silverman and Torode (1980), especially Chapters 1-2.

Foucault's work is discussed at greater length in Chapter 4, pp. 82-91. The issue of the historical origins of modern individualism is a matter of contemporary debate between MacPherson (1962) and Macfarlane (1978).

3 The articulation of elements: the parts and the whole

Language is a system of interdependent terms in which the value of each term results solely from the simultaneous presence of the others. (Saussure 1974: 114)

A thinker is very much like a draughtsman whose aim is to represent the interrelations between things. (Wittgenstein 1980: 12)

In this chapter, I seek to outline a way of reasoning which, I believe, is equally applicable to such diverse topics as the micro sociology of the classroom and the macro sociology of inter-war Fascism. Given this diversity, the structure of what follows differs somewhat from other chapters in both organisation and substance. First, there is more extended discussion of a few helpful research studies. Second, my analysis happens to take me much more directly towards political themes than elsewhere, except in Chapter 9. I make no apology for this and would merely remind the reader of the interconnectedness of sociological and social perspectives noted in the conclusion of the last chapter.

INTRODUCTION: THE ISSUE OF STRUCTURE

Paul Atkinson (1981) has written about the illusion of security that tape-recorded data can give. It is tempting to feel that, once the data have been transcribed, the battle has almost been won. However, he adds, inexperienced observers who believe this are likely to experience 'profound disappointment'. He goes on:

They often expect, if only at a subconscious level, to 'find' educational, sociological or psychological concepts staring them in the face or leaping out at them from the data. It is a common enough misconception to expect to stumble across 'authoritarianism', 'social control', or whatever, and to be disappointed — even to feel betrayed — when such things are not given to direct observation. (1981: 101)

What mistake are such observers making? First, as Atkinson points out, they have probably tended to assume that the material speaks for itself. Consequently, they may have rushed at the analysis and failed to stand back in order to allow what appears obvious to become problematic or, in Garfinkel's (1967) words, 'anthropologically strange'. Second, they may have imposed an interpretive framework and treated the talk as a mere expression of sociological concepts. But the talk is itself socially organised. Using an example of a classroom, Atkinson once again makes the point: 'there are long strings of talk in which each utterance, by either teacher or pupil, displays some sort of relevance to the preceding utterance: the talk is not made up of random utterances, and the participants do not just pursue their own line of talk with no reference to that of any other participant' (Atkinson 1981: 102–3)

Atkinson is saying that talk does not consist of isolated units or 'random utterances' but has a structure. Following Garfinkel, he implies that this structure is organised by the speakers themselves as they attend to such issues as the sequential organisation and topical coherence of their turns at speaking. However, the preference for analysis of talk in terms of structures is not the prerogative of ethnomethodologists. Michael Stubbs (1981), for instance, from a more conventional linguistics perspective, has argued against the *ad hoc* or unprincipled selection of linguistic units to analyse (like pronouns or questions). Instead of directly reading off social–psychological or sociological categories from such units, Stubbs believes that we need to relate them to the linguistic and sociolinguistic structures in which they are located.

Atkinson and Stubbs share a position which is central to the argument proposed in this chapter. To say that talk is socially organised or has a linguistic structure is to imply that analysis can never begin with a single unit or element. Instead, it must always be concerned with how such elements are organised or articulated.

A simple example may convey the point. For some years, many women have refused to identify themselves as 'Mrs' or 'Miss' and have used the title of 'Ms'. Considered as isolated units, there is, of course, nothing wrong with the title 'Mrs' or 'Miss', both are in common usage and both express clearly identifiable concepts. The problem resides not in the units themselves but in the system of identifying people of which they are a part. Within this system, there is a gender difference which arises at two levels. Men and women are differently identified. But while there are two terms for women ('Mrs' or 'Miss'), there is only one term for men (we exclude other terms, like 'Doctor' which may apply to both men and women or 'Lord' and 'Lady' which are single, gender-specific alternatives). These two terms allow women to be distinguished by their marital status. There is no way of similarly distinguishing men. Some women, then, object to using 'Mrs' or 'Miss' because it singles them out in terms of their availability on the marriage market. The problem, in short, is not the unit but the system. If there were two terms for men, then the objection to 'Mrs' or 'Miss' would cease, or certainly begin to look very different.

So far, I have been concerned entirely with linguistic examples. However, the concern with the articulation of elements is certainly not confined to analysts of natural language. I next show how an explanation of the vast political event of inter-war Fascism can only properly be developed through a method which identifies the articulation of relevant elements. None the less, the distinction between elements and their articulation does have a linguistic origin even if it has a far wider explanatory power. Consequently, I then explain its origin within the work of the Swiss linguist, Ferdinand de Saussure. Having surveyed Saussure's work, I show its heritage in structuralism and discuss two sets of oppositions which it leaves unresolved. I then return to the theme of politics, examining how the concept of articulation can help explain situations as diverse as the Left's strategies against Fascism and the political appeal of the Conservative Party in the 1983 British general election. I conclude by returning, via the work of Hugh Mehan, to the issue with which we began: explaining the orderly character of talk in the classroom.

THE SUCCESS OF FASCISM

In this section, I rely entirely on Ernesto Laclau's account of 'Fascism and Ideology' which is the long, central essay in his *Politics and Ideology in Marxist Theory* (1977). Following Laclau, I begin by contrasting traditional accounts of the return of Fascism — liberal, Marxist and psychological — with the important argument put forward by Nicos Poulantzas in his *Fascism and Dictatorship* (1974). I then present Laclau's critique of Poulantzas, his own argument about the triumph of Fascism, and his account of the failure of the Left in the 1930s. Finally, I show how Laclau's method of analysis depends precisely upon an understanding of the articulation of elements.

Traditional explanations

Laclau points out how liberal scholars, like Ortega y Gasset and Croce, see Fascism as an enigma, containing contradictory elements. It is an interruption in the normal course of historical development brought about by what Croce sees as a moral sickness. This psychological reduction of Fascism is also favoured by people as far apart as the historian Meinecke (Fascism as a breakdown of psychic balance), and neo-Marxists like Reich (Fascism as an expression of cruel impulses) and Fromm (Fascism as the opposite of love).

Even when such psychology is avoided, Laclau notes how writers have tended to favour reducing Fascism to one simple contradiction. For Hannah Arendt, both Fascism and Communism are dependent, in large part, upon the atomisation of the individual in modern mass society. Coming from an opposite political perspective, the Comintern shared with Arendt a desire to separate Fascism from its particular national contexts. For them, Laclau notes it was simply an expression of the direct dictatorship of monopoly capital over the rest of society.

Poulantzas's argument
Laclau notes how Poulantzas avoids reducing Fascism to a simple contradiction. Instead, he favours viewing it, in Althusserian lánguage, as a complex set of 'over-determined' contradictions. Briefly, Poulantzas uses an economic–political–ideological notion of an 'imperialist chain', implying that Fascism will appeal to the weakest links in the chain. Moreover, politics itself cannot be reduced to clear-cut class interests. Thus, for Poulantzas, Fascism succeeded because of (i) internal conflicts between the bourgeoisie over the control of the state; (ii) an acute ideological crisis of the *petit-bourgeoisie* which disassociated itself from the dominant bourgeois capitalist discourse; and (iii) a failure of the political strategy of the working class through an economistic dependence upon trade unionism and reformism.

Laclau's critique
Despite Poulantzas's rejection of simplistic mono-causal explanations, Laclau argues that his analysis remains reductivist. Poulantzas still assumes that social classes have 'pure' or 'necessary' ideologies. Thus, for him:

> Marxist–Leninist ideology is the ideology of the working class. Liberalism is bourgeois ideology in the stage of competitive capitalism . . . [and] as for the petty-bourgeoisie, since it is not one of the basic classes in social formations dominated by the capitalist mode of production, its ideology can only comprise 'elements' incorporated into the ideological discourse of the dominant class. (Laclau 1977: 94)

One implication of Poulantzas's position is that, since nationalism is an element of bourgeois ideology, it can only function as a tool of the established order. For the Left in Germany or Italy to have taken up a nationalist line could only be, at best, a logical contradiction and, at worst, a concession to the adversary. By seeing ideological elements as class-determined, Poulantzas is forced to treat the articulation of political strategy in terms of a preconceived theoretical scheme.

This account, in terms of theoretically 'right' and 'wrong' political lines, arises from a language which Poulantzas shares with orthodox Communist Party theoreticians. Although presented as the purest '*logic*', it is none the less, as Laclau shows, an entirely *arbitrary* interpretative framework:

the process of pronouncing the class belonging of elements of class ideologies is a purely arbitrary one; . . . it not only fails to theoretically construct its object but, on the contrary, *presupposes* empirical knowledge of it, and operates taxonomically on that knowledge. (ibid.: 97)

For instance, we have seen that Poulantzas treats 'liberalism' as, in modern times, the ideology of the bourgeoisie. Yet, as Laclau points out, in Latin America it was 'the characteristic ideology of the feudal land-owners' (ibid.: 98). We cannot *presuppose* the essential character of any ideological element, like liberalism. Elements have no *essential* meaning. Their meaning only arises in the way they are articulated with other elements in specific historical situations.

Laclau's analysis of Fascism
We are now in a better position to understand Laclau's own analysis. Fascism was not simply a ruling-class ideology. It involved an intervention into widely-shared popular elements, re-articulating them in a particular direction:

> Fascism, far from being the typical ideological expression of the most conservative and reactionary sectors of the dominant classes was, on the contrary, one of the possible ways of articulating popular–democratic interpellations [i.e. identities] into political discourse. (ibid.: 111)

From Laclau's rich analysis I shall only pick out two elements: (a) the appeal of Nazi ideology and (b) the failure of the Left in the arena of ideological struggle.

(i) Nazi ideology was successful in Germany, according to Laclau, because it managed to articulate (in its own direction) the prevailing sentiments (or ideological elements). Thus it incorporated *petit-bourgeois* anger against inflation and foreign occupation into a language of race and racial conflict. It retained the working class's language of class but re-articulated it into a national class (i.e. the *German* worker). The class struggle was denied, and a corporativist language, geared to both class and national elements, replaced it. This skilful re-articulation of real sentiments was shown to its best effect in the Nazi takeover of significant historical symbols. Laclau quotes a perceptive comment to this effect by Dmitrov, a communist of the 1930s:

> The Fascists are rummaging through the entire history of every nation so as to be able to pose as the heirs and continuators of all that was exalted or heroic in the past, while all that was degrading or offensive to the national sentiments of the people they make use of as weapons against the enemies of fascism. (ibid.: 139)

(ii) The success of the Nazis was balanced by the failure of the Left which, Laclau shows, 'abandoned the arena of popular–democratic struggle' (ibid.: 124). Although Poulantzas correctly diagnoses the disease in his critiques of the economism of the Left, he fails to explain why the Left was economistic. Laclau's answer to this problem is that economism arises in a perspective which Poulantzas shares with the Left of the 1930s: a tendency to reduce all ideological elements to a class belonging. As he puts it: 'The answer is that socialist political discourse had been structured in such a way that it excluded as a matter of principle its articulation with any interpellation [i.e. identity] which was not a class interpellation' (ibid.: 125). Consequently, the working class had to be separated from popular sentiments, like nationalism, because 'the working class had frequently been mobilised . . . by the populism of bourgeois politicians' (ibid.: 126). The strategy of the Left, therefore, blandly and inexorably, isolated itself from the very identities which were so powerful among workers and non-workers alike. Faced with a national crisis, the German Left (like the British Left in the period 1979–83) preferred sectarianism to getting its hands dirty in the difficult arena of popular sentiments.

The articulation of elements

Laclau's analysis highlights the need to locate ideological elements in relation to their articulation within a particular system: 'ideological elements taken in isolation have no necessary class connotation, and . . . this connotation is only the result of the articulation of these elements in a concrete ideological discourse' (ibid.: 99). How does this articulation take place? or, to put it in Laclau's own terms, 'what comprises the unity of an ideological discourse?' (ibid.: 100)

We may abstract three elements from Laclau's answer to this question:

(i) Following Althusser's theory of the subject (as briefly sketched out in Chapter 2), Laclau suggests that ideological discourse constitutes individuals into subjects who believe that they are acting freely. For instance, Nazism constitutes a 'German' subject by re-articulating nationalist, racist, economic and class themes. The unity of the discourse is expressed in the (constructed) identity of such subjects.

(ii) This unity has nothing to do with logical consistency. Within an articulation, each element comes to evoke another element which becomes treated as an equivalent. So, for instance, within Nazism being a worker = being a German worker = being a racist = being a Nazi.

(iii) Finally, ideological discourses try to incorporate the past and present in order to tell a story which disconnects the articulation forged by other discourses. Each ideology thus has what Laclau calls a particular 'system of narration' (ibid.: 103).

I have used Laclau's analysis of Fascism to reveal important aspects of the method with which this chapter is concerned. In doing so, we have seen Laclau's use of Althusser's theory of the subject. However, both Laclau and Althusser are, in turn, intellectually indebted to an apolitical Swiss linguist who lived in the early years of this century, for it is Saussure's work that allows us to talk in terms of elements, articulation and the constitution of subjects. Consequently, it is to that work that we now turn.

SYSTEMS OF SIGNIFICATION

Much earlier, I discussed Stubbs (1981) criticism of the *ad hoc* selection of linguistic units for study. Before Saussure, however, such an approach was the accepted form of analysis. Linguistics viewed language as an aggregate of units (words), each of which had a separate meaning attached to it. Linguistic research concentrated on historical changes in the meaning of words.

In the early years of this century, Saussure revolutionised this approach. Hawkes (1977) has identified the two crucial aspects of Saussure's reform of linguistic research:

(i) His rejection of a substantive view of language — concerned with the correspondence between individual words and their meanings — in favour of a relational view, stressing the system of relations between words as the source of meaning.

(ii) His shift away from historical or diachronic analysis towards an analysis of language's present functioning (a synchronic analysis). No matter what recent change a language has undergone, it remains, at any given point of time, a complete system. As Hawkes puts it: 'Each language has a wholly valid existence *apart* from its history as a system of sounds issuing from the lips of those who speak it now' (1977: 20).

We can now see how these two distinctions provided the framework for Laclau's analysis of Fascism. A relational view of language shows how nationalism only gets a meaning in relation to other terms — hence the Nazi success in identifying a relation between nationalism and Fascism (e.g. National Socialism). A synchronic analysis implies that terms have no fixed meaning derived from their past use. So, as Laclau shows, liberalism is not essentially a bourgeois ideology (even though it might have that connotation in a particular articulation of elements).

Saussure now makes a distinction between language (*langue*) and speech (*parole*). We need to distinguish the system of language (*langue*) from the actual speech acts (*parole*) that any speaker actually utters. The latter are not determined by language which solely provides the system of elements in terms of which speech occurs. Saussure uses the analogy of a chess game to explain this. The rules and conventions of chess constitute a language (*langue*) within which actual moves (*parole*) take place. For Saussure, the linguist's primary concern is not to describe *parole* but to establish the elements and their rules of combination which together constitute the linguistic system (*langue*).

At this point, the astute reader may recognise a point of conflict between Saussure's emphasis on the linguistic system and Laclau's concern with the actual articulations of elements in Fascism. Doesn't Laclau analyse actual moves in a game (*parole*) much more than its abstract conventions (*langue*)? Of course the answer is yes, and we shall shortly see how this points to a tension in Saussure's work which he left unresolved. But first, I must return to an exposition of Saussure's analytical scheme.

Having identified *langue* as the concern of linguistics, Saussure now notes that language is comparable to other social institutions like systems of writing, symbolic rites and deaf-sign systems. All these institutions are systems of signs and can be studied systematically. Saussure calls such a science of signs semiology (from the Greek *semeion* = 'sign'). Signs have four characteristics:

 (i) They bring together a concept and an image (e.g. 'horse' and a pictorial image — as in a road sign — or a written English word or a spoken English 'sound-image').

 (ii) Signs are not autonomous entities — they derive their meaning only from their place within an articulated system. What constitutes a linguistic* sign is nothing but its differences from other signs (so the colour red is only something which is *not* green, blue, orange, etc.).

(iii) The linguistic sign is arbitrary or unmotivated. This, Saussure says, means that the sign 'has no natural connection with the signified' (Saussure 1974: 69). Different languages simply use different terms for concepts. Indeed they can generate their own concepts — for instance, the multiple words that Eskimos have for describing different kinds of snow.

(iv) Signs can be put together through two main paths. First, there are combinational possibilities (e.g. the order of courses that constitute a meal, or the prefixes and suffixes that can be attached to a noun — for example, 'friend' can become 'boyfriend' 'friendship',

---

*I say a *linguistic* sign because certain pictorial images *may* actually picture an object rather than signal it. Compare two road signs: one pictures a level crossing, the other signals 'danger' by an exclamation mark in a circle.

'friendly',etc.). Saussure calls these patterns of combination *syntagmatic* relations. Second, there are contrastive properties (e.g. choosing between dishes on a particular course; saying 'yes' or 'no'). Here the choice of one term necessarily excludes the other. Saussure calls these mutually-exclusive relations *paradigmatic* oppositions.

An example may help to pull these various features of signs together. Think of traffic-lights: (i) they bring together concepts ('stop', 'start') with images ('red', 'green'); (ii) these images are not autonomous: red is identifiable by the fact that it is not green, and vice versa; (iii) they have no natural connection with what they signify: red has simply come to mean 'stop' and green to mean 'start'; finally (iv) they express syntagmatic relations (the order in which the traffic-lights can change: from red to green and back again but much more complicated in the UK where there is also an amber). They also express paradigmatic oppositions: imagine the chaos created if red and green light up simultaneously!

For Saussure, then, as Culler (1976) has pointed out, no meaning can ever reside in a single term. Linguistics thus shares with economics a concern with the relation of elements in a system. Both disciplines, as Barthes has noted, are primarily concerned not with 'essential' meanings but with 'value.'

> From the point of view of the language, the sign is like a coin which has the value of a certain amount of goods which it allows one to buy, but also has value in relation to other coins, in a greater or lesser degree. (Barthes 1967: 14)

In order to explain this relation of signification and value, Saussure uses the analogy of a sheet of paper. If we cut the sheet into shapes, each has a value in relation to its neighbour. Each also has a front and a back cut out at the same time but which may appear differently according to which side we lay them on. As Barthes suggests, this moves us away from Saussure's original notion of a fixed relation between a concept and an image towards an interest in human or social practices of fixing (or 'cutting out') meaning:

> language is the domain of *articulations* and meaning is above all a cutting-out of shapes. It follows that the future task of semiology is far less to establish lexicons of objects than to rediscover the articulations which men impose on reality. (ibid.: 57)

Barthes' concern with articulation takes us back to the main theme of this chapter and forward to an analysis of some of the hidden tensions in Saussure's semiological project. But, first I want to refer briefly to some examples of the structuralist project which Saussure inspired.

THE STRUCTURALIST PROJECT

Saussure's model of a synchronic science of signs, concerned with the forms of articulation which give meaning to elements or units, was the inspiration for modern structuralism. Its point of departure from other approaches is its focus on the combinational possibilities of signs and their contrastive properties, i.e. syntagmatic relations and paradigmatic oppositions.

Structuralism has been much criticised for its supposedly 'anti-humanist' stance. This criticism has arisen because structuralists refuse to give any explanatory weight to human intention. We can now see that the reason for this is quite clear. Following Saussure, structuralists refuse to privilege any unit in a particular sign system. Naturally, this must include man. Indeed, following Benveniste and Althusser, I showed in Chapter 2, how the human subject is constructed within such a system. This does not mean that structuralists are opposed to human freedom or believe that people may never change their conditions. It does mean that we have to understand the precise articulation of units like the 'subject' and 'intention' within particular signifying systems and to avoid *a priori* formulations depending on versions of the 'essential' features of human beings and their intentional life.

Now we have already encountered, in Chapter 1, an elegant expression of structuralist work in Mary Douglas's debate with Lévi-Strauss about the nature and function of entities which mediate between what we can now call paradigmatic oppositions. However, it would be wrong to assume that the structuralist impulse has limited itself to anthropological data. The reader may recall that the third of Laclau's methods for identifying an ideological discourse arose in how it told a story in order to disconnect the articulations forged by other discourses. This involves what Laclau calls a particular 'system of narration' (1977: 103). The organisation of such systems of narration, within literature and elsewhere, has been a constant interest of structuralists. I shall briefly discuss V.I. Propp's study of the *Morphology of the Folktale*, written in Russia in 1928 (Propp 1968) and its subsequent development by the French sociologist A.J. Greimas (1966).*

Propp argues that the fairytale establishes a narrative form which is central to all story-telling. The fairytale is structured not by the nature of the characters that appear in it, but by the function they play in the plot. Despite its great detail and many characters, Propp suggests that 'the number of functions is extremely small' (1968: 20). This allows him to

---

*I am here indebted to Terence Hawkes's discussion in his book *Structuralism and Semiotics* (1977).

attend to a favourite distinction of structuralists between appearances (massive detail and complexity) and reality (a simple underlying structure repeated in different ways).

Propp's analysis suggests that *all* fairytales share the same form: they consist of 31 'functions' (actions like 'prohibition' or 'violation') in an identical sequence. These functions are played out in seven 'spheres of action': the villain, the provider, the helper, the princess and her father, the despatcher, the hero and the false hero. Although any one character may be involved in any sphere of action, and several characters may be involved in the same sphere, we are dealing with a *finite* sequence: 'the important thing to notice is that the *number* of spheres of action occurring in the fairytale is finite: we are dealing with discernible and repeated *structures*' (Hawkes 1977: 69).

Writing in 1960, Greimas agrees with Propp about the need to locate narrative form in a finite number of elements disposed in a finite number of ways. However, following Barthes' reading of Saussure, he argues that the articulations between the elements rather than the elements themselves are primary. He shows these articulations within narratives in two ways:

(i) Propp's list of seven spheres of action can be reduced into three sets of structural relations: subject versus object (this subsumes 'hero' and 'princess' or 'sought-for person'); sender versus receiver (includes 'father' and 'despatcher'); and helper versus opponent (includes 'donor', 'helper' and 'villain'). As Hawkes shows, this reveals the simple structure of many love stories, i.e. involving relations between both subjects and objects and receivers and senders.

(ii) Propp's 31 functions may be considerably reduced if one examines how they combine together. For instance, although Propp separates 'prohibition' and 'violation', Greimas shows that a 'violation' presumes *a priori* prohibition. Hence they may be combined in one function: 'prohibition versus violation'. Hawkes points out that this allows Greimas to isolate several distinctive structures of the folk narrative. These include: contractual structures (relating to establishing and breaking contracts); performative structures (involving trials and struggles); and disjunctive structures (involving movement, leaving, arriving, etc.).

This summary presentation of the work of Propp and Greimas has underlined two useful arguments. First, the structuralist method can be an important aid to what C. Wright Mills called 'the sociological imagination'. It reminds us that 'meaning never resides in a single term' (Culler 1976) and consequently that understanding the articulation of elements is our primary task. Second, more specifically, it shows some aspects of how narrative structure works. When one reflects how much of sociological data (interviews, documents, conversations) takes a narrative form, as indeed do sociological reports themselves, then the analysis of the fairy-tale stops to look like an odd literary pursuit. I take up this second argument in the discussion of ethnography in Chapter 5. For the moment, we must return, as promised, to the hidden tension present in Saussure's work and, consequently, in modern structuralism.

THEORY AND PRACTICE IN SAUSSURE

Curiously, Saussure's work is a combination of authoritarianism and anarchism. Like his contemporary, Durkheim, Saussure argued that social systems, like language, were 'fixed' by society. For both theorists, social (= linguistic) facts were to be recognised by their external and constraining character. Yet, at the same time as indicating this massive constraint imposed by language, Saussure insists on the *arbitrary* character of the sign, thereby appearing to link authoritarianism with pure anarchy. Put another way, for Saussure, signs are natural facts but the link between any item (signifier) and reality (what is signified) is purely arbitrary. In this contest between constraint and freedom, constraint wins out. For although the link between any signifier and its signified is arbitrary, the system of signs is, for Saussure, a socially given, natural fact of life (see Figure 3.1).

Given system
$\left\{ \begin{array}{l} \text{Sign 1:} \quad \text{signifier} \rightarrow \text{signified} \\ \text{Sign 2:} \quad \text{signifier} \rightarrow \text{signified} \\ \text{Sign 3:} \quad \text{signifier} \rightarrow \text{signified} \\ \text{Sign 4:} \quad \text{signifier} \rightarrow \text{signified} \end{array} \right\}$
Related arbitrarily within a given system

Figure 3.1: The dual character of the sign in Saussure

This would appear to leave no room for human practice (hence the humanist critique of structuralism to which I have already referred). However, there is a further element in Saussure's model of the sign which is more hopeful. It will be recalled that item (ii) in the earlier presentation of his concept of the sign stated that signs are not autonomous — they derive their meaning only from their relations with and differences from other signs. This implies that the meaning of signs cannot be finally fixed. It is always possible to extend the signifying chain.

Two examples may help to explain this. Colours, as already noted, are constituted by their differences. Hence red is not orange (or any other colour). Now think of the way in which some great artists use pallettes which make us rethink the way in which particular colours stand in relation to others. So although the spectrum of colours is fixed, the relation between particular colours can be endlessly re-articulated. This process is, however, not limited to aesthetics. We have already seen the signifying power of linking nationalism with socialism in the context of twentieth-century Fascism. But this re-articulation of signs extends to much more mundane political practices. Think of the symbolic potential of two examples from the 1980s: 'People's Airline' (flying = everybody's right) and, from an attempt by the Greater London Council to gain support for its cheap fares policy, 'Fares Fair' (payment : equality). These examples reflect only some of the myriad connections that have been made between these elements: compare 'People's Airline' with 'People's Republic'. The connotation of such articulations and their popular success are entirely dependent on the particular historical and cultural context in which they are deployed. However, they emphasise that Saussure's concept of the sign does allow an understanding of (political, aesthetic) practice consisting of a struggle over the articulation of the relation between elements.

Let me summarise the argument so far about the link between practice and the sign:*

(i) The relation between signs has no unity defined from the outside (say by the 'economy' or 'history'). Instead there are likely to be various practical attempts at unification.

(ii) There is thus no originary point which is the source of signs ('society', say, or 'nature'). Although some connections or insulations between signs may reflect the hidden needs of a social order (think of Mary Douglas's (1975) attempt to link exchange relations and response to anomaly), it would be wrong to assume that signifying systems as a whole have some general overall pattern. As Wittgenstein (1968) has noted, meaning usually arises in *use*.

(iii) However, this does not mean that there is no relation between signs. The only arbitrary aspect of the sign is the relation of signifier to signified. Without *some* fixing, the sign would not exist.

(iv) But no sign is totally fixed. Politics is not an expression of the 'hidden' movement of history (or of anything else). It is concerned with the articulation and disarticulation of the ensemble of signs and sign-systems (or discourses).

'POLITICS AS THE CONSTRUCTION OF THE UNTHINKABLE'

In this section, whose title is taken from a paper by Laclau (1981), two examples are used to exemplify this version of politics. Laclau (1981) examines some debates between communists over the proper response to Fascism in the 1930s. Moloney (1983) compares the political strategies of

*Here as elsewhere in this chapter I am indebted to the work of Ernesto Laclau.

the British Conservative and Labour Parties during the general elections of 1983 and 1945. Taken together, they provide what I call at the end of this section a *materialist* model of both analysis and practice.

The communist response to Fascism

Laclau (1981) points out that Marxists generally have tended to refer to 'nationalism' and 'patriotism' as part of the ideological superstructure of society. These conceptions have no clear relation to an ideology of class solidarity and hence must be dismissed as 'petty bourgeois deformations', 'class residues', and so on. The trick is to appeal to an extra-discursive causal chain (class structure as revealed by Marxist theory) which reduces nationalism to a reactionary residue. This is illustrated in Figure 3.2.

Figure 3.2: An economistic Marxist interpretation of Nationalism

We have already come across this political line in Laclau's discussion of the 'economism' of the Left in the 1930s. Note how the line implies that certain relations between signs are natural (i.e. nationalism = reactionary), while others are unthinkable (e.g. nationalism = communism). If we reject the economistic assumption that the relation between signs is reducible to an external logic, then this suggests that (i) a political strategy which distinguishes 'natural' and 'unnatural' relations is 'idealist', and (ii) political strategies in general, as I shall show, consist in rendering certain articulations between signs unthinkable.

Laclau provides a good example of the political strategy produced by economism in a quotation from a speech made by Trotsky in 1931. Here Trotsky criticises the nationalist line of the German Communist Party:

> 'As a slogan it [nationalism] displays an inept charlatanism, it enters into a competition in the marketplace with the Fascists, whose only prize is the sowing of confusion in the mind of the worker. . . .
>
> To make the nation capable of being reconstructed round a new class nucleus, it must be ideologically reconstructed and that can only be achieved if the proletariat is not dissolved within the 'people' or within the 'nation' but, on the contrary, develops a programme of *its* proletarian revolution and forces the *petit-bourgeoisie* to choose between the two regimes. (Trotsky, quoted by Laclau 1981: ms. 4–5)

Laclau shows how, in the speech, by criticising the 'marketplace' of ideas, Trotsky presents a picture of the Marxist theorist who shows to the fascist worker that what he believes in ('the people', 'the nation') are only appearances or 'charlatanism'. Consequently, Trotsky never addresses the extent to which nationalism and the subject to whom it appeals are entirely real, constituted in real political situations (like the response to the Treaty of Versailles). In short, Trotsky is asking communists to become educators ('professors of sociology'), teaching fascist workers to dissolve themselves as ideological subjects.

The palpable implausibility of this line was implicitly recognised by those European communist parties who participated in popular fronts during the 1930s and, thereby, involved themselves in the territory of popular symbols. Although out of power and persecuted by the Fascists, the Italian Communist Party, in the tradition of Gramsci, pursued a populist, anti-economistic line. Laclau quotes from an apposite speech made by Togliatti, its General-Secretary, on Radio Moscow in 1941. Note how, in this extract, Togliatti, unlike Trotsky, appeals to subjects in terms of how they currently see themselves. He refers to a nineteenth-century nationalist hero, Balilla, whose name was used on fascist uniforms:

> I would like to say some words to you the young Italians . . . you people who wear a black shirt and a black beret and wear with pride the name of Balilla. I would like to say to you above all that the pride with which you wear that name is fully justified because Balilla is a hero of the Italian people. (Togliatti, quoted by Laclau 1981: ms. 6)

Togliatti goes on to point out that Balilla, in his day, struggled against a foreign power (the Austrians). Therefore, 'young Italians' who wear his name 'with pride' should today also struggle against foreign oppressors (the Germans) and those who support them (Mussolini). In this way Togliatti accepts the material reality of the discourse of nationalism and re-articulates it to construct a new discursive object as shown in Figure 3.3.

Patriotism ≠ Fascism
Patriotism = Opposition to foreign rule =
Opposition to those who ally themselves with foreigners

Figure 3.3: Togliatti's re-articulation of nationalism (Laclau)

Laclau draws two implications from his analysis. First, Togliatti's practice implies that Marxism need *not* be read as defining the 'truth' of society but as 'a site of discursive interventions' (ibid.: ms. 11). Second, and more relevant for our present analytic concerns, political struggle can be analysed as an attempt to create or to deny equivalence between discourses like 'nationalism' 'fascism' and 'socialism'. So,

Togliatti tries to create . . . the unthinkability of the referent 'Fascist and patriot'. Trotsky seeks to do the same for the relation 'Marxism' and 'Socialism in one Country' . . . any discourse is neither innocent nor indifferent to the presence of other discourses: it can only constitute the conditions for the thinkability of certain objects through the construction of the unthinkability of other objects. We can thus speak of discursive intervention, which is to say *politics*, as the process of the construction of the unthinkable. (ibid.: ms. 12–13)

Political strategy in Britain: 1983 and 1945 (Moloney)

Populism is not restricted to the Left. Movements as diverse as the Italian Fascists and the British Conservative Party have successfully used populist strategies. A recent study of Conservative Party texts prior to the 1983 British general election shows how this form of discursive intervention was used with great success. Moloney comments on the consistency of the themes used by Prime Minister Thatcher after the Falklands War of 1982 up to the election one year later: 'These elements are identifiable as follows: the people, the nation, the people's historical/traditional virtues and qualities and . . . freedom as an agency of . . . social unification' (Moloney 1983: ms. 2). Moloney further notes how Thatcher's speeches skilfully create a link between the Conservative Party and the nation. This is achieved through an appeal to their presumed common concern for 'freedom' and articulated through an ambiguous use of the pronoun 'we'. For instance, in a speech at Cheltenham in July 1982, Moloney quotes Thatcher as stating, in the context of the Falklands War: 'We have proved ourselves to ourselves. It is a lesson we must not now forget' (ibid.: ms. 3). Using a simple method of counting the subjects that appear in her text, Moloney also shows how fully two-thirds of such subjects are constituted by reference to the 'nation' or the 'people', almost always in terms of their national or traditional qualities or virtues.

Conversely, references to the opposition Labour Party imply its alien relation to the British people, as in this quote from the General Election campaign:

> I think we have altered the balance between the person and the state in a favourable way and in a way which is much more in keeping with the character of the people of Britain. So that really was a total change of philosophy, away from the all-embracing dominance of socialism. (Thatcher, quoted ibid.: ms. 7)

As Moloney comments, while Conservative policies are equated with 'the character of the people of Britain', the Labour Party is not mentioned. Instead we have the equation shown in Figure 3.4.

$$\text{Labour} = \text{Socialism} \neq \text{British people}$$

Figure 3.4: Thatcher's discourse

Throughout the election campaign, Moloney shows how this theme is maintained. Equating socialism with coercion, Thatcher's speeches successfully construct the Labour Party as 'an increasingly alien and unpatriotic object' (ibid.: ms. 10).

Conversely, Moloney shows how the Labour Party's campaign repeatedly fails to enter the arena of popular symbols. In its Manifesto, for instance, almost four-fifths of the subjects constituted are political objects (e.g. parties, politicians). While two-thirds of the subjects of Thatcher's Cheltenham speech were constituted by reference to the 'nation' or the 'people', these categories account for only 5 per cent of Labour's Manifesto.

By contrast, in its 1945 Manifesto, Labour specifically entered the marketplace of popular symbols. Moloney shows how this was done partly by challenging Churchill's version of freedom as 'abstract'.

'Does freedom for the profiteer mean freedom for the ordinary man and woman?. . . . There are certain so-called freedoms that Labour will not tolerate: freedom to pay poor wages and to push up prices for selfish profit, freedom to deprive the people of the means of living full, happy, healthy lives. (1945 Labour Party Manifesto, quoted ibid.: ms. 11–12)

In this extract, Labour speaks for 'the people' and shows that freedom is many different things. It manages to re-articulate the meaning of freedom and to identify it with the Labour Party.

Of course, it would be foolish to suggest that Labour's success in 1945 and failure in 1983 can wholly or even largely be explained in terms of the character of its discursive interventions, i.e. in purely ideological terms. However, Moloney's study does underline two themes we found in Laclau's treatment of Fascism and the Left. First, political strategies which deny or down-grade popular discourses only succeed in handing over that ideological territory to their opponents. Second, analytic strategies which limit themselves to the documentation of single elements or which conceive of society as a naturalised unit are condemned to ignore the processes of articulation through which social relations and their subjects are reproduced and changed.

The material reality of discourses
In Laclau's terms, in 1945 Labour succeeded in constructing the equivalence between freedom and the Conservative Party as 'unthinkable'. In 1983, the Conservatives silenced any perceived equivalence between patriotism (the 'British people') and Labour. At both elections, the defeated party lost, in part, by failing to take seriously popular discourses. In 1945, the Conservatives spoke, in patrician terms, of maintaining cultural standards (i.e. 'what is splendid and glorious in life and

art' — 1945 Conservative Party Manifesto quoted ibid.: ms. 6). In 1983, Labour largely spoke a language of 'socialist' principle articulated in relations between institutional subjects — the trade unions, the government, and so on. In both cases, the party concerned stayed within its own political language and failed to enter popular discourses. Preferring doctrinal purity to what Trotsky dismissively entitled 'the marketplace', it abandoned the ideological arena to its opponents. At issue here is what I shall call the 'material reality' of discourses. Trotsky, Churchill (in 1945) and the Labour Party (in 1983) shared an *idealist* conception of discourse. They spoke as if it were possible to ignore popular conceptions or to dissolve them through re-education. Consequently, in their own way, each constructed his own language as the medium of instruction, and each, thereby, failed to take seriously the material reality and power of existing popular discourses. Each was inevitably élitist. The only relation they proposed between the politician and the public was that of professor to student. No possibility was provided for a dialogue with subjects constituted in terms of existing discourses (e.g. as family members, as patriots, etc.).

A *materialist* conception of discourse involves a recognition of the power of existing discourses and seeks to understand how these are articulated. A materialist political practice seeks to intervene in these articulations, revealing contradictions and suggesting combinations of elements denied by political opponents. Just as Togliatti turned patriotism against the Fascists, so the contemporary Left, operating on a very different political terrain, can re-articulate patriotic sentiments with popular belief in fair play and pride in national institutions which exemplify it. An example from the British context, based on the populist strategy of 1945 is illustrated in Figure 3.5 below.

Freedom ≠ Freedom for the speculator =
Freedom from want of the old and the sick

Patriotism ≠ High arms spending =
Pride in national institutions which are the envy
of the world (the British National Health Service)

Figure 3.5: A Populist strategy for the Left

Contrary to what rigid Marxists believe, politics is not the pre-defined working-out of a class struggle. It consists of a series of clashes upon particular terrains in which discursive relations are reproduced and challenged. Because particular elements have no significance in themselves, all depends on how they are articulated. Consequently, the most successful political strategy is likely to be the most eclectic, incorporating popular elements from a wider variety of fields. For instance, the original politics of a patriotic hero is irrelevant, as long as (s)he can be incorporated into such a discursive strategy. So, Togliatti could identify his movement with the nationalist Balilla, Margaret Thatcher could appeal to the spirit of Queen Elizabeth I, the Nicaraguan regime to the nationalist Sandino and Neil Kinnock could, in his first speech as Labour Party leader in 1983, call upon the spirit of Winston Churchill to justify his critique of a Conservative government.

CONCLUSION

I began this chapter by looking at the problems of explaining talk in the classroom. We have moved a long way away from that topic since then. But the previous discussion of political discourses has sought to maintain the same theme. Just as classroom talk has a structure which gives meaning to its units, so I have tried to show that politics is not about individual ideas but about their structural organisation, i.e. what I have called, following Laclau, the articulation of the relation between discourses. Equally, Stubbs' (1981) argument against the *ad hoc* selection of linguistic elements is applicable to political strategies which are fixated on a single unit (e.g. internationalism). So the classroom, no less than the political arena, is best understood in terms of articulated elements which provide structured relations.

For instance, Mehan (1979) reports the discovery of a set of sequential and hierarchical structural arrangements in the classroom. Teacher-student behaviour is organised into interactional sequences with the order (1) teacher topic initiation, (2) student reply, (3) teacher evaluation of the reply. This last feature is used by Mehan to illustrate a recurrent sequential form:

> The teacher evaluated the completion of initiation–reply sequences with a positive comment (like 'good') often while repeating a student's reply. While I would not necessarily expect the exact vocabulary of this classroom to be duplicated (another teacher might nod or say 'fine'), I would predict that equivalent structural arrangements would be duplicated . . . in other classrooms. (Mehan 1979: 178)

Mehan points out that he is specifically *not* talking about the duplication of actual words ('elements', in my terms) but of a particular sequential organisation ('articulation'). The concern is not with the statistical reproducibility of the elements in a range of settings but with the comparison of structures:

The phenomena in constitutive ethnography are structural not statistical. Therefore, the concern is whether the structural arrangements located in this classroom will be recapitulated in other classrooms, or even in other kinds of international events. (ibid.: 177)

Although their substantive concerns vary widely, the analytic framework of Mehan and Laclau remains structural. Their work shows a common method for the analysis of micro and macro social relations. Both exemplify the mode of thought recommended in this chapter, expressed most clearly in the statement by Wittgenstein with which I began: 'A thinker is very much like a draughtsman whose aim is to represent the interrelations between things' (Wittgenstein 1980: 12).

FURTHER READING

A simple introduction to Saussure's work is provided by Culler (1976). Hawkes (1977) takes structuralism beyond Saussure to Propp, Lévi-Strauss and Barthes.

An example of a contemporary semiotic analysis of a text is Barthes' (1975) reading of a short story by Balzac. Norris (1982) gives a brief overview of this and other 'deconstructionist' work.

The papers by Atkinson and Stubbs discussed in this chapter are taken from Adelman (ed.) (1981). This collection provides a good source book for the research issues that arise in micro sociology. All the papers use the classroom as their focus.

4 Macro and micro relations

In this chapter, I shall be developing an argument with four related strands:

1. The opposition between macro and micro perspectives (between sociologies of large-scale social structures and of interaction, respectively) has been fundamental to how many sociologists have conceived and located their work.
2. It is misleading to assume that a fundamental choice must be made between these perspectives. While research data are often mainly gathered at either a structural or at an interactional level, sound analysis and intelligent conceptualisation requires that *both* levels (and their relations) should be addressed.
3. The *rapprochement* between macro and micro perspectives cannot be achieved by approaches which assume that micro phenomena can be reduced to macro structures, or vice versa. None the less, although the levels cannot be reduced to one another, each *presupposes* the other.
4. As argued in the last two chapters, there is no future in 'pure' sociologies of meaning or of structure. Individual elements need to be identified but analysis always centres on their articulation within a network of relations. In this respect, Michel Foucault's work on the relations between power and knowledge offers a valuable example of a *rapprochement* between macro and micro concerns. In the context of this book, it has the added advantage of being based on extensive research and yet remaining sensitive to the problematic status and consequences of social science 'knowledge'.

The organisation of the chapter falls naturally into two main sections. In the first half, I show how many research studies have remained at purely a micro or macro level of analysis. I examine the limits of such studies and return to the work of Roy Bhaskar and of Mary Douglas as examples of constructive synthesis. The second half is entirely concerned with a brief exposition of some of the principal themes of Foucault's work as it bears on this issue. Using his work on law and systems of punishment and on the construction of sexuality, I argue that a focus on networks of power relations offers a useful means of bridging the macro/micro divide.

Before commencing, however, I want to give the reader a taste of Foucault's concerns. Here is what he has written in one of his relatively rare programmatic statements:

> I believe one's point of reference should not be to the great model of language [*langue*] and signs, but to that of war and battle. The history which bears and determines us has the form of a war rather than that of a language: relations of power, not relations of meaning. History has no 'meaning', though this is not to say that it is absurd or incoherent. On the contrary, it is intelligible and should be susceptible of analysis down to the smallest detail — but in accordance with the intelligibility of struggles, of strategies and tactics. ('Truth and Power' in Foucault 1980: 114)

In Chapter 3, we examined Saussure's account of signs. This provides 'the great model of language' to which Foucault refers here. I noted then that, like Durkheim, Saussure tends to limit himself to a model of structural determinants which leaves little place for practice. This is why, I think, in this passage Foucault rejects a model of language in favour of the more active model of 'war and battle'. Having disposed of a purely structural or macro account of reality in his first sentence, Foucault now seems to dismiss the micro alternative, at least in its interactionist form. He is not concerned, he tells us, with 'relations of meaning' but with 'relations of power'.

At first sight, this looks like a retreat — after all 'power' is usually understood as a macro variable, while Foucault's stress on 'history' as a determinant supports the interpretation that he is emphasising structural relations. However, in the third sentence, Foucault makes it clear that he is implacably opposed to any monolithic theory of history. 'History has no "meaning" ' — at least as understood within a rigid Marxist dialectic of contradictions.

So far it looks like Foucault is saying something like 'a plague on both your houses'. The macro categories of 'language' and 'history', it would seem, are just as limited as the micro category of 'meaning'. However, the fact that he does have a constructive alternative to this polarity is made clear in the final sentence of this passage. History, he tell us, is 'intelligible'. How? By careful research ('analysis down to the smallest detail') rather than by using purely theoretical schemes and by a focus on the variety of settings where definitions of reality and the rewards associated with those definitions are constituted and contested ('struggle . . . strategies and tactics'). As we shall later see, Foucault is adamant that these 'struggles' cannot be reduced to any single logic. Only by a precise understanding of the network of relations within which such struggles are positioned can we develop a good piece of research and, incidentally, bridge the gap between macro and micro perspectives.

It is now time to turn away from Foucault for a while. In the first part of the chapter, I shall be looking at the macro/micro opposition within more conventional sociological territory.

THE MACRO/MICRO OPPOSITION IN SOCIOLOGY

Using examples from appropriate research studies, I want now to explore the limits of purely interactionist (micro) or structural (macro) work. This part will break down into four sections:

1. interactionist research and its limits,
2. structural research and its limits,
3. a theoretical synthesis of the macro/micro opposition,
4. the continuing gulf between the two perspectives: a case-study.

1 Interactionist research

Two examples must suffice to show some of the limits of such work. Intentionally, the examples are chosen from two very different kinds of micro perspectives.

The Hawthorne studies

These studies were carried out in the 1920s at the Western Electric plant at Hawthorne and are reported, at length, in Roethlisberger and Dickson (1939). Today, they have mainly a historical interest. They indicate a period in which American social science was in the grip of pre-social accounts of human behaviour and of a rigid pro-management ideology. None the less, they reveal the emergence of an early interactionist perspective and show some of its limits.

The researchers' topic was unashamedly managerialist. They were interested in discovering the working conditions which were most conducive to high productivity. In the 1920s, the relevant newly fashionable theory was F.W. Taylor's 'scientific management'. Taylor was an engineer whose ideas had been used, apparently with some effect, to boost production during the first world war. His theory split into two simple units. First, it was management's job to organise manual tasks on a sound time-and-motion basis so that work could take place within an efficient pre-planned structure where nothing would be left to chance. The assembly-line was the examplar of this kind of job design. Inside this structure, manual tasks were to be classified and workers employed according to their relevant physical capacities. Within Taylor's engineering perspective, this ensured that the production machine was built from the right parts. The second unit of Taylor's theory was designed to provide the fuel to ensure that the parts functioned properly. This fuel came in the form of economic incentives. Piecework methods of payment, Taylor believed, would ensure that workers would work at optimum efficiency.

Using Taylor's engineering model, the Hawthorne researchers began by conducting a simple study to discover whether workers assembling electrical relays would produce more if the lighting was increased. The findings of the 'Illumination Study' were ambivalent. Productivity increased as the light grew brighter but it also remained high when the light was subsequently reduced.

The researchers reasoned that they needed to build economic variables into subsequent research, and to try to design a more closed laboratory-like experimental setting. Consequently, the 'Relay Assembly Room' study isolated six workers in a special observation room and sought to vary their wage incentives as well as light and other working conditions. Once again, however, regardless of the presence or absence of these conditions and incentives, output rose continuously over the two-year period of the study.

At this point, the researchers began to move away from Taylor's non-social conception of behaviour towards a position which had the germs of an interactionist perspective. First, they recognised that, in studying the workers, they had had an effect on their behaviour. Although this 'Hawthorne' effect had long been recognised in the physical sciences, they now saw that it had a special twist in the social world, where human researchers study human subjects. Hence the first 'interactionist' element in their new approach stemmed from the recognition that social science research follows a subject–subject model rather than the subject–object model of the physical sciences.

Two further things arose from this understanding. First, it suggested to the researchers that individual workers responded well to a management who took an interest in their feelings (as expressed in the interviews carried out during the study). Second, it became clear that this favourable reaction to the situation was a group phenomenon. Over the two years, the workers had come to know each other. The workgroup had developed norms which supported each individual in her favourable reaction to the situation. Thus, although the work physically consisted of operations performed individually, rather than as a team, something like a tiny society had developed. So the second 'interactionist' element in the new approach arose from the newly-recognised importance of 'definitions of the situation' and a social rather than a calculative version of human behaviour.

I shall not detain you with an account of the later studies carried out by the Hawthorne researchers, except to point out that they discovered a less cooperative workgroup but explained its attempts to restrict production as having a psychological function to maintain group solidarity *vis-à-vis* an unsympathetic management. In many respects, this research is more relevant today as originating a managerial ideology — 'human relations' — than as serious interactionist research. Its pro-management bias and assumption of the irrationality of worker behaviour severely limit its value.

None the less, we should not entirely dismiss the Hawthorne studies. The researchers' preparedness to learn from their mistakes and to attempt to avoid spurious correlations was praiseworthy. In a context where engineering models of the workplace were predominant, it was also a minor breakthrough to switch to a minimally interactionist view of human behaviour. However, as Landsberger (1958) has pointed out, this micro concern with group behaviour considerably limited the data analysis. The Hawthorne researchers seem to have almost totally ignored the macro industrial framework of the study. The Great Depression had commenced towards the end of the research but no mention is made of the fact that the study was forced to end when the workers were laid off — so much for the irrationality of restricting production! Again no account was taken of the social background of the workers — some were first-generation immigrants who were perhaps more likely to respond to human relations techniques than hardbitten second-and third-generation 'instrumental' workers. Nor is overall industrial relations seriously considered — according to Landsberger, there is only one passing reference to trade unions in the whole 600-page report by Roethlisberger and Dickson. The Hawthorne studies thus serve as an early example of what follows when even reasonably rigorous micro research ignores structural realities.

The 'negotiated order'

This term is taken from the approach adopted by Strauss et al. (1964) in their account of the social organisation of some American psychiatric hospitals. It involves the assumption that all social order depends on negotiation, and that organisational structure and rules reflect no more than the constant reconstitution of this negotiated order. Six years later in The Theory of Organizations (Silverman 1970), I developed an approach to organisational analysis which paralleled Strauss's perspective, but built on concerns stemming from Weber and Schutz. The aim was to attack the notion that organisations could be seen as self-maintaining 'systems' and to establish the interactional parameters of organisational behaviour. In brief, I stressed the definitions of the situation and the typifications, or habituated expectations, through which actors viewed themselves and others. I argued that these perceptions influenced the types of attachment (e.g. instrumental, moral) which they had to the organisation. The concern then became with the strategies and tactics of action which flowed from actors' attachments, definitions and typifications. Finally, it was necessary to look at the interactional consequences (e.g. for the organisational 'rules of the game') of these strategies.

Like many approaches, what I called the 'action framework' was stronger on critique than in providing a workable alternative. As Clegg and Dunkerley (1980) point out, it had a number of deficiencies, most of which stemmed from its purely micro frame of reference. First, it reduces the wider society simply to a meaningful environment of Schutzian 'stocks of knowledge': for it, 'the environment is now no longer a deterministic constraint under which people labour' (Clegg and Dunkerley 1980: 277). Second, although it has a great deal to say about organisational processes, it cannot say very much about organisational structures, except, like Strauss, by reducing them to face-to-face processes. Third, in denying the direct impact of external structures like technology, it tends to become purely subjectivist. Although, as Clegg and Dunkerley show, technology is not simply an objective, neutral variable, it none the less must be understood within an organisational structure as a 'historically locatable practice of production and re-production focused on the control of the labour process' (ibid.: 297).

The validity of these kind of criticisms of purely micro sociology was recognised by Strauss when he returned to his own 'negotiated order' model in a later work called *Negotiations* (Strauss 1978). As Strong and Dingwall (1983) have pointed out, Strauss now tried to take account of the social context of negotiation, including structural factors, like the labour market, as well as particular local factors. Fifty years on from the Hawthorne studies, micro researchers were at last taking seriously the need to pay attention to the wider social structure. The question remained, however, whether they might have replaced a flawed but consistent theory by a more widely applicable but none the less atheoretical bundle of variables.

2 Structural research

In Chapter 2, we encountered a classic example of structural research — Durkheim's study, *Suicide*. I stressed then that this study should not be underrated, not least because of its principled avoidance of psychological explanations of sociological phenomena. None the less, as all the standard critiques point out, Durkheim too readily explains suicide in terms of purely structural correlations, e.g. between divorce and suicide. By doing so, he is forced to ignore or to infer the interactional processes through which structural regularities are reproduced, e.g. following Atkinson (1978), the processes of practical reasoning through which coroners come to the conclusion that a sudden death is a suicide, for instance through their interpretation of the meaning of a recent divorce.

Perhaps the most famous contemporary example of a theory of society which has the sweep of Durkheim's work is that of Talcott Parsons. In his attempts to synthesise earlier social theories extending from political economy to Durkheim, Parsons (1949) claimed to have produced a 'voluntaristic' theory of social action. This sought to encompass both macro and micro perspectives, acknowledging the constraining character of social facts, while being sensitive to the subjective processes of interpretation through which they are reproduced.

Although Parsons' intent was praiseworthy, the standard critique is again correct in noting the inadequacy of Parsons' treatment of interaction. Put crudely, this amounts to an ill-conceived blend of Freud and Weber. Parsons explains conformity in terms of a model of learning (socialisation) leading to the development by the actor of a conscience (internalisation of norms). However, as Wrong (1967) has pointed out, this is really a caricature of Freud's theory, leaving out all the inner conflicts which intervene in and often interrupt this process. Again, even if a norm is successfully internalised, this need not mean that the actor will conform but only that he will feel guilty when he does not.

Parsons is no more successful in incorporating Weber's account of social action. Weber had stressed an active process of interpretation of social norms in which people adapted common understandings to their own needs. He gives a good example of this in the sermons of eighteenth-century Protestant clergy who skilfully twisted Luther and Calvin's anti-capitalist rhetoric into a wholehearted support of unrestrained money-making. In Parsons' hands, however, interpretation is reduced to a passive process in which people more or less blindly play out their lives according to the norms and roles into which they have been socialised. Parsons does talk about choices available to actors, for instance the choice between defining someone in terms of achieved or ascribed characteristics. Nevertheless, in his theory what the actor chooses seems always to be defined in advance by 'society'. Consequently, the 'central value system' which Parsons attributes to society is not so different from Durkheim's 'collective conscience'. Although Parsons calls his work a theory of 'social action', the action, as C. Wright Mills (1958) has noted, is always *about* to take place and finally turns out to be pre-defined.

Parsons' neglect of processes of interpretation is reflected in a great deal of structural research which, in its atheoretical concern with the quantitative measurement of 'variables', has otherwise very little in common with him. For instance, Blauner in his book *Alienation and Freedom* (1964) quite arbitrarily defines alienation in terms of work satisfaction and then seeks to show how this varies according to the technological form of the workplace. Although he is quite correct in arguing that Marx's original conception cannot be readily reduced to a measurable variable, he is not prepared to abandon the theoretically highly-embedded concept of 'alienation' in order to construct his own theory. Consequently, he is successful in showing that job satisfaction is lowest in assembly-line production and highest in craft technology. But this 'finding' is obtained at the cost of an adequate theory of either job satisfaction or of alienation.

What seems to have happened in Blauner's case is that the logic of measurement has developed its own dynamic and displaced careful, theoretically-sensitive concept formation. This is clearly revealed when he treats workers' responses, obtained from questionnaires, as implying a critique of Marx's assumption that alienation is inevitable under capitalism. The limits of such an interpretation are obvious if you reflect upon the fact that, for Marx, the person who was the most satisfied would, in a capitalist society, be just as alienated as a dissatisfied individual. In short, for Marx, alienation was not a psychological category. This need not imply that there is nothing wrong in Marx's concept — for instance, the notion of 'false consciousness' is clearly highly problematic. But it does mean that if one wants to say something about concepts like 'alienation', then it is essential to grasp the theory in which they are embedded. Conversely, if you are simply concerned with the effects of a structural variable like technology upon people's perceptions, then it is worth recognising that multiple-choice questionnaires can only produce a very partial understanding of the processes of interpretation through which such structural factors are subjectively understood.

3 A theoretical synthesis

We have seen some of the limits of purely micro and macro studies. A narrow concern with social structures precludes a proper understanding of the processes of interpretation through which they are reproduced and, sometimes, changed. Conversely, interactional sociology has constantly to be aware of the real structures which constrain and enable social action. There is an urgent need to synthesise both approaches. Once again, I turn to Bhaskar's (1979) perceptive formulations which, I shall present, in summary form, via three propositions:

(i) Interpretive procedures are central to the reproduction of social structures:

> one must insist, against Durkheim, that the range of social facts depends upon (though it is irreducible to) the intentional activity of men. The individualist truth that people are the only moving forces in history — in the sense that nothing happens, as it were, behind their backs; that is everything that happens, happens in and through their actions — must be retained. (Bhaskar 1979: 50)

(ii) Social structures are real, constraining and enabling forces:

> all activity presupposes the prior existence of social forms. Thus consider *saying, making* and *doing* as characteristic modalities of human agency. ... Speech requires language; making materials; actions

conditions; agency resources; activity rules. Even spontaneity has as its
necessary condition the pre-existence of a social form with . . . which the
spontaneous act is performed . . . society is a necessary condition for any
intentional human act. (ibid.: 43)

(iii) Social structures are the condition of social action and are reproduced and changed by it:

> people, in their conscious activity, for the most part unconsciously
> reproduce (and occasionally transform) the structures governing their
> substantive activities. . . . Thus people do not marry to reproduce the
> nuclear family or work to sustain the capitalist economy. Yet it is never-
> theless the unintended consequence . . . of their activity . . . as it is also a
> necessary condition for [it]. (ibid.: 44)

Lest this synthesis appear too abstract, a research study which seems to
fit very well Bhaskar's prescription lies close to hand. In Chapter 1,
I briefly discussed Mary Douglas's work on the pangolin cult among
the Lele. You may remember that Douglas (1975) shows how the Lele's
celebration of this spiny anteater reflects their preparedness to look
favourably upon anomalous entities, like a creature which had a mixture
of animal, human, land and water characteristics. In turn, this reaction to
anomaly was based upon their favourable experience of exchange with
other tribes. This had suggested that movement across categories could be
valuable.

Now, if we reformulate her research in terms of my three propositions
(as adapted from Bhaskar), it will be seen from Table 4.1 that there is a

Table 4.1: Structures and interaction in Bhaskar and Douglas

Theoretical proposition	Douglas's research
1. Interpretive procedures are central to the reproduction of social structures.	An ethnography of the Lele's perceptions and actions.
2. Social structures are real, con-straining and enabling forces.	Revealing the cultural forms which constitute anomalies favourably.
3. Social structures are the condition of social action and are reproduced and changed by it.	Showing the Lele's relations of exchange with other tribes. These encourage and are sustained by their celebration of anomalies.

close congruence. Douglas's work only neglects to match these propositions in her failure to identify how Lele social structure has been changed
by social action (proposition 3). However, this omission is understandable
in what was, presumably, a relatively unchanging social structure. Apart
from this, her research sensitively explores both the macro and micro
dimensions of social life. Unlike much purely structural research, she sets

out to discover structural forms rather than presuming them. Although this is clearly the only way in which research can discover anything new, it is not always recognised, particularly by investigators who accept uncritically crude Marxist notions like 'false consciousness' or 'hidden contradictions'.

Equally, Douglas's work goes beyond a purely interactionist perspective. She is not content simply to describe how the Lele perceive the world and act in it. She goes beyond by asking 'why' questions and finding answers in cultural forms which, in turn, are the unintended consequences of structural arrangements.

4 The continuing gulf between macro and micro perspectives: a case-study

Unhappily, Douglas's research is, I believe, untypical of how contemporary investigators have handled the macro/micro conceptual dimension. I shall conclude this section by examining briefly how the study of organisations continues to be split into warring camps of interactionists and structural sociologists, each of whom imperialistically claim, by fiat, to incorporate the other. To do this, I shall look in turn at structuralist and ethnomethodologically-inspired interactionist accounts of organisational processes.

The structuralist argument

Structural sociologies of organisations are split between neo-positivist/functionalist and neo-Marxist schools. They share in common a desire to explain organisational behaviour in structural terms, reducing interpretive procedures to a minor or non-existent status.

The work of Peter Blau is a good example of the functionalist tradition. In an early work, he had argued (mistakenly) that Weber's account of bureaucracy was limited to objective or formal structures. Instead, there was a need to look at 'informal organisation', like the bending of rules by employees, and to examine the functions it served for the organisation (Blau and Scott 1963).

To this functionalist approach, he later added an empiricist, neo-positivist dimension by arguing, with Richard Schoenherr, that organisational research should seek to isolate and to measure 'structural' variables like levels of hierarchy and specificity of job definition (Blau and Schoenherr 1971). By means of statistical correlations between such variables, he hoped to discover how organisations really functioned, as opposed to how their employees perceived them.

As I have argued elsewhere, this position contained two flaws (Silverman 1975). First, it assumed that structures could be conceived separately from interpretations and interactions. In practice, this meant that it treated organisational wall-charts as *sui generis* realities. This led to the second flaw in the approach. When Blau and Schoenherr wanted to measure their variables, they were forced to define the meaning of such wall-charts in their own terms. Through a series of essentially *ad hoc* decisions, they read a meaning into these charts. Their practice here, of course, mirrored the practices of employees who themselves had to find a meaning in the charts for their own practical purposes. Unwittingly, they revealed the inseparability of social structures and processes of interpretation. Consequently, their correlations tell the reader more about their own interpretations than about the organisations being studied.

For neo-Marxists students of organisations, structural analysis cannot be confined to purely organisational variables, such as levels of hierarchy. Thus, in advocating research designs 'which are sensitive to . . . macrostructural phenomena', Clegg and Dunkerley (1980: 480) want to extend the analysis to the socioeconomic system in which the enterprise functions: 'a crucial issue within organisations involved in the immediate reproduction of the capitalist mode of production will be one which affects the ideal of profitability as it is manifested in the organization's mode of rationality' (ibid.). However, they speedily imply that a still broader macro perspective must ultimately be adopted since the capitalist enterprise operates within 'the environment of the world economy' (ibid.: 481).

It is easy to see that this kind of macro work, which proceeds to ever higher levels of generality, will tend to treat interaction in a reductionist manner, explaining it as the mere outcome of some more general system. The links with more sensitive accounts of interaction via notions like 'forms of life' (Wittgenstein) and 'hegemony' (Gramsci), to which Clegg and Dunkerley appeal in their final chapter, appear highly tentative within such an over-determined structural context.

The interactionist response

We have already seen the problems that arise within an 'action' framework on organisations (Silverman 1970). Although it can be used to demolish the claims of purely structural sociologies, showing the way in which they ignore interpretive processes, it is less effective in proposing an alternative. It would seem that the whole cannot be deduced from knowledge of the parts, or vice versa.

A more recent micro approach to organisational analysis has arisen from a paper by a colleague of Garfinkel's, Egon Bittner. Bittner (1965) argues that organisations exist mainly as 'normative idealisations' or rhetoric which provide 'a generalised formula to which all sorts of problems can be brought for solution' (Bittner 1965: 76). Instead of treating organisational structures as realities in their own right, the aim instead is to examine 'the sense of organisational structure' with which people operate.

This was the programme which I recommended in my paper 'Accounts of Organizations', published five years after my earlier book. In this (Silverman 1975), I suggested research which examined how people display the rational character of their activities by appealing to a rhetoric of organisational rules and structures. I then documented how these concerns had been developed in studies by Garfinkel (1967) on jurors' decision-making. Cicourel (1968) on the social organisation of juvenile justice, and Zimmerman (1974) on how welfare workers check the tales of their clients. In Chapter 1, we encountered a further example in Sudnow's (1968) research on how lawyers decide what is a proper charge to bring against a defendant. More recently, Strong and Dingwall (1983) have, in a similar vein, called for research which investigates 'how members constitute organisations', in particular by attributing actions and motives to institutions (such as 'the university', 'the Vatican').

Although there is clearly a rich vein of data here, the status of such neo-ethnomethodological work is unclear. Sometimes it appears only to claim to be able to explain small-scale structures. In this case, it would be adopting a defensible position but at the cost of having to ignore the macro structures within which its data are located. However, more frequently, its exponents make a more general claim, like Mehan and Wood (1975: 194–7) to treat social structures as well as members' structuring activities. However, the tendency then is to reduce social structures simply to such structuring activities: 'showing', as Mehan (1979: 18) puts it, 'how the social facts of the world emerge from structuring work to become external and constraining.' This wider claim only achieves an integration between macro and micro levels by reducing one to the other: it is the mirror image of Parsonianism.

Our inspection of contemporary sociology has come to rather disappointing conclusions. The polarity between macro and micro perspectives seems to be highly entrenched and institutionalised in academic settings. The student has only to look through the teaching offered in any sociology department to discover, in all likelihood, the provision of separate courses in social structure and in micro sociology, or interactional sociology. The split is usually as rigid and institutionalised as that between courses in theory and in research methods.

In fact, I have tried to show that not all sociologists work rigidly within the macro/micro polarity. Unfortunately, we have seen how their attempts at synthesis, with some honourable exceptions, are largely unsatisfactory. Table 4.2 reviews the three principal responses to this issue that have been considered so far.

Table 4.2:   Three responses to the macro/micro polarity

Approach	Examples	Criticism
Polarised (micro *or* macro)	Much interactionist sociology Demography	Limits its claims but also limits its potential.
Reductionist	Parsons Ethnomethodology	Treats all phenomena as the product of macro *or* micro processes.
Empiricist	Later Strauss Survey research	Seeks to include all relevant variables but loses theoretical consistency.

OVERCOMING THE MACRO/MICRO POLARITY: POWER AND KNOWLEDGE IN FOUCAULT

As promised, the remainder of this chapter will focus on the recent work of Michel Foucault. My reason for doing so is because I believe his work exemplifies *one* useful way of overcoming the polarity that we have been considering. Unfortunately, the value of Foucault's work has been partly obscured by its reception in the context of the trendiness usually associated with the latest Paris (intellectual) fashions. This means that we have to disentangle it from overblown theory dressed up in unnecessary jargon. My present concerns could not be more different. I want to treat two of Foucault's studies as examples of perceptive empirical research. They are relevant because they show us a helpful way to proceed in our own research rather than simply giving us a new language in which to carry out armchair theorising. After setting out sufficient material from these studies to give a taste of Foucault's methods, I shall conclude by assessing the methodological value of Foucault's approach in the light of some standard critiques that are made of it.

Law and punishment

Foucault's *Discipline and Punish* (1977) begins with a terrifying account of a public execution in 1757. To modern eyes, the pulling off of flesh, the burning and quartering are hideous enough. The fact that the whole thing had the atmosphere of a public spectacle — as street theatre — seems incomprehensible. Foucault contrasts this grisly scene with details of a prison timetable 100 years later. The tasks of each prisoner are set out in minute detail. Each is designed to achieve a specific purpose; a careful balance between the elements is intended. So a rational calculus, bounded and balanced, has replaced an apparently limitless display of the vengeance of the sovereign.

As in all his work, Foucault wants to make us look again at our assumption that what we see in history is progress. Is indeed the 'human-ised' prison an example of a 'freer' society in which arbitrary power is controlled? To answer this question we must observe, says Foucault, three changes in the system of punishment since the eighteenth century: (1) punishment now takes place outside the public gaze — it is enclosed; (2) the body is no longer the major target of penal repression; and (3) The 'soul' or mind of the prisoner is now the major focus, and scientific knowledge of men now becomes a central resource in legal and penal processes. These changes imply that we must look at punishment as a complex social function not tied to its repressive aspects. Methods of punishment cannot be understood in terms of enlightened or unenlight-ened legislation. Nor can they be reduced to mere expressions of simple or complex social structures. Foucault insists that punishment is one among many techniques of exercising power. Punishment is a 'political tactic'.

Evolutionists like Durkheim made the mistake of interpreting systems of punishment in terms of a simple schema whereby repression is replaced by restitution. By reducing tactics of punishment to the overall form of social structure, Durkheim wanted to treat greater apparent leniency as a simple product of increasing individualisation. For Foucault, on the contrary, individualisation is one of the effects of new tactics of power. Leniency is but a technique of power.

Consider the following: in punishment-as-spectacle (the public execution), the legal violence of the state is publicly revealed. While this could serve to frighten would-be troublemakers, it could also provide an occasion when the authority of the state is publicly challenged — for instance, the demonstrations or riots that could accompany the execution of a popular figure or the uncertainties provoked by a botched attempt at execution.

In modern times, public interest shifts away from the punishment and towards the trial. The state no longer takes public responsibility for the violence that is bound up with its practice (compare public executions in the eighteenth century to the enclosed executions behind prison walls today). Now, when the state kills, it is not as a glorification of its strength but as a necessary evil. The legitimacy of its violence is hidden away from the public gaze. Instead of a simple display of the vengeance of the sovereign, punishment takes the form of society expressing its hurt at this breakage of a social contract. But its response, although sometimes using the language of 'humanity', is, in reality, a calculus of punishments — what Foucault calls 'an economy of power' — punishing exactly enough to avoid repetition, 'an art of effects'. Moreover, the powers of judicial bodies now extend *beyond* the sentence. The practical implication is that, with a view to the humanitarian end of parole, the prisoner must be continually observed and must appear to internalise 'appropriate' standards of remorse and desire for betterment.

In all these changes, the locus of attention of the state is no longer the body, but the soul. A whole new set of scientifically-trained workers (psychologists, social workers, penologists) legitimate state action on the soul through the work of the law. Penal judgement now works within a framework of scientifically and morally-grounded procedures of assessment, diagnosis and prognosis. Foucault makes clear that the humanitarian language of these new professionals and of the law coexists with a regime of permanent observation or surveillance:

> Today the question is no longer simply Has the act been established and is it punishable? but also What is this act . . . is it a fantasy, a psychotic reaction, a delusional episode?. . . . No longer simply who committed it? but How can we assign the causal process that produced it? Instinct, unconscious, environment, heredity? It is no longer simply: What *law* punishes this offence? *but* What would be the most appropriate measures to take? How do we see the future development of the offender? What would be the best way of rehabilitating him? (Foucault 1977: 19)

Rather than being a simple hand-maiden of penal reform, the human sciences share a common matrix with penal practice. The technology of power, Foucault argues, is the principle underlying both the humanisation of the penal system and of the knowledge of men. The common entry of the soul into penal justice and of scientific knowledge into legal practice is related to a transformation of the way in which the body is constituted in power relations. The body has always been important as a force of production — as labour power. But the body can only be utilised if it is caught up, as Althusser shows, in a system of subjection. (see Chapter 2, pp. 36–7.) Consequently, the body becomes a useful force only if it is both productive and subjected. Foucault argues that psychology and sociology provided the language of that subjection in the modern prison. The means of subjection is continual surveillance, disguised as in the prisoner's best interests. Penal leniency is no more than a technique of power. Prison revolts, Foucault believes, are fundamentally not about conditions but about the material character of the modern, rational, scientific prison as an instrument and vector of power.

As in his other studies, Foucault shows that careful historical research can overturn many of the preconceptions built into monolithic theories of society (whether Marxist or evolutionary). Power in prisons, as elsewhere, is not reducible to one factor but is a network of relations. It is not the privilege of a dominant class but 'the overall effect of its strategic positions' Moreover, there is no 'pure' revolutionary class — for Foucault power is also transmitted through the activities of classes who are dominated. (I shall take up the political consequences of this argument at the end of the chapter.)

The social construction of sexuality

Foucault quite rightly stresses that no power relationship simply reproduces general societal forms. So we cannot deduce legal forms from knowledge of government or economy. Instead we must carefully delineate the specific relations of institutions to one another without assuming one single logic. Above all, we must be wary of simplistic categories like 'progress' or 'humanisation'. Nothing cannot be utilised within strategies of power.

The same message is repeated in Foucault's *The History of Sexuality, Volume 1* (1979). This time the assumption that is questioned is that the twentieth century is the era in which sexual repression has been exploded. This assumption depends on a contrast between three historical periods. Prior to the seventeenth century, it is assumed that sexuality was open and unrepressed. Subsequently, especially in the Victorian age, sexuality was firmly smothered — one popular argument mentioned by Foucault is that this tied in with the needs of capitalism (the new labour force must concentrate on work, hence sexuality must be limited to reproduction). Finally, according to the conventional wisdom, new critics like Freud and Reich brought into the open the sexual hypocrisy that lay beneath polite society. Consequently, it is now assumed that we must pursue speech where in the past there has only been silence and that any remaining sexual codes are only there to be transgressed.

Foucault raises two problems with this position: (i) Do the workings of power and its mechanisms really belong primarily to the category of repression? (ii) From what institutional and discursive base does this position claim to reveal the 'truth' about sex? May it not be part of the same historical network as what it denounces?

His own approach proceeds from the assumption that sexuality is not one 'thing' or one 'truth'. Instead, he tries to examine the various ways in which sex has been put into discourse in modern times. As I argued in Chapter 3, any element only derives meaning from its articulation with others: following Saussure, the point is always the relative *value* of a sign within a sign system (or economy of signs). Likewise, Foucault's interest is in the study of the general economy of discourses on sex. Such a study raises two overall questions: (i) Who does the speaking? From which institutions? How do these institutions store and distribute the things said?; and (ii) What are the forms of power involved, the discourses it permeates, the everyday pleasures it penetrates and controls?

Modern societies have seen an explosion of discourses on sexuality: in religion (via the confessional), in literature (pornography), in demography

(Malthus), in education (morality particularly in relation to boarding and to mixed-sex schools), as well as in the more modern territories of psychiatry and psychology. Much of this has been going on since at least the seventeenth century. Thus, Foucault argues that there was no golden age followed by a period of repression: 'What is peculiar to modern societies . . . is *not* that they consigned sex to a shadow existence, but that they dedicated themselves to speaking of it *ad infinitum*, while exploiting it as *the* secret' (1979: 35).

This babble of voices had the result of erecting ever-new categories and specifications of human sexuality. For instance, while in the past adultery and rape had been publicly considered as deviant as sodomy and incest, now we make a distinction between marital and non-marital relations (especially those involving children), and between 'natural' and 'unnatural' practices. Specialists have come to focus on non-marital relations and on 'unnatural' practices, placing them in classificatory schemes, thereby giving them identity and unity and subjecting them to surveillance, based on continual questioning and monitoring of sexual behaviour. A science of sexuality, Foucault argues, has developed new forms of the confessional based on the postulation of a general and diffuse causality. Because sex, following Freud, is presumed to be present in everything, anything might be relevant to the investigator. 'Sin' is replaced by notions of the 'normal' and the 'pathological'. But these notions are even more elastic than sin, and consequently extend the professional's opportunity for surveillance. Moreover, because sexuality is held to be 'latent' and the ways of sex to be obscure, an exhaustive, delicious enquiry into people's habits becomes entirely proper. Finally, the layman is now no longer in a position to comprehend the meaning of his own actions. While at least the concept of sin allowed you to know when you had erred (because you felt guilty), the modern science of sexuality removes expertise from ordinary hands. Only the specialist will know how to interpret a statement or an act. Confession is now no longer a test, but a sign to be placed by an expert in a scientific discourse which monopolises truth.

However, my presentation so far probably overstresses the degree of unity in these processes. Foucault repeatedly emphasises that no single strategy operates in the discourses of sexuality. There is no overall attempt at repression or even at reducing sexual activity to reproduction or to heterosexual adult partners. Instead, different sexual politics may be observed in relation to the two sexes, to different age groups and to social classes. In particular, Foucault suggests that four great 'strategic unities', beginning in the eighteenth century, formed specific mechanisms of 'knowledge and power centring on sex' (1979: 103):

1. The hysterisation of women's bodies — the female body is treated as thoroughly replete with sexuality. It is to be integrated into society through medical practice (because of its intrinsic pathology) and through agencies of the state which intervene in child care and family life.
2. The pedagogisation of children's sex — all children are held to be prone to indulge in sexual activity. This is curiously both 'natural' and 'unnatural'. Hence parents, educators, doctors and psychologists must join forces, especially in a war against masturbation.
3. The socialisation of procreative behaviour — state intervention in birth control and in the provision of financial support for large families.
4. The psychiatrisation of perverse pleasure — the clinical analysis of all anomalies of sexuality; the definition of pathological forms and the provision of corrective technologies.

Each of these 'strategic unities' is associated with a specially defined subject: respectively, the 'hysterical woman', 'masturbating child', 'Malthusian couple' and the 'perverse adult'. The process does not involve a repression of sexuality but its production, deployment and control through a special strategy. It is based on an interpenetration of scientific and institutional discourses sharing a common matrix in the field of the 'social'.

Foucault's analysis of the scientific and institutional discourses of sexuality and of the prison allows him to develop an account of power which incorporates a macro sweep with micro particulars and is theoretically well developed but research-based. The traditional theory of power, as we have seen, implies that power works through outright repression and, in the case of more modern, complex societies, through censorship and concealment. Foucault suggests that this simplistic view neglects the varying strategies of power in different contexts: it overlooks: 'everything that makes for its productive effectiveness, its strategic resourcefulness, its positivity' (1979: 86). Instead, we need to analyse power other than as an excluding, silencing activity based only on state apparatuses. Power does not arise in domination, in the law, or in any *central* point — these are only the *terminal* forms power takes. Power is not exterior to economic, scientific or sexual relations but is immanent in all of them. The old hierarchical model of power had stressed legal constraints and prohibitions based upon a single sovereign authority. Foucault's new strategic model analyses how power works through disciplines which adopt the viewpoint of 'objectivity', through discourses which provide new ways of talking rather than silencing or prohibiting talk and through a multiplicity of strategies, grounded not by a single principle but through a standard of 'tactical efficacy'.

Foucault's method
So far I may have convinced the reader that there is something of
substantive interest in Foucault's discussions of the law and of sexuality.
However, you may still be unclear about how all this directly relates to the
issue of macro and micro analysis with which I began. After all, this
chapter started with the language of structure and interaction. How, if at
all, do these concepts relate to the new language of 'strategic unities' and
'discursive formations'? In these concluding sections, I shall try to draw
these threads together. First, I shall present my principal claim: that
Foucault offers an original way of overcoming the macro/micro split
which is non-reductionist and research-directed. Next, I shall briefly
review and criticise a few of the standard critiques of his work.

Where does power reside? For Foucault, power does not work primarily at either the level of institutions (structures) or of individuals
(interactions). In a paper, translated as 'Prison Talk', Foucault (1980)
writes about the 'capillary' form of existence of mechanisms of power.
This arises outside changes in regimes, institutions or hierarchies. It is
concerned with the exercise of power *within* society rather than from
above it:

> the point where power reaches into the very grain of individuals, touches their
> bodies and inserts itself into their actions and attitudes, their discourses,
> learning processes and everyday lives. (Foucault 1980: 39)

This point is overlooked by both structural and interactional analyses of
power. Using a lecture given by Foucault in 1976 (reproduced ibid.:
92-108), I shall list some of his observations on where power resides.

Not institutions but techniques
An institutional analysis of power is concerned with power in its central
locations — kings, parliaments, corporations. It implies that power
works in a centralised, uniform way. Instead, Foucault is concerned with
'multiple forms of subjugation' which extend beyond formal rules and
become embodied in particular techniques and equipped with particular
instruments (ibid.: 96). As he shows in *Discipline and Punish*, the structural
organisation of the prison — the design of the buildings and the rules
which govern behaviour — exemplifies the workings of power. To
understand power within the legal system, one must focus at these
'extreme points of its exercise'.

Not intentions but practices
Foucault argues that it is fruitless to speculate about the motives of individuals who are thought to 'possess' power. Far more relevant is what we can
observe about the nature of certain practices and about their real effects:

Let us not, therefore, ask why certain people want to dominate, what they seek, what is their overall strategy. Let us ask, instead, how things work at the level of ongoing subjugation, at the level of those continuous and uninterrupted processes which subject our bodies, govern our gestures, dictate our behaviour, etc. (ibid.: 97)

Not classes but webs of power

Power is never the simple property of one group or class. People simultaneously may exercise power and be governed by it. Rather than a deductive procedure, whereby we deduce everything from one phenomenon like the domination of the bourgeois class, we must investigate how mechanisms of power actually function and their unintended as well as intended consequences.

Not individuals but constructed subjects

As I argued in Chapter 2, analysis can never begin by treating individuals as the primary point of reference. Likewise, Foucault argues that individuals are not 'primitive atoms' who are 'subdued' or crushed by power. In fact 'it is already one of the prime effects of power that certain bodies, certain gestures, certain discourses, certain desires, come to be identified and constituted as individuals' (ibid.: 98).

Not ideologies but knowledge

Although Foucault acknowledges that ideologies are found in social institutions, he is unhappy with attempts to relate power to ideology. First, it carries the implication that there is a simple opposition between 'ideology' and 'truth', and that the former can be dissolved into the latter. Foucault rejects this implication and we shall return to his argument (and its critics) shortly. Second, relating power to ideology can imply that ideas are somehow the hand-maiden to material practices. Conversely, Foucault wants to show how knowledge itself consists of a set of material practices. At the level of practice, there is thus no opposition between ideas and reality. When we examine institutions we simply find: 'the production of effective instruments for the formation and accumulation of knowledge — methods of observation, techniques of registration, procedures for investigation and research, apparatuses of control' (ibid.: 102).

'An ascending analysis of power'

All the above implies that Foucault is recommending research rather than grand theory. Instead of formulating a global theory of the social system, we ought 'to analyse the specificity of mechanisms of power, to locate the connections and extensions [in order] to build, little by little, a strategic knowledge' (ibid.: 197, 145). Power relations are never simple projections of class or political relations. For instance, although relations between men and women, and within families, work and educational institutions, do make it possible for the state to function, they are not projections of the state's power. Each has its own pattern and relative autonomy (here Foucault implicitly criticises Althusser's unitary theory of the subject): 'Fathers, husbands, employers, teachers do not simply "represent" a state power which itself "represents" the interests of a class' (ibid.: 188). Rather than deducing power from the centre,

> 'One must rather conduct an *ascending* analysis of power, starting . . . from its infinitesimal mechanisms, which each have their own history, their own trajectory, their own techniques and tactics, and then see how these mechanisms . . . have been . . . invested, colonised, utilised, involuted, transformed, displaced, extended etc, by ever more general mechanisms and by forms of global domination. (Foucault 1980: 99)

We have already seen how both Parsonians and neo-Marxists try to reduce everything to the demands of the system (functional prerequisites and the world economic system respectively). Here Foucault is criticising both this approach and that of interactionists who can never explain the unintended consequences of action. We need to retain a concern with 'forms of global domination' but build up towards it via precise analysis of diverse institutional practices.

In this passage, dealing with his work on madness and on sexuality, Foucault provides his own illustration of the kind of research that is required:

> it was not the bourgeoisie itself which thought that madness had to be excluded or infantile sexuality repressed. What in fact happened instead was that the mechanisms of the exclusion of madness, and of the surveillance of infantile sexuality, began from a particular point in time, and for reasons which need to be studied, to reveal their political usefulness and to lend themselves to economic profit. . . . Only if we grasp these techniques of power . . . can we understand how these mechanisms come to be effectively incorporated into the social whole. (ibid.: 101)

Three criticisms

Since I am concerned in this chapter with how Foucault's work relates to the macro/micro polarity, rather than with a general exposition of his approach, I shall deal very briefly with some criticisms of it.

'The displacement of man'

This is the standard critique of neo-structuralist work which, it is claimed, replaces an analysis of human action with a purely external, mechanistic approach. We have already seen how Foucault is, in fact, very concerned with the *deployment* of human action and intention. What he rejects is not 'man' but 'humanism' as an approach which blinds itself to how human subjects are constituted in material practices. Moreover, 'humanism' is the very ideology of the 'human sciences' which are principally involved in the practices of surveillance and discipline which so constrain us.

Relativism

Since Foucault rejects the distinction between ideology and science, one can immediately see how he could be subject to a charge of relativism. I believe, however, that he is mainly concerned not with an abstraction like 'truth', but with careful research on the social effects of knowledge by: 'seeing historically how effects of truth are produced within discourses which in themselves are neither true nor false' (ibid.: 118). Personally, I believe such research has more potential than armchair agonising about 'truth'.

Pessimism

This is the strongest charge. Certainly, Foucault is quite clear that power is coextensive with society. For him, there are 'no spaces of primal liberty' from which revolutionaries can struggle. However, since his theory does not envisage any *centre* of power and power relations depend upon multiple strategies, the exercise of power may be subject to multiple points of resistance. Indeed, it is wrong to assume that resistance is *external* to power. As we saw in Chapter 3, populist strategies can mobilise elements in the very discourses that rule us. As Foucault puts it: 'Discourse transmits and produces power; it reinforces it, but also undermines and exposes it, renders it fragile and makes it possible to thwart it' (ibid.: 101).

If there is an effective critique of Foucault, I believe it lies in his occasional failure to follow his own methodological injunctions. Despite his justified calls for careful research, he limits himself to written texts, excluding any significant analysis of actual encounters. Even within such a textual analysis, he sometimes jumps rather too speedily from a passage to his interpretation. Finally, he probably over-generalises the global significance of what can be read into French social history. (It is doubtful, for instance, whether what he calls the 'Malthusian family' had the same relevance in British social policy.)

Issues like these, raising problems of description and comparative method, form the basic concern of the second part of this book. For the moment, I hope to have said enough to convince the reader that there is a problem in integrating macro and micro levels of analysis and that Foucault offers one helpful solution.

FURTHER READING

Foucault's later work (1977, 1979) is quite approachable in translation, although the beginning student is advised to stay clear of his earlier excursions into epistemology. A useful collection of his essays and discussions which examine the politics of his approach is found in Foucault (1980).

Donzelot's (1979) book on the surveillance of family life has many Foucaultian themes. The overall issues involved are discussed in a book by Bauman (1982) and, on a regular basis, in the journal *Ideology and Consciousness*.

PART THREE:
THE PRACTICE OF
QUALITATIVE
RESEARCH

5 Descriptions: the process of ethnography

The reader may be puzzled by the title of this book. Why refer only to 'describing' the social world? Surely sociological analysis, like any other scientific analysis, is concerned with *both* description and explanation?

One kind of response, which I don't share, would be to stress that these questions presume the scientific status of sociology and that such a status cannot be achieved or is not worth achieving. In O'Neill's (1975) 'wild sociology', for instance, we are urged to reject the vain pursuit of science in favour of a celebration of the 'conversation of mankind'.

O'Neill, of course, is out on a limb. Few practising sociologists would want to relinquish scientific standards — providing that 'science' is defined in minimalist terms, say as the rigorous development of generalisations using methods appropriate to the data. So, if we retain a scientific framework, the question still remains: what has happened to 'explanation'?

The answer lies in two related observations. First, this book is concerned with qualitative methodologies. Here questions of adequate *description* have always been at the forefront. Second, the qualitative tradition in sociology has been largely informed by two approaches both of which presume that their special kind of descriptions are not a preliminary to explanations but are, in themselves, adequate scientific explanations.

The approaches to which I refer are interactionism, with its concern for the interpretation of meaning along the lines of Weber and Mead, and ethnomethodology which follows Garfinkel's (1967) interest in the everyday practices through which (societal) 'members' make visible ('observable–reportable') the orderly character of social relations. Both approaches reject the positivist assumption that descriptive concepts are simply a first stage towards the test of explanatory hypotheses.

This point is well made in Peter Halfpenny's (1979) depiction of 'interpretivism' (or interactionism):

> in contrast with the sharp distinction drawn between concepts and explanatory hypotheses within the positivist approach, in the interpretivist approach

'understanding' the actions and interactions of respondents, by virtue of grasping and comprehending the culturally appropriate concepts through which they conduct their social life is the way in which explanation is achieved. (1979:808)

Ethnomethodologists are not concerned with what people are *thinking* (their 'concepts') but with what they are *doing*. However, they share with interactionists a belief that proper description is, in itself, explanatory, part of 'a naturalistic observational discipline that [can] . . . deal with the details of social action[s] rigorously, empirically and formally' (Schegloff and Sacks, in Turner (eds.) 1974: 233)

Cuff and Payne (eds) (1979) have succinctly outlined this linkage between description and explanation within ethnomethodology:

Instead of trying to produce 'deductive causal explanations' (Popper) or sets of law-like propositions, they aim to produce *descriptions*. These descriptions concern the methods members use to accomplish the world for what it is. In the description and analysis of these methods, ethnomethodologists, like other social scientists, are attempting to generalise about social life. In their case, these generalisations are about the sort of 'apparatus', the 'sense assembly equipment', that human beings use to construct and sustain their everyday lives. (1979: 178)

In this chapter and the next, I shall examine critically the methods through which qualitative sociologists attempt to generate 'adequate' descriptions. Chapter 7 is concerned with the work of conversational analysts who, like Schegloff and Sacks, attempt to develop accounts of the formal structures of talk. In this chapter, I look at another way of describing the social world which focuses on the interactional particulars of a range of social settings. As we shall see, some of the difference between conversational analysis (c.a.) and interactionism is caught by the former's concern for form rather than content. Thinking back to Michael Moerman's (1974) work, discussed in Chapter 2, c.a. aims to go beyond interactional particulars to describe universal forms of conversational organisation.

Not only the title of this book but also the title of this chapter may strike some sociologists as odd. Why call this chapter 'Ethnography' when this is a method principally associated with anthropology? In sociology, the usual term used to refer to methods for describing interactional particulars is 'participant observation' or simply 'observation'. However, I believe that sociologists have much to learn from anthropologists' long experience of attempts to describe whole cultures. Their concept of 'ethnography' involves a recognition of the interdependence of theoretical and methodological issues. Conversely, thinking of description in terms of participant observation can trivialise the issues involved to ones of mere technique (e.g. the discussions of how to obtain access and/or to remain concealed that figure so large in discussions of participant observation).

Consequently, I begin now by describing the version of ethnography found in cognitive anthropology which is particularly concerned with what Halfpenny calls 'grasping and comprehending the culturally appropriate concepts through which [actors] . . . conduct their social life'. I then turn to the theory and practice of ethnographic description in interactionist sociology and go on to compare its approach to what Dingwall (1981) has called 'ethnomethodological ethnography'. For each approach I introduce some illustrative case-studies.

These three approaches to ethnography — anthropological, interactionist and ethnomethodological — share, I believe, a common method of grounding and validating their observations. Following Robinson (1951), I then discuss this method in terms of 'the logic of analytic induction'. Finally, taking up some implications of a recent work by Hammersley and Atkinson (1983), I conclude that the practice of ethnography should not limit itself to interactionist concerns and can usefully incorporate (not too indigestibly) aspects of ethnomethodology, structuralism and even neo-positivism.

COGNITIVE ANTHROPOLOGY

Cognitive anthropology is concerned with formal ethnographic descriptions. These are conceived as adequate and replicable accounts of routine social events within specific cultures. For these purposes, culture is defined in terms of communicative competence. It is 'Whatever it is one has to know or believe in order to operate in a manner acceptable to its members and to do so in any role that they accept for any one of themselves' (Goodenough, in Hymes 1966:36).

In their search for a theory of *communicative competence*, cognitive anthropologists seek to develop an *ethnography* of *communication*. Both these concepts are briefly explained below.

1. *Ethnography of communication* is concerned with

> the ethnographic analysis of the communicative habits of a community in their totality, determining *what counts* as communicative events, and as their components, and conceiving no communicative behaviour as independent of the set framed by some setting or implicit question. (Hymes, in Giglioli (ed.) 1972: 22)

Hymes points out that this includes the analysis of (what counts as) communicative events; the kinds of participants (senders and receivers, addressors and addressees, interpreters and spokesmen); the settings in which communication is permitted, enjoined, encouraged, abridged; the various codes shared by the participants (linguistic, paralinguistic, kinesic, musical); and the events themselves, their kinds and characters as a whole.

2. *Communicative competence* is a concept formulated out of Chomsky's distinction between *competence*, the speaker-hearer's implicit knowledge of his language, and *performance*, his actual use of language in concrete settings:

> the notion of communicative competence: what a speaker needs to know to communicate effectively in culturally significant settings. Like Chomsky's term . . . communicative competence refers to the ability to perform. An attempt is made to distinguish what the speaker knows — what his inherent capacities are — and how he behaves in particular instances. However, whereas students of linguistic competence seek to explain those aspects of grammar believed to be common to all humans independent of social determinants, students of communicative competence deal with speakers as members of communities, as incumbents of social roles, and seek to explain their use of language to achieve self-identification and to conduct their activities. (Gumperz and Hymes, in Gumperz and Hymes (eds) 1972:vii)

The notion of communicative competence provides a basis to develop higher-level generalisations, based on native knowledge: 'The advantages of such an approach in providing a criterion against which to appraise participants' own explanations and conceptualizations of their behaviour, their "home-made models", should be obvious' (Hymes, in Giglioli 1972: 24).

I now turn to two illustrations of cognitive anthropology in practice.

'To give up on words': Silence in western Apache culture
(Basso, in Giglioli 1972)

Communicative competence involves more than being able to formulate utterances that will be recognisably 'correct' to native speakers. Communicative competence implies the ability to recognize culturally-defined settings and to bring off utterances that are recognisably *appropriate* to such settings.

Being silent is itself an activity and may be appropriate on certain occasions from the point of view of natives. Following the case-study discussed here, we should not assume that the apparent predilection of the American Indian for remaining silent is other than a response to these kind of occasions. As Basso quotes from a saying: 'It is not the case that a man who is silent says nothing.' He goes on, 'For a stranger entering an alien society, a knowledge of when *not* to speak may be as basic to the production of culturally acceptable behaviour as a knowledge of what to say' (ibid.: 69).

'*When not to speak*' — Basso outlines six 'situations':

1. 'Meeting strangers' — people who have not been previously seen or

who have not been engaged in face-to-face interaction. This happens most frequently at gatherings, like fairs and rodeos, and the appropriate response is silence. Strangers are not introduced — it is assumed that they will find their own time and place to begin conversing. Strangers who are quick to launch into conversation are believed to have ulterior motives.

2. 'Courting' — courting couples are typically 'strangers' to each other as rules of exogamy discourage courtship between members of the same clan. Consequently, 'sweethearts' are not expected to converse until they 'know each other'. Women who engage in conversation early on are regarded as particularly immodest.

3. 'Children coming home' — when children return home to the reservation from boarding school, very little is said. Almost invariably, the child breaks the silence first. The parents are concerned that their children may have developed unfavourable views towards their parents and the Apache way of life during their absence from home. Instead of interrogating the child, they listen — hoping that the child will indicate whether he has changed.

4. 'Getting cussed out' — people who get angry and swear at you should be regarded as temporarily crazy and ignored:

   People like that don't know what they are saying, so you can't tell about them. When you see someone like that, just walk away. If he yells at you, let him say what he wants to. Let him say anything. Maybe he doesn't mean it. But he doesn't know that. He will be crazy and he could try to kill you. (Apache interviewee)

5. 'Being with people who are sad' — when meeting mourners, it is inappropriate to engage in conversation. They may be too tired to speak, speech is unnecessary since everyone knows how the other feels, and the mourner, like the enraged person, may not be himself and is best left alone.

6. 'Being with someone for whom they sing' — in the context of curing ceremonials, it is inappropriate to speak to the patient who, during the ceremony, becomes both holy and potentially harmful to others.

Basso suggests that in all these cases the status of at least one focal participant is characterised by ambiguity. Non-focal participants (those who refrain from speech) are consequently uncertain about how the focal participant will behave towards them. In such a situation of unstable role expectations, it is safest to remain silent.

How to ask for a drink in Subanun (Frake, in Giglioli 1972)

To ask for a drink among the Subanun it is not enough to know how to construct a grammatical utterance in Subanun translatable into English as a request for a drink. Rendering such an utterance might elicit praise for one's fluency in Subanun, but it would probably not get one a drink. To speak appropriately it is not enough to speak *grammatically* or even *sensibly*. Our stranger requires more than a grammar or a lexicon; he needs what Hymes has called an *ethnography of communication*. (Frake, ibid.: 87)

As Frake points out, such an ethnography could not *predict* what natives might do, but would specify the *appropriate* alternatives in a given situation and the consequences of each. Subanun 'beer' is drunk with bamboo straws inserted into a jar filled with a fermented drink topped up with water.

The significance of drinking — since Subanun society contains 'no absolute, society-wide status positions or offices which automatically entitle their holder to deference from and authority over others', one's role in the society at large (especially for the adult male) depends greatly on *verbal performance* during drinking encounters. To elicit deference through skill in the use of speech during drinking is to display one's right to decision-making positions in legal and economic domains. Since within any drinking group there are likely to be cross-cutting ties of kinship, friendship and residential proximity:

> The strategy of drinking talk is to manipulate the assignment of role relations among participants so that, within the limits of one's external status attributes, one can maximise his share of encounter resources (drink and talk), thereby having an opportunity to assume an esteem attracting and authority-wielding role. (ibid.: 91)

Stages of drinking talk — Frake outlines four distinct *discourse stages* within the drinking talk of the encounter:

1. Invitation–permission — the provider of the jar invites someone to participate. Deference can be claimed by the manner in which the newcomer addresses the other participants: he can vary the order in which he addresses others and the form of address.
2. Jar talk — after an initial round of short tasting, turns become longer and some of the participants are cut out. Prestige is gained now in two ways: by competitive drinking and by gaining strong responses to his comments about the taste and strength of the beer and the performances of the other drinkers. Those who receive little encouragement drop out.
3. Discussion — as the gathering gets smaller, the topics switch outward into the community, from gossip to seeking to settle disputes. Success in settling quasi-legal problems is status-conferring.
4. Display of verbal art — finally, the discourse shifts from litigation to displays of verbal artistry, through song and verse. 'The most prestigious kind of drinking songs require the mastery of an esoteric

vocabulary be means of which each line is repeated with a semantically equivalent but formally different line' (ibid.: 93).

Frake's account can be compared to his discussion of a nearby tribe's (the Yakan) concept of litigation which is more formalised than that of the Subanun, although still very different from the western pattern ('Struck by Speech: The Yakan Concept of Litigation', in Gumperz and Hymes 1972: 106–29).

INTERACTIONIST SOCIOLOGY

Cognitive anthropology has much to recommend it. As we have seen, it is able to offer ethnographies of whole cultures which avoid getting bogged down in details because of its concern with *forms* of communication. Conversely, if one had to characterise much interactionist ethnography, it would be precisely by its concentration on limited, often minor, aspects of cultures and very limited concern for formal relations. In a sense, then, interactionism has the worst of both worlds, being often unable to benefit from its limited topics by exploring form rather than simply content. However, this critique presupposes an examination of interactionist theory and practice. Using Denzin's (1970) influential text, I shall now present a summary view of interactionist theory and methodology. This will be followed by a brief case-study of one interactionist ethnography about marihuana users (Becker 1953).

As we shall shortly see, interactionist theory is concerned with the creation and change of symbolic orders via social interaction. This has an important implication for how interactionists view methodology. While positivists can view methods as mere techniques of more or less efficient data-gathering, the interactionist is bound to view research itself as a symbolic order based on interactions. Consequently, Denzin properly points out that for him, as an interactionist, 'Methodology . . . represents the principal ways the sociologist acts on his environment' (1970: 5).

For Denzin, each theoretical perspective represents a particular way of looking at and acting on society. Methods cannot be neutral instruments because they define how the topic will be symbolically constituted and how the researcher will adopt a particular definition of self *vis-à-vis* the data. For instance, interactionists are likely to define themselves in a subject-to-subject relation to their data, while positivists pursue an object-to-object model.

Such an attempt to fix methodology within the symbolic order is perceptive and appropriate to Denzin's analytic model of social order. Curiously, however, he chooses to defend his selection of that model in entirely positivist terms, as follows: 'This selection is deliberate because in my judgement interactionism best fits the empirical nature of the social world' (ibid.). Here Denzin is appealing, as positivists do, to the 'empirical world' *prior to* its appropriation by any perspective. Yet, as an interactionist, he would surely want to argue that social reality is perceived via symbols and is established through symbolic interaction. Consequently, it is entirely inconsistent to appeal to a prior 'empirical world' as the support for an interactionist perspective since that perspective constitutes the world it perceives. So, of course, interactionism 'fits the empirical nature of the social world'. It could not do otherwise since it constitutes the world it describes (as does positivism or any other perspective viewed in terms of an interactionist model). Thus Denzin's defence of his position turns out to be entirely tautological, reflecting a failure of analytic nerve. Even in non-interactionist terms, Denzin's defence looks bizarre. Paradigms, like interactionism, cannot be true or false as he seems to assume. They can only be more or less useful, elegant or economical.

Denzin is much more convincing in his exposition of the interactionist model. He presents seven methodological principles which stem from the perspective. I have amalgamated some of his points in Table 5.1, while citing some examples that he uses for each principle.

*Table 5.1: Interactionism's methodological principles**

Principle	Implication	Example
1. Relating symbols and interaction.	Showing how meanings arise in the context of behaviour.	Behaviour of marihuana-users in the presence of non-users (Becker 1953).
2. Taking the actors' point of view.	Learning everyday conceptions of reality; interpreting them through sociological perspectives.	Becker's observation of a drug culture.
3. Studying the 'situated' character of inter-action.	Gathering data in naturally-occurring situations.	Observing people in their own environments.
4. Studying process as well as stability.	Examining how symbols and behaviour vary over time and setting.	Studies of 'moral careers' (Becker *et al.* 1961; Goffman 1968).
5. Generalising from descriptions to theories.	Attempting to establish universal interactive propositions.	Goffman 1981 on the 'forms' of interaction.

*Adapted from Denzin (1970:7–19)

A case-study: becoming a marihuana-user (Becker 1953)
Two references to Becker's study have been used in this account of interactionist methodology. Some further details may give some flesh to Denzin's schematic account.

In accord with principle 1, Becker observed the relationship between the marihuana smoker's own understandings and the interactions in which he was involved. He discovered that the individual's participation in groups of users taught him how to respond to the drug. Without such learning, a novice would not understand how to smoke marihuana nor how to respond to its effects. Consequently, he would not get 'high' and so would not continue to use it.

Becker outlines a number of stages through which the novice passes on his path to become a regular smoker. These include:

1. Direct teaching — e.g. being taught the difference between how to smoke marihuana and how to smoke tobacco; learning how to interpret its effects and their significance.
2. Learning to enjoy the effects — through interaction with experienced users, the novice learns to find pleasure in sensations which, at first, may be quite frightening.
3. Resocialisation after difficulties — even experienced users can have an unpleasant or frightening experience either through using a larger quantity or different quality of marihuana. Fellow users can 'cool them out', explaining the reasons for this experience and reassuring them that they may safely continue to use the drug.
4. Learning connoisseurship — through developing a greater appreciation of the drug's effects, becoming able to distinguish between different kinds and qualities of the drug.

Becker stresses that it is only in the context of a social network, which provides a means of interpreting the effects of the drug, that people become stable marihuana users. It is unlikely, however, that such a network could have been identified by, say, survey research methods concerned with the attitudes of marihuana users. Observation allowed Becker to take the actors' point of view (principle 2) but, more important, to understand its situated and processual character (principles 3 and 4). Finally, it allowed the possibility of the generation of a formal interactive theory (principle 5) about stages in 'moral careers' from 'novice' to 'old hand'.

Returning to Denzin's statement of the methodological implications of interactionism. It has, as I see it, one key insight and one problem. The insight arises in what I have called principle 5. Unlike much interactionist work which, as I have suggested, fails to improve upon good descriptive journalism, Denzin proposes that a description of content serves only as a prelude to analytic work. Basing himself on Glaser and Strauss's (1967) distinction between 'substantive' and 'formal' theory, he reminds us that the intrinsic fascination of much ethnographic data should be a stepping-stone towards the attempt to establish 'universal interactive propositions' (Denzin 1970:19). In this respect, his approach shares the analytic breadth that we found in cognitive anthropology.

The problem that I mentioned stems from principle 2 with its injunction to treat the actors' point of view from within a sociological perspective. This carries the further implication for him that: 'An irreducible conflict will always exist between the sociological perspective and the perspective of everyday life' (ibid.: 9).

Now the recognition of such a conflict has some value as we saw in Chapter 2 when considering Bloor's critique of methods of 'member validation' and Moerman's distaste for 'trusting the native'. However, there is a danger that Denzin's formulation in terms of 'an irreducible conflict' goes altogether too far. After all, without mobilising 'the perspective of everyday life' how can a sociologist understand social reality at all? Denzin seems to be confusing the *content* of everyday understandings with *formal practices* for generating understandings. While the sociologist need not identify with the former, he cannot but adopt the latter. The nature and consequences of this confusion is well illustrated in Denzin's debate about ethnomethodology with Zimmerman and Pollner (in Douglas (ed.) 1970).

Following a practice common to interactionists, Denzin uses the term participant observation rather than ethnography to index the research methodology most appropriate to his perspective. Such a method involves sharing in people's lives white attempting to learn their symbolic world. They way it is used will depend on the precise role carved out by the researcher, varying from a 'complete participant' to the 'complete observer'.

Denzin rightly suggests that participant observation embodies the principles as set out in Table 5.1. It involves taking the viewpoint of those studied, understanding the situated character of interaction, viewing social processes over time, and can encourage attempts to develop formal theories grounded in first-hand data. Unlike survey research, Denzin points out: 'the participant observer is not bound in his field work by pre-judgements about the nature of his problem, by rigid data-gathering devices, or by hypotheses' (ibid.: 216). Denzin also notes that participant observation is not without its own difficulties. First, its focus on the present may blind the observer to important events that occurred before his entry on the scene. Second, as Dalton (1959) points out, confidantes or informants in a social setting may be entirely unrepresentative of the less open participants. Third, the observer may change the situation just by his presence and so the decision about what role to adopt will be fateful. Finally, the observer may 'go native', identifying so much with the participants that, like a child learning to talk, he cannot remember how he found out or articulate the principles underlying what he is doing.

Given these difficulties, Denzin offers two related solutions. The first is non-contentious. It involves using multiple sources of data as part of the methodology. Thus Denzin defines participant observation: 'as a field strategy that simultaneously combines document analysis, respondent and informant interviewing, direct participation and observation and introspection' (ibid.: 186).

Now, as an assembly of reminders about the partiality of any one context of data-collection, such a 'field strategy' makes a great deal of sense. However, it seems that Denzin wants to go beyond a recognition of the partiality of data, for his second solution to the difficulties of participant observation is to suggest that a more general practice of 'method triangulation' can serve to overcome partial views and present something like a complete picture.

Underlying this suggestion is, ironically, once more, elements of a positivist frame of reference which assumes a single (undefined) reality and treats accounts as multiple mappings of this reality. Interestingly, Denzin talks about 'measuring the same unit' (ibid.: 308) and quotes from a text which supports multiple methods within a logic of hypothesis testing. Conversely, from an interactionist position, one would not expect a defence of hypothesis-testing nor, more importantly, of social 'units' which exist in a single form despite their multiple definitions.

Halfpenny (1979) has neatly pointed out the positivist assumptions behind this kind of method triangulation. Positivism, for Halfpenny, seeks to obtain reliable measures of mental states or social events. Triangulation helps to validate findings from this point of view because, by enabling the comparison of a number of accounts, it serves to eliminate bias.

For an interactionist, on the other hand, without bias (in this case a range of symbolic orders generating different accounts) there would be no phenomenon. Consequently, as Denzin noted earlier but now seems to forget, actions and accounts are 'situated'. The sociologist's role is not, as Dingwall (1981) reminds us, 'to adjudicate between participants' competing versions' but to understand the situated work that they do.

Of course, this does not imply that the sociologist should avoid generating data in multiple ways. As already noted, this can serve as an assembly of reminders about the situated character of action.* The 'mistake' only

*This is how Cicourel (1973) uses his method of the 'indefinite triangulation of accounts'.

arises in using data to adjudicate between accounts. For, as briefly discussed in Chapter 1, this reduces the role of the researcher to what Garfinkel (1967) calls an 'ironist', using one account to undercut another, while remaining blind to the sense of each account in the context in which it arises.

Fortunately, Denzin does not confine his discussion of the problem of validation to the confused concept of method triangulation. He also provides a fruitful discussion of the method of generalisation known as 'analytic induction'. Because I believe this method is central to the logic of any ethnography, whether anthropological, interactionist or ethnomethodological, I shall return to it after I have discussed the way in which ethnomethodology has reformulated the nature of ethnography.

ETHNOMETHODOLOGY AND ETHNOGRAPHY

Earlier in this chapter, I quoted Cuff and Payne's statement that ethnomethodology was concerned with the 'sense-assembly equipment' people use 'to construct and sustain their everyday lives' (Cuff and Payne 1979: 178). This suggests a crucial difficulty with Denzin's injunction to take the actors' point of view. Although actors use 'sense-assembly equipment' in order to understand what is happening, they rarely have any motive to focus upon it as a topic. So the actors' point of view takes for granted how they come to assemble the sense they do. Consequently, sociologists who adopt the actors' viewpoint run two related dangers. First, they will, like the actors, fail to topicalise the sense-assembly equipment through which the actors are able to attribute meanings. Second, they are likely to remain unconscious of their own dependence on such equipment in order to attribute meanings to action. Unless these problems are grasped, no appeal to sociological concepts (like 'role' 'labelling' or 'status-passage') can serve to hide the interactionists' failure to topicalise the procedures through which researchers and subjects alike make sense of situations (see Cicourel 1968).

Because interactionists can rely on their readers' tacit knowledge of sense-assembly procedures, they tend to produce research reports which are convincing precisely because of that reliance. This accounts for the anecdotal quality and truncated presentation of data in some ethnography.

In a passage already cited in Chapter 1, Mehan points out these methodological failings of ethnographic field studies:

> Firstly conventional field reports tend to have an anecdotal quality. Research reports include a few exemplary instances of the behaviour that the researcher has culled from field notes. Second, these researchers seldom provide their criteria or grounds for including certain instances and not others. . . . As the researcher abstracts data from raw materials to produce summarised findings, the original form of the materials is lost. (Mehan 1979: 15)

These methodological problems in field-studies reflect what ethnomethodologists see as crucial *analytic* weaknesses which interactionism
shares with many other varieties of sociology. Their argument implies
that such weaknesses are not overcome simply by a change of topic. So
interactionists' claims to offer a distinctive focus by concentrating on the
actor's point of view are severely weakened if it can be shown that their
methods for depicting the actor's point of view and for relating data to
sociological concepts are little different from, say, Durkheim's methods
for depicting 'social facts'.

Table 5.2: The ethnomethodological critique of Interactionism

Assumptions shared by Interactionism and 'traditional' sociology*	*Example from Denzin*	*Dingwall's critique**
'Sociology is capable of producing descriptions and explanations of social phenomena which correspond to actual events.'	His defence of interactionism as 'best fitting the empirical nature of the social world'.	Descriptions can be 'indefinitely extended'. Like lay descriptions and explanations, they make sense only in context.
'Sociological accounts of the social world are different from, and superior to, those of lay members.'	Non-problematic movement from everyday to sociological perspectives: 'the irreducible conflict' between the two.	'The ethnographer trades on his cultural competence like any other witness.' Like laymen he is fasci-nated by the exotic or unusual and 'dis-counts the mundane or everyday'.
'Lay members' procedures for making sense of their world are flawed and must either be modified or avoided in doing sociology.'	Use of 'method triangulation' as a means of presenting a 'complete picture'.	'Adjudicating between the participants' competing versions', instead of seeing their sense in context.

*Adapted from Dingwall, in Payne *et al.* 1981:124–30.

Dingwall, in Payne *et al.* (1981), has neatly summarised some of these analytic failings. In Table 5.2 above, I have indicated the three 'basic assumptions' which he suggests interactionists share with conventional sociology. I then illustrate how Denzin's account of ethnography provides examples of this lack of radical challenge in interactionism. Finally, I have summarised some of Dingwall's critique of these assumptions.

Obviously, it is far easier to offer convincing criticisms of other approaches than to deploy successfully your own approach. I now turn, then, to the kind of concerns expressed in ethnomethodologically-inspired ethnography. Once more, I shall use Dingwall's account of the issues, concentrating on five of the features that he distinguishes in what he calls 'ethnomethodological ethnography' (EE).

1. Accomplishing social order

The reader may recall the discussion in Chapter 1 of Mehan's (1979) study of classroom behaviour. Mehan sought to show how apparently 'objective social facts' (like intelligence or routine patterns of behaviour) are produced or accomplished in the everyday ways that actors talk and act. Again in Chapter 2, I discussed how Moerman's (1974) anthropological field-study revealed how the Lue only became a 'tribe' through such everyday activities. As Dingwall puts it: 'The ethnomethodological ethnographer starts from the question of how the participants in some event find its character and sustain it, or fail to, as a joint activity' (Dingwall, 1981:134).

2. Specifying actors' models

As Dingwall points out, sustaining the character of social order depends upon the use of conceptual models and interpretive procedures in order to behave in an 'acceptable' way. He appeals to the work of the cognitive anthropologist Goodenough here, revealing strong links with the kind of concerns found in the work of Basso and Frake discussed earlier in this chapter. 'Remaining silent' or 'asking for a drink' are accomplished and understood by actors through an appeal to taken-for-granted conceptual models which are equally the concern of cognitive anthropology of EE.

3. Suspending a moral stance

It is undoubtedly true that many interactionists have adopted an underdog perspective. As I tried to show in Chapter 1, such a perspective tends to direct attention away from the forms of social organisation which must be understood in order to grasp the relation between 'top dogs' and 'bottom dogs'. Predictably, then, EE tries 'to suspend that moral stance and to concentrate on recovering the situated rationality of events' (ibid.: 135). However, Dingwall does not point out the other danger to which EE's position is prone. Moral neutrality may go hand-in-hand with a functionalist, social-order model, where everything that exists is held to have a necessary function. In Chapter 8, I shall return to this point in the context of a more general discussion of ethnomethodologists' treatment of interview data.

4. Creating 'anthropological strangeness'

Dingwall argues that the interactionists' notion of 'empathy' (with actors) is 'woolly'. Instead, in EE, the aim is deliberately to stand 'on the margins' of some collectivity in order to 'interchange cultural frames' (ibid.: 136). Sometimes the observer assumes the perspective of a member, sometimes he distances himself from such everyday understandings (making them 'anthropologically strange') in order to understand how they function.

Dingwall refers to this as 'an acculturation experience' and as an 'internal dialogue' which is a 'reflexive creation' (ibid.). However, these abstract terms, in my view, fail to mask that what he is describing is the standard procedure in most other forms of ethnography. Cognitive anthropologists have discussed at length these issues of 'going native', while Denzin, in his discussion of the social role of the observer, shows how this topic is common ground in interactionism. Creating 'anthropological strangeness' is then, I believe, the weakest of these five ways of specifying the special concerns of EE.

5. Depicting 'stocks of knowledge'

Although interactionism, as Denzin notes, does seek to generate 'universal interactive propositions' (Table 5.1), its fascination with the exotic or unusual tends to work against this. Conversely, EE is firmly rooted in an analytic posture oriented to the mundane or everyday. Based on Schutz's (1970) account of the 'natural attitude', it expressly aims to depict local 'stocks of knowledge' and their relation to what may turn out to be universal interpretive procedures. Unfortunately, however, this concern with formal generalisations is still largely programmatic. Individual studies within the orbit of EE have tended to veer between particularistic accounts of commonsense procedures within organisational contexts (e.g. Zimmerman 1974), and very general listings of universal interpretive procedures which advance very little on Schutz's insights (e.g. Cicourel 1964). An example of the former will reveal some of the uses of this perspective.

'TALK-IN-THE-WORK': AN EXAMPLE OF EE

Johnson and Kaplan (1980) have noted how much sociology depends on data derived from 'artificial' settings. In interviews concerned with work experiences, for instance, the researcher generates 'talk-about-the-work'. However, this excludes three other areas about which data might be sought:

1. How people talk to one another about their work in 'natural' settings ('narrative talk-about-the-work').
2. How people organise their work by talking to each other, e.g. giving orders ('talk-*as*-the-work').
3. What accompanies 'talk-as-the-work', e.g. the 'mutterings' that people make while accomplishing their working tasks ('talk-*in*-the-work').

Johnson and Kaplan take 'talk-in-the-work' as their topic, defining it 'as the reflexive talk that is embedded in the actual work process' (1980: 353). They investigate such talk via audio-tapes of encounters between programmers and users at a computer centre. Using one transcript drawn from such an encounter, they show that programmers tend to impute responsibility for errors in programmes. Programmers, they write,

> are engaged in deciding *who* should be held accountable when the computer does not do what was intended . . . a routine and problematic aspect of the interaction is that the imputations of the programmer may not be accepted by the user. (ibid.: 356)

The data show that an error is treated by both parties as implying a potentially negative statement about the competence of the user. However, the programmer is jointly recognised as 'agent of the machine'. This allows him to resolve any dispute in his favour by appealing to the character of the machine (in particular its inability to generate its own errors): 'In a sense, the programmer functions in social interaction much like the priest of a cult by embodying the authority of a super-human entity as he interprets its messages to the novices and non-initiates' (ibid.: 358). This has many interesting consequences:

1. The programmer appears more interested in demonstrating his own special knowledge than in whether the user understands the source of his errors.
2. Users tend to bluff, pretending that they understand the computer's 'messages' as transmitted by the user.
3. The programmer sees through this bluff but still follows the users' illogical instructions.
4. Thereby 'by conspiring to reveal only certain signs to the user, while withholding others, the programmer . . . [is able] to impute

responsibility to the user without having to worry that the user will be put in a position in the ever to *assume* it' (ibid.: 360). This allows the programmer to maintain control over the programme.

Johnson and Kaplan reveal how, by encouraging users to continue to run badly-designed programmes, the programmer gains in two ways. In the short run, he is increasing his earnings and prospects of overtime. More important, in the long run, he is protecting his job by ensuring that users do not become so competent that programmers become redundant. So programmers work to maintain the dependency of users.

This study reveals some of the strengths of EE. By taking everyday knowledge seriously, it provides a method that, as Johnson and Kaplan write, 'amplifies, deepens and reveals the knowledge that is available to the . . . [participants] as a practical resource' (ibid.: 353). Further, by commencing with an analytically-defined phenomenon ('talk-in-the-work'), it provides a far sounder theoretic basis for description than is offered by a simple concern for 'spectacle' or the 'underdog perspective'. Finally, perhaps because it is so well anchored in everyday processes, it is able to make links between the details of face-to-face encounters and changes in technological and employment structures.

One should not exaggerate, however, the claims and potential of EE. Within ethnomethodology itself, the current fashion is concerned much more with the invariant speech-exchange systems depicted by conversation analysis (c.a.) than with situated, commonsense knowledge of social structures depicted by EE. Indeed, the very possibility of ethnography has come to be questioned because of its apparent dependence on what Moerman calls 'trusting the native' (see Chapter 2, pp. 45–7).

I shall return to c.a.'s critique and alternative in Chapter 6. I want to conclude this chapter by trying to locate points of contact between the three forms of ethnography that I have been considering. Consonant with the argument deployed throughout this book, researchers have more to learn by exploring the interstices between analytic positions than by dwelling on one side of fine-sounding polarities. The logic of analytic induction adds rigour and comparative flavour to a variety of forms of ethnography.

THE LOGIC OF ANALYTIC INDUCTION

Ethnographers, whatever their theoretical presuppositions, share a common problem — they appear to lack a sound means of developing and validating generalisations. For survey researchers and, to a great extent, users of laboratory methods, the problem does not arise so directly. Experimenters can use a control group which is not exposed to the assumed causal variable. Survey researchers can use statistical tests of significance to assess the explanatory power of different variables.

Analytic induction is a method by which the qualitative researcher or ethnographer tries to formulate generalisations that hold across all his data. Although originally formulated by Robinson (1951) and Lindesmith (1952), it has been discussed at length by Denzin (1970), Bulmer (1979), Hammersley and Atkinson (1983) and Mitchell (1983). I shall discuss here only Denzin's exposition of the method and Mitchell's examination of its theoretical logic. Finally, as an example of the application of the method, I shall briefly refer to Dingwall and Murray's (1983) study of categorisation in hospital accident departments.

Denzin (1970) notes how Lindesmith based analytic induction on the researcher's attempt to discover negating evidence for any generalisation he proposed. The aim was to find a 'decisive negative case' (Lindesmith 1952: 492). As described by Denzin, the method involves six stages:

1   A rough definition of the phenomenon to be explained is formulated.
2   A hypothetical explanation of that phenomenon is formulated.
3   One case is studied in light of the hypothesis, with the object of determining whether or not the hypothesis fits the facts in that case.
4   If the hypothesis does not fit the facts, either the hypothesis is reformulated or the phenomenon to be explained is redefined so that the case is excluded.
5   Practical certainty may be attained after a small number of cases has been examined, but the discovery of negative cases disproves the explanation and requires a reformulation.
6   This procedure of examining cases, redefining the phenomenon, and reformulating the hypotheses is continued until a universal relationship is established, each negative case calling for a redefinition, or a reformulation. (Denzin 1970: 195)

Denzin shows how Lindesmith (1947) had used this method to great effect in explaining the social basis of opiate addiction. Negative cases led Lindesmith to reject both his initial hypotheses that addiction was associated with (i) knowledge of the drug being used, and (ii) a sufficient history of use to produce withdrawal distress. Finally, he revised his hypotheses to relate addiction not to withdrawal distress *per se* but to the use of the drug after this had occurred for purposes of alleviating the perceived distress. No negative cases which might cast doubt on this hypothesis were found. Lindesmith could now confidently state that:

Addiction rests fundamentally upon the effects which follow when the drug is removed, rather than on the positive effects which its presence in the body produces. . . . If the individual fails to conceive of his distress as withdrawal distress brought about by the absence of opiates, he cannot become addicted. (Lindesmith 1947: 165)

We may note, in passing, how Lindesmith's model of the social processes involved in drug use closely parallels Becker's study discussed earlier in this chapter. More importantly, it is based on a method which, as Denzin points out, 'forces the sociologists to formulate and state his theories in such a way as to indicate crucial tests of the theory and to permit the explicit search for negative cases' (Denzin 1970: 197). Denzin adds that this process enables fact, observation, concept, proposition and theory to become closely articulated. Furthermore, it encourages the development of 'processual' theories which, like Lindesmith's theory of the development of opiate addiction, view interaction over time. Finally, it allows the researcher to be more confident about moving from substantive theories to what Glaser and Strauss (1967) call 'formal theories' — Lindesmith claimed that his model might apply to other forms of addiction, such as alcoholism.

Denzin also notes that analytic induction relies on theoretical sampling rather than statistical sampling models: 'While Lindesmith made use of prior statistical studies of opiate addicts, his main strategy was to *sample theoretically* in a continual effort to find crucial cases that would invalidate his theory' (ibid.; my emphasis). This points to a weakness in the argument that case-studies (like ethnographies) are not to be taken seriously because single cases cannot be *representative*. As Mitchell (1983) has demonstrated, the logic of case-studies is theoretically rather than statistically defined. I have summarised Mitchell's observations on the difference between the logic of survey research and case-studies in Table 5.3. I shall briefly expand on what Mitchell says about each of the three areas indicated in this table.

Table 5.3:   The logic of case-studies (based on Mitchell 1983)

	Survey research	*Case-studies*
Claim to validity	Depends on representativeness of sample	Only valid if based on articulated theory
Nature of explanations	Correlations not causes	Logical/causal connections
Relation to theory	Theory-neutral	Theory-dependent

Claim to validity
Quantitative survey research takes great care to select a sample in a way to ensure that no bias is present. The aim is to try to reflect accurately the characteristics of the parent population. Conversely, in a case-study, the analyst selects cases only because he believes they exhibit some general theoretical principle. His account's claim to validity depends entirely on demonstrating that the features he portrays in the case are representative not of a population but of this general principle. As Mitchell points out,

the aim is not to select a *typical* case, but a deviant or compelling case.

Nature of explanations
Statistical analysis can only demonstrate concomitant variation of two characteristics. Therefore, it reveals correlations not causes. Only by the use of theory or logic, can the analyst go beyond his significance tests and impute a causal relationship between his variables. Conversely, inference from case-studies cannot be statistical. We can extrapolate from case-studies to like situations by logical inference based on the demonstrated power of our theoretical model to account for initially negative instances. The claim, therefore, is not to representativeness but to faultless logic.

Relation to theory
Quantitative research can be theory-neutral or theory-free. Conversely, generalisations from case-studies may only be made if the underlying theory involved is adequate and, consequently, if the case is deviant or compelling in significant ways. What Mitchell calls 'the cogency of the theoretical-reasoning' is the basis of inference rather than the typicality or representativeness of the case.

Implicit in Mitchell's account of the validity of case-studies is an appeal to the logic of analytic induction. In 'enumerative induction', found in quantitative research, the researcher seeks 'to discover some final truths about a certain class of empirical data, circumscribed in advance, by studying a number of cases belonging to this class' (Znaniecki 1934: 222). However, in analytic induction, 'No definition of the class precedes . . . the selection of data to be studied as representatives of this class . . . enumerative induction abstracts by generalisation, whereas analytical induction generalises by abstracting' (ibid.: 249–51).

One further example must suffice of how the logic of analytical induction is concretely reflected in research. Dingwall and Murray (1983) show how theoretical abstraction provides the basis for the selection of a case to study. They begin from Jeffery's (1979) account of how doctors in accident departments distinguish between 'good' and 'bad' patients. 'Good' patients allow medical staff to practise their chosen specialty or to practise skills necessary for passing professional examinations. 'Bad' patients are responsible for their own illness or are non-cooperative.

Dingwall and Murray point out two problems with this analysis. First, it is logically inconsistent. It is possible not to be a 'bad' patient but still not to be a 'good' patient. Furthermore, many patients are viewed as neither 'good' nor 'bad' but as 'legitimate but routine'.

They now seek to generate an explanation of such categorisation by two steps which follow from the logic of analytic induction. First, they treat Jeffery's propositions as a set of 'programming rules' in order to 'make predictions about the ways patients will be treated' (Dingwall and Murray 1983: 132). Second, they select a sample of child patients because of their theoretical interest, given the likelihood that although children will tend to have the features of 'bad' patients, they will not be defined as such by doctors.

Using this deviant case, selected precisely because of its theoretical interest, Dingwall and Murray extend and modify Jeffery's model of medical categorisation, showing that childhood allows patients to be defined as not responsible for much 'bad' behaviour and that 'bad' and 'good' patients 'are not in practice contrasted with each other' (ibid.: 141).

TOWARDS AN INTEGRATED MODEL OF ETHONOGRAPHY

One valuable feature of analytic induction is that it is not specific to any one theoretical model. In terms of the argument I am proposing in this book, analytic induction is no respecter of polarities.

I shall conclude this discussion by examining a recent account of ethnography which shares my enthusiasm for non-sectarian versions of research practice. Hammersley and Atkinson (1983) point out how socio-logical theory and research have been polarised between positivism and naturalism (i.e. which is concerned with studying the meanings that arise in natural settings):

> Positivism treats the researcher — by virtue of scientific method — as having access to superior knowledge. The radical naturalist . . . views the social scien-tists as incapable of producing valid accounts of events that compete with any provided by the people being studied. (Hammersley and Atkinson 1983: 243)

Now, since the observer is part of the soical world, many of the pretensions of positivism must clearly be resisted. However, as we saw Moerman pointing out in Chapter 2, this need not mean that the inter-actionist concerns of naturalism are free from criticism. I shall mention five of Hammersley and Atkinson's criticisms (1983: 11-14).

1. Observation is not a pure, 'uncontaminated' activity. The observer may influence the setting and/or may miss the effects there of tem-poral cycles. Hence his conclusions may be contingent and invalid for that setting at other times and/or for other settings.
2. Naturalism's aim to 'observe things as they really are' is uncritical and atheoretical. It makes a misleading distinction between 'natural' and 'artificial' settings.
3. It limits research to 'cultural description'. Although members check claims and make causal assertions, the naturalist is debarred from so doing. While this may provide a defence in terms of not 'distorting reality', it precludes the kind of rigour introduced by methods like analytic induction.

4. Unconsciously, naturalism shares with positivism a desire to eliminate the effects of the observer upon the data. The former recommends the standardisation of research procedures, while the latter asks the ethnographer to surrender to or embrace the culture
   studied. Yet, as Hammersley and Atkinson note, all data are theory-
   impregnated.
5. Although participants' understandings should not be dismissed: 'they
   are certainly not immune to assessment, nor to explanation' (ibid.:
   234).

Hammersley and Atkinson rightly show that the tired polarity between
positivism and naturalism (or interactionism) is more or less played out.
Central to it is the assumption that commonsense knowledge must either
be avoided or exalted. Instead, they recommend that 'We must work with
what knowledge we have, while recognising that it may be erroneous and
subjecting it to systematic inquiry where doubt seems justified' (ibid.: 15).
The programme that they recommend involves an iconoclastic appeal to
elements of both positivism and ethnomethodology. They are positivists
to the extent that they rightly argue that the function of research, as
opposed to journalism, is to develop and test theories. Consequently, they
are happy to recommend analytic induction and, in certain cases, quantification as means of depicting valid relations between variables. This
defines their 'experimentalist mentality' (ibid.: 18). However, they also
make a notion of 'reflexivity' central to their programme. This derives
from Schutz and ethnomethodology's observation that common sense is
the ineradicable basis for any understanding. Consequently, they argue
that social research is *not* primarily based upon paradigms but upon
refinements of methods used in everyday life (ibid.: 15). As a result, rather
than try to eliminate the observer, they aim to make research practices a
central topic for investigation. At this point, somewhat confusingly but, I
believe, justifiably, they appeal to neo-structuralist accounts of narratives,
as in the work of Propp (see Chapter 4, pp. 59–60), as useful means of
understanding the structure of research accounts.

Atkinson and Hammersley offer a heady brew. Occasionally, this leads
them to logical inconsistencies. For instance, they treat participants'
responses as *both* a source of data (Bloor's line; see Chapter 2, pp. 43–5)
and as a 'threat to validity' (a purely positivist suggestion). Again,
Denzin's method of triangulation becomes, in their hands, an attempt to
recognise context-boundedness (the ethnomethodological position) *and* as
a way to 'counteract various possible threats to validity . . . of analysis'
(ibid.: 199) — Denzin's line, which I have tried to demonstrate is mistaken.

These inconsistencies serve as a useful reminder that the alternative
to rigid polarities in social research cannot be 'anything goes'. In

ethnography, as elsewhere, our attempts to describe the social world must be based on critical analysis which avoids both polarised concepts and sloppy thinking.

FURTHER READING

Among many texts on this subject, I would recommend Hammersley and Atkinson (1983) for a sympathetic view, and Schwartz and Jacobs (1979) for a basically critical view.

Mehan (1979) and Dingwall, Eekelaar and Murray (1983) provide two fascinating ethnographies informed by the ethnomethodological critique. An earlier, important work in this tradition is Cicourel (1968). Cognitive anthropology is introduced via a number of useful papers in Gumperz and Hymes (1972).

Mitchell's (1983) paper offers the best defence I know of the value (and potential rigour) of case-studies in sociology and anthropology.

6 Conversational analysis: the description of forms of understanding

In a lecture given in 1971 at a meeting of the American Anthropological Association, Michael Moerman and Harvey Sacks pointed out that anthropology, like sociology, is fundamentally concerned with 'culture'. Culture can be defined as 'a system of common understandings' (Moerman and Sacks 1971: 2). Like other fundamental social activities, like food-gathering and socialisation of new members, understanding is likely to be accomplished through socially-organised means.

The existence of such forms of social organisation should, Moerman and Sacks argue, be made a topic in its own right. The question is not so much why people understand one another, or even what they understand, but the organisational forms through which they achieve that understanding. Or, as they put it:

> What forms of social organisation secure the recurrence of understanding among conversation, the central institution of language use? What forms of social organisation get participants to occasions of talk to do the work of understanding the talk of others in the very ways and at the very times at which they demonstrably do that work? (ibid.: 3)

Three observations are in order about Moerman and Sacks' two questions. First, their insistence, in the second question, that understanding is somehow present in what people are perceived to do in concrete situations, involves a direct rejection of psychological accounts of understanding. Like Durkheim, they appeal only to forms of social organisation as explanatory factors. Unlike Durkheim, however, they demand that such factors should be visible in observable practices — not hidden, say, as in suicide statistics. Consequently, and this is my second observation, the character of any activity, such as understanding, is inseparable from — indeed is constituted by — what people do in a particular situation. There is thus, for these writers, no split between any activity and what people say and do in relation to it, for what they say and do will constitute the character of that activity — as, for instance, 'doing understanding' (or 'doing description' or 'doing sociology', and so on). This is Garfinkel's (1967) phenomenon of 'reflexivity'. Consequently, Moerman and Sacks write as ethnomethodologists.

My third observation is that 'conversation' is selected as 'the central institution of language use'. This raises a number of questions about the role of *non-verbal* behaviour and the *other language uses* (like lectures, interviews, trials, and so on) relative to natural conversation. A major part of this chapter will be devoted to addressing this question via powerful critiques from Dingwall (1980) and Goffman (1981). For the moment, by way of introducing some of the themes raised by conversational analysis (c.a.), I want merely to note some of Moerman and Sacks' comments on the social organisation of conversation.

Speakers generally appear to be able to take turns at talking without gap or overlap, even when their turns are of widely varying length and composition. Although gaps, overlaps and silences do occur, no-gap/no-overlap transitions are, according to Moerman and Sacks, the rule. This suggests, they say, that forms of social organisation are employed to achieve these features and therefore to provide for gaps and overlaps as recognisable 'violations'. 'Many occasions of violation can be shown to be consequences of the very system that accomplishes proper speaker transitions' (Moerman and Sacks 1971: 4). People manage to maintain 'proper speaker transitions' in the course of their talk. The social order that is obtained is not based on what they call 'retrospective editing' (ibid.: 5). Neither is it usually necessary to use outside social control agencies (policemen, referees, etc.) to recognise and punish violations. Instead,

> There is . . . a social organisation to turn-taking which has as one of its proper products that one person talks at a time. Achieving this product requires participants to encounter and solve at least two tasks: the collaborative location of transition points, and the collaborative use of means for arriving at who speaks after any current speaker. These are tasks which, on the situated occasions of their solution, are tasks of understanding. And participants so interpret them: they take failing to talk when one has been selected to and another stops as evidence of failing to understand what has been said. (ibid.: 5)

Sacks and Moerman suggest that such 'understanding' is broadly achieved by a current speaker *selecting* the next speaker or, if (s)he fails to do so, on completion of the utterance, the next speaker is self-selected. The information relevant to the selection and identity of the next speaker is embedded into utterances in a number of ways. These ways influence both *who* is to speak next and the *form* which their utterance should take. For instance, 'What do you think, John?' requires a recognisable answer on the proper topic from the person named. This means that hearers must attend to and analyse current utterances to yield an understanding of who is to speak and what they should 'do' with their 'turn'. The embarrassment of pupils who have not followed their teacher's talk is only a slightly exaggerated version of the interactional problems of the inattentive adult listener in even very informal social gatherings.

Sacks and Moerman conclude by a modest statement of their argument but this is followed by a very broad claim about its significance:

> We are not proposing that what is called understanding consists entirely of what it takes to accomplish proper speaker transition. . . . We can demand, however, that any forms of understanding which are said to be important be shown to matter as natural phenomena in conversation. (ibid.: 10)

So even though they acknowledge that more than 'proper speaker transition' is involved in understanding, forms of understanding are basically located, they claim, in conversation. The significance of this claim cannot be overestimated. Sacks and Moerman are implying that the whole Weberian-cum-interactionist problematic of understanding finds its proper home within the analysis of natural conversation. If Chapter 5 was concerned with the attempt by ethnographers to take on the research mantle of Weber's method of *verstehen* (understanding), then this chapter documents the parallel claim by ethnomethodology and, more specifically, c.a.

The rest of this chapter falls into four parts. First, I shall consider in rather more detail the sequencing rules described by c.a. In the next two sections, I shall examine, in turn, two criticisms of the approach and the response from c.a. — both criticisms have been clearly stated by Dingwall (1981). The first relates to the limits of an appeal to apparently universal rules of speaker transition. How far, for instance, Dingwall asks, can this explain findings that women's intervention in conversation is systematically limited (Zimmerman and West 1975)? As he puts it: 'Can one speak of this just as a rule of speech-exchange or must one elaborate it into some notion like commonsense knowledge of social structure?' (Dingwall 1981: 134). It is clear that this line of criticism will, as Dingwall seems to intend, highlight the merits of ethnographic analysis of social contexts, albeit in the mode he describes as ethnomethodological ethnography (EE).

The same return to ethnographic concerns is suggested by Dingwall's other line of criticism which complains that c.a. can assume the existence of the very 'cultural dopes' whose existence was denied by Garfinkel: 'Conversational analysis can risk lapsing into a 'cultural dope' model by virtue of its stress on context-free mechanisms, which come to look like programming rules' (ibid.: 137). Again, the implication is that the perspective of c.a. needs to be broadened by approaches which do not reduce understanding to a competence to follow universal rules of talk. Reference should also be made to members' sensitivity to context through their selection of the content of what they say as well as their use of gestures and other forms of body language. This argument will be considered via Goffman's (1981) important comments and the recent attempts by c.a. to incorporate video-taped data into their analyses (e.g. Heath, forthcoming).

Finally, I shall conclude by looking at a neglected part of Sacks' apparatus for analysing 'understanding' — his account of 'membership categorisation devices'. Through Sacks' own empirical work and that of Baruch (1982), I shall assess the explanatory power of these devices and return to the theme which unites this chapter with the previous one — 'description'.

SEQUENCING RULES

Using papers by Schegloff (1972) and by Sacks, Schegloff and Jefferson (1974), I shall now outline some further features of c.a.'s account of the role of sequencing rules in the social organisation of turn-taking. This is necessarily a summary presentation of early work. More recent work in this area is discussed in the papers in *Sociology* (January 1978) and in Atkinson and Drew (1979).

Schegloff: conversational openings

Schegloff's study is based on data drawn from the first five seconds of around 500 telephone calls to and from an American police station. He begins by noting that the basic rule for two-party conversation, that one party speaks at a time (i.e. providing for a sequence *ababab* where a and b are the parties), 'does not provide for the allocation of the roles "a" and "b" ' (1974: 350). Telephone calls offer interesting data in this regard because non-verbal forms of communication — apart from the telephone bell — are absent. Somehow, despite the absence of visual cues, speakers manage an orderly sequence in which both parties know when to speak. How? 'A first rule of telephone conversations which might be called 'a distribution rule for first utterances' is: *the answerer speaks* first' (ibid.: 351; original emphasis). In order to see the force of the 'distribution rule', consider the confusion that occurs when a call is made and the phone is picked up, but nothing is said by the receiver of the call. Schegloff cites an anecdote by a woman who adopted this strategy of silence after she began receiving obscene telephone calls. Her friends were considerably irritated by this practice thus indicating the force of the rule 'the answerer speaks first'. Moreover, her tactic was successful: 'However obscene her caller might be, he would not talk until she had said "hello", thereby obeying the requirements of the distribution rule' (ibid.: 355).

Although answerers are expected to speak first, it is callers who are expected to provide the first topic. Answerers, after all, do not normally know who is making the call, whereas callers can usually identify answerers and answerers will assume that callers have initiated a call in order to raise a topic — hence the embarrassment we tend to feel when somebody we have neglected to call, calls us instead. Here we may convert ourselves from answerers to hypothetical callers by using some formula like: 'Oh, I'd been trying to reach you.' Having re-allocated our roles, we are now free to introduce the first topic.

On examining his material further, Schegloff discovered only one case (out of 500) which did not fit the rule: answerer speaks first. Using the method of analytic induction (see Chapter 5, pp. 111–5), he reworked all his data to try to find rules which would account for this apparently deviant case. He concluded that this could be done by seeing the distribution rule as 'a derivative of more general rules' (ibid.: 356).

The person who responds to a telephone bell is not really answering a *question*, but responding to a *summons*. A summons is any attention-getting device (a telephone bell, a term of address — John? — or a gesture, like a tap on the shoulder or raising your hand). A summons tends to produce answers. Schegloff suggests that summons–answers (SA) sequences have the following features which they share with a number of other linked turns (e.g. questions–answers, greetings) classed as 'adjacency pairs':

1. Non-terminality
They are preambles to some further activity; they cannot properly stand as final exchanges. Consequently, the summoner is obliged to talk again when the summoned completes the SA sequence.

2. Conditional relevance
Further interaction is conditional upon the successful completion of the SA sequence.

3. Obligation to answer
If we do not answer a summons, then this allows a set of inferences to be drawn (e.g. being asleep, or purposely ignoring the summons).

4. Obligation to further the sequence
Answers to a summons have the character of questions (e.g. What? Yes. Hello.). This means that, as in question–answer (QA) sequences, the summoner must produce an answer to the question he has elicited. Furthermore, the person who has asked the question is obliged to listen to the answer he has obligated the other to produce. Each subsequent nod or 'uh huh' recommits the speaker to attend to the utterances that follow. Through this 'chaining', 'provision is made by an SA sequence not only for the coordinated entry in a conversation but also for

its continued orderliness' (ibid.: 378–9).

Schegloff is now able to explain his deviant case as follows: Summons (phone rings) — no answer; further summons (caller says 'Hello') — answer (recipient says 'Hello'). The normal form of a telephone call is: Summons (phone rings) — answer (recipient says 'Hello'). In the deviant case, the absence of an answer is treated as the absence of a reply to a summons. So the caller's use of 'Hello' replaces the summons of the telephone bell. The failure of the summoned person to speak first is heard as an incompleted SA sequence. Consequently, the caller's speaking first makes sense within the 'conditional relevance' of SA sequences.

The power of these observations is suggested by two examples. The first is mentioned by Cuff and Payne (1979): 'The recipient of summons feels impelled to answer. (We note that in Northern Ireland, persons still answer the door and get shot — despite their knowledge that such things happen)' (1979: 151). The second example arises in Schegloff's discussion of a child's utterance; first discussed by Sacks (1974): 'You know what, Mommy?' This establishes an SA sequence, where a proper answer to the summons is 'What?' This allows the child to say what he wanted to at the start, but as an obligation (because questions must produce answers). Consequently, this utterance is a powerful way in which children enter into conversations despite their usually restricted rights to speak.

Sacks, Schegloff and Jefferson: the structure of turn-taking

While Schegloff is concerned with the interactional consequences of initial turns at talk, these writers set out to provide a more general model of the sequencing of conversations. Turns, they argue, have a three part structure. This involves:

1. How the speaker makes a turn relate to a previous turn (e.g. 'Yes', 'But', 'Uh huh').
2. What the turn interactionally accomplishes.
3. How the turn relates to a succeeding turn (e.g. by a question, request, summons, etc.).

Where turn-taking errors and violations occur, the authors note that 'repair mechanisms' will be used. For instance, where more than one party is speaking at a time, a speaker may stop speaking before a normally possible completion point of a turn. Again, when turn-transfer does not occur at the appropriate place, the current speaker may repair the failure of the sequence by speaking again. Finally, where repairs by other than the current speaker are required (for instance because another party has been misidentified), the next speaker typically waits until the completion of a turn. Thus the turn-taking system's allocation of rights to a turn is respected even when a repair is found necessary. Turn-taking and repair can now be seen to be embedded in each other.

> The compatibility of the model of turn-taking with the facts of repair is thus of a dual character: the turn-taking system lends itself to, and incorporates devices for, repair of its troubles; and the turn-taking system is a basic organisational device for the repair of any other troubles in conversation. The turn-taking system and the organisation of repair are thus 'made for each other' in a double sense. (Sacks, Schegloff and Jefferson 1974: 723)

The authors conclude by stating three consequences of their model which are of general interest:

1. *Needing to listen.* The turn-taking system provides an 'intrinsic motivation' for listening to all utterances in a conversation. Interest or politeness alone is not sufficient to explain such attention. Rather, every participant must listen to and analyse each utterance in case (s)he is selected as next speaker.
2. *Understanding.* Turn-taking organisation controls some of the way in which utterances are understood. So, for instance, it allows 'How are you?' to be usually understood not as an enquiry but as a greeting (for an example of the important consequences that may flow from this, see the case of the medical consultation discussed in Chapter 2, pp. 37–9).
3. *Displaying understanding.* When someone offers the 'appropriate' form of reply (e.g. an answer to a question, or an apology to a complaint), (s)he displays an understanding of the interactional force of the first utterance. The turn-taking system is thus the means whereby actors display to one another that they are engaged in *social* action — action defined by Weber as involving taking account of others.

The depiction of sequencing rules is dependent upon the preparation of very detailed transcripts of conversation which overcome the tendency of transcribers to 'tidy up' the 'messy' features of natural conversation. Sacks, Schegloff and Jefferson (1974) offer an Appendix which provides a detailed description of the notation they use and the interested reader is recommended to study it.

However, it should not be assumed that the preparation of transcripts is simply a technical detail prior to the main business of analysis. As Atkinson and Heritage (1982) point out, the production and use of transcripts are essentially 'research activities'. They involve close, repeated listening to recordings which often reveal previously unnoted recurring features of the organisation of talk. The convenience of transcripts for presentational purposes is no more than an added bonus.

So far, c.a. has been presented, albeit in summary form, as an empirically-oriented research activity, grounded in a basic theory of social action and generating significant implications from an analysis of previously unnoticed interactional forms. It is time now to examine two major criticisms of it, and the responses that have offered from within c.a. I begin with the criticism that its focus on natural conversation tends to underplay the significance of the range of settings and contexts which give meaning to interaction. In a classroom, for instance, the form of the encounter may be relatively more shaped by the specific purposes and interactional resources of the teacher than by any supposedly universal rules of turn-taking. Moreover, even if such rules are universal, do they not need to be supplemented by reference to what Dingwall calls 'a continuing stock of knowledge of social life which carries through from one situation to another, although locally modified in the same fashion as conversational organisation' (Dingwall 1981: 137)?

THE CRITIQUE THROUGH CONTEXT

The question that Dingwall poses raises the central issue of whether c.a. can entirely replace the traditional attempts by ethnographers to map cognitive systems (see Chapter 5). Now writers like Sacks, Schegloff and Jefferson are not unaware of the role of context in making sense of interaction. They acknowledge that 'turn-taking systems can be workably built in various ways' (1974: 696). They also note that such systems must adapt to the properties of the activities in which they operate. However, they affirm that their interest is in 'the organisation of turn-taking *per se*' (ibid.: 699) and not in its application in particular contexts.

At best, then, all they would offer is the suggestion that context will be illuminated by an analysis of formal — presumably universal — processes. The claim is that these processes are both 'context-free and capable of extraordinary context sensitivity' (ibid.: 699). Using instances of context as the places and times of interaction and the identities of the parties, they put their argument most precisely in a footnote:

> major aspects of the organisation of turn-taking are insensitive to such parameters of context and are, in that sense, 'context-free'; but it remains the case that examination of any particular materials will display the context-free resources of the turn-taking system to be employed, disposed in ways fitted to particulars of context. *It is the context-free structure which defines how and where context sensitivity can be displayed*; the particularities of context are exhibited in systematically organised ways and places, and those are shaped by the context-free organisation. (ibid.: footnote 699; my emphasis)

It is clear from this elegant response to the 'critique through context' that they are treating what they call the 'context-free' structure as *prior* to particular contexts. Although the dispute about whether such formal structures or contexts are primary may turn out to have a 'chicken and egg' character, by electing structures as primary, Sacks, Schegloff and

Jefferson leave themselves open to the charge of reducing all interactions to a single form. As Dingwall puts it, using a classroom example,

> there may well be certain kinds of encounter which resolve around the assumed or imputed right of *one participant* to mediate the formal apparatus of speech-exchange rather than each participant having *equal access* to it. One member, in other words, is preferentially able to decide the sense of rules or the appropriateness of descriptions. How can we account for this and the grounds on which the choice is made? (1981: 134; my emphasis)

Dingwall makes it clear that c.a. has trouble in handling differential rights based on locally available resources. Consequently, he claims c.a. runs the risk of presenting dialogue as 'an empty skeleton of formal procedures' (ibid.). Let us examine his important argument in a little more detail.

Dingwall attacks c.a. on two fronts. First, if we accept its claim to depict a 'trans-situational' apparatus of speech-exchange, why should we assume that such a context-free cultural apparatus is limited to sequencing in natural conversation? For instance, Schutz's (1964) work on everyday structures of allocating type-concepts or attributing relevance suggests the existence of much more general interpretive schemes. So Dingwall's first claim is that c.a. deals only with a limited part of commonsense knowledge.

However, and this is his second point, even if we assume that speech-exchange is central to social life, why limit ourselves to natural conversation? Interviews, tutorials and trials all seem to offer significant variation from such conversation. Consequently, the interactional problems which c.a. has identified may be resolved by using one of a range of speech-exchange systems. Which system or apparatus is chosen and how it is used will depend on context:

> The choice of that apparatus is determined by reference to contextual features and at the same time embodies and displays those features. Problems are resolved by reference to some interpretive scheme or body of commonsense knowledge available to the members of the collectivity which is constituted by the ability to invoke that scheme or body of knowledge. (Dingwall 1980: 154)

Dingwall illustrates the use of such an interpretive scheme by data drawn from his work on tutorials in a school for health visitors in the British National Health Service. He points out that in conversations it is assumed that parties all have the right to contribute more or less equal amounts of speech. Hence, as Sacks has noted, speakers use particular devices (like 'story prefaces') to retain the floor by indicating that the story is not yet complete. However, Dingwall shows that, in these tutorials, the closure of a story and the opening of a discussion requires the tutor's authorisation. Hence the tutor may intervene and demand further documentation of the facts reported in a student's story.

The sequencing of talk here is based on an interpretive scheme which differentially allocates conversational rights:

> Since the students are, by definition, not certificated as competent occupation members, they cannot *know* what will constitute a good story which can be heard as complete. Indeed one aim of the tutorial is to instruct them on precisely that point. (ibid.: 161; original emphasis)

If students cannot know when a story is complete, neither can they know when the tutorial as a whole is complete. Dingwall points out that students are torn between their demands for an agreed summary of what the tutorial 'was all about', and their desire to leave, especially when tutorials extend into inconvenient times like lunch hours. However, tutorials never end until the tutor indicates that (s)he has heard the tutorial as complete.

Dingwall proposes that, unlike natural conversation, such tutorials are 'orchestrated encounters' in which the right to organise speech-exchange is ceded to one of the parties. These kinds of encounters are organised 'to sustain a particular thematic orientation and to keep the other addressing that theme, rather than introducing themes of his own' (ibid. 169).

Orchestrated encounters serve to sustain an orientation to joint action by appealing to the interpretive context of the encounter and by using what Goffman calls 'locally realised resources', including the assumed identities of the participants. These identities are often located, as in these tutorials, by an appeal to the concerns of the 'organisation'. (For a further discussion of the use of the concept of 'organisation' as a generalised formula for solving interactional problems, see Bittner (1965), discussed in Chapter 4, pp. 80–1.) However, we need not assume a consensus about these concerns. As Dingwall points out, a merit of focusing on a more broadly-based conception of commonsense knowledge, rather than on universal forms of speech-exchange, is the ability of the former 'to cope with dissensus by mapping the interpretive schemes used by dissenting parties as orienting principles' (ibid.: 172).

One recent attempt to incorporate studies of 'non-casual' conversation within c.a. has been made by Atkinson (1982). Dingwall's tutorials may be seen as an instance of what Atkinson calls a 'professional–lay encounter'. Unlike natural conversation, one would expect to find a single topic in focus. Moreover, sequencing would be achieved through a chain of questions and answers, with the professional doing most of the former. By behaving in this way, the professional displays his status. As Atkinson observes: 'television reporters who marked receipt of news with "Oh", or doctors who told second stories about their own ailments would not be regarded by other participants (or observers) as "proper professionals" ' (1982: 113). Professional encounters may only involve two people. They depart from the forms of natural conversation because of the professional 'work' that is being done. Multi-party conversations, whether or not professional in nature, may also depart from these forms.

Atkinson suggests that, in such conversations, practical solutions must be found to the problem of achieving and attaining shared attentiveness to turns at talk. The turn-taking system is less effective for five reasons:

1. In a large group, there will be less opportunity for everybody to have a turn.
2. Any current speaker will find it more difficult to monitor the attentiveness of all his recipients.
3. Without shared monitoring, more than one concurrent conversation is likely to occur.
4. Monitoring is limited by physical distance from the speaker, the direction in which (s)he is looking and the presence of obstacles, whether people or objects.
5. Limited opportunities for speaking may diminish the chance of understanding checks where difficulties of interpretation arise (*ibid.*: *passim*, 99–101).

How may these problems be overcome? Sacks, Schegloff and Jefferson (1974) offer a general solution. Instead of one turn-allocation at a time, as in natural conversation, all turns may be *pre-allocated* (as in debates) or chairpersons may pre-allocate turns and have the right to talk first (as in meetings). This suggests, for them, a continuum or 'linear array' of turn-taking systems:

> The linear array is one in which one polar type (exemplified by conversation) involves 'one-turn-at-a-time' allocation, i.e. the use of local allocational means; the other pole (exemplified by debate) involves pre-allocation of all turns; and medial types (exemplified by meetings) involve various mixes of pre-allocational and local allocational means. (1974: 729)

Atkinson takes up the pre-allocation of turns as a solution to the interactional problems of multi-party conversations. Using his study of courtroom procedures (Atkinson and Drew 1979), he adds a further three solutions:

1. *Turn-type pre-allocation*: the pre-allocation of specific *types* of turns to different participants in a particular sequence (e.g. proposing and seconding, praying and responding).
2. *Turn mediation*: allocating special rights to decide the speaker and the topic to a particular person (e.g. a chairperson or judge).
3. *'Situated particulars'*: this (my term not Atkinson's) refers to his discussion of how the organisation of seating or the wearing of special garments may indicate specific speakers and their rights. Alternatively, speakers may claim the floor by standing up to speak.

Atkinson's paper indicates a significant broadening of the concerns of c.a. in the direction of a comparative study of how people organise their talk in a range of settings. He seems to accommodate the ethnographic thrust behind Dingwall's insistence on the need to study situationally-located particulars. The consequence is that both Dingwall and Atkinson *may* be moving c.a. away from its concern with an empty formal skeleton of 'programming rules' and towards something like a sociology of occupations. As Atkinson puts it: 'findings from conversation analysis enable more precise and confident claims to be made about just what is special or particular to certain sorts of work' (1982:113).

I say *may* be moving because there is little evidence that c.a. has abandoned its search for context-free universals despite its rediscovery of contexted practices. Discussing the developments of studies of 'specialised' interactional settings, Atkinson and Heritage have recently emphasised their logical subservience to the study of natural conversation:

> While such developments are beginning to demonstrate that the potential of adapting a conversational analytic approach for researching a wider variety of interactional settings, they also serve to emphasise the central and continuing importance of studies of conversation . . . in so far as the practices found in these other settings may be understood to involve deletions, modifications or transformations of those operative for conversation, such studies . . . support . . . suggestions . . . that *small-scale conversational interaction may have a fundamental 'bedrock' status in relation to other types of interaction.* (Introduction to Atkinson and Heritage 1982; my emphasis)

This position turns out to be wholly in line with that of Sacks, Schegloff and Jefferson (1974) who insist that 'conversation should be considered the basic form of speech exchange system' and that other forms do not possess independent or equal status (ibid.: 730). It seems, then, that we are left with a genuine disagreement about the priority to be attached to a context-free speech-exchange system. For Sacks and Atkinson, the limits on such a universal system are largely formal — for instance, the problems which multi-party conversations create for turn-taking systems. Conversely, for Dingwall, 'The strains on speech-exchange may . . . be environmental and organisational as much as reflecting the practical limits of some context-free system' (1980: 169). The implication is that we cannot reduce interactions to deviations from a universal model and that much more conventional notions of 'role', 'culture' and even 'power' need to be mobilised. None the less, as Atkinson's recent work on the diverse character of 'professionalism' suggests, that is some common ground. Perhaps the happiest *rapprochement* could be organised around constructive comparison of research findings rather than purely theoretical paradigm construction.

TALK, COMMUNICATION AND RITUAL

> Instead, then, of merely an arbitrary period during which the exchange of messages occurs, we have a social encounter, a coming together that ritually regularises the risks and opportunities face-to-face talk provides, enforcing the standards of modesty regarding self and considerateness for others generally enjoined in the community, but now incidentally doing so in connection with the special vehicles of expression that arise in talk. (Goffman 1981: 19)

Dingwall (1980, 1981) implies that c.a. should seek a *rapprochement* with ethnography based on Schutz's concern with socially-distributed stocks of knowledge. Similarly, in the quotation above, Goffman is arguing that an account of communication must extend beyond a description of the formal procedures through which we exchange 'messages'. For Goffman, c.a. must be supplemented by an account of the interactional accomplishment of the moral order via rituals regarding self and other. While Dingwall shows that speech-exchange is not limited to natural conversation, Goffman reveals that even conversation cannot be reduced to the enactment of a set of formal rules.

Goffman notes that c.a. is concerned with what arrangements facilitate the extended flow of talk. It shares with a communications engineer an optimism about 'the possibility of culture-free formulations' (Goffman 1981: 14). Consequently, its model of communication, implying 'a two-way capability for transceiving acoustically adequate and readily interpretable messages' (ibid.), is a model of *system* requirements and constraints.

However, Goffman argues that any inspection of naturally-occurring conversation should suggest that more is going on than an attempt at mutual understanding in the framework of a communication system. For instance, when one asks a stranger for the time, one has to guard against 'the potentially offensive consequence of encroaching on another with a demand' (ibid.: 16). Consequently, a complex sequence is often enacted involving a 'remedy' (for a demand), 'relief' for potential offence, 'appreciation' for the service rendered and 'minimisation' of the effort involved. Hence:

    (i)   A: 'Do you have the time?' (remedy)
    (ii) B: 'Sure. It's five o'clock' (relief)
    (iii) A: 'Thanks' (appreciation)
    (iv) B: '(Gesture) 'T's okay' (minimisation) (ibid.)

Although the exchange can be reduced to a question–answer sequence (QA) (utterances (i) and (ii)) which allows the questioner to speak again, this conceals the essentially *ritual* practices within which QAs are enacted.

In what Goffman calls 'ritual interchanges', speakers not only convey information but attend to the 'social acceptance' of what they are conveying. Social acceptance involves whether what is being said is compatible with recipients' views of the speaker and of themselves. Goffman's 'ritual frame' thus allows analysts to account for what occurs in talk as a response to both communication and ritual constraints. Further, it encourages a move away from empty formalism to a recognition of cultural variety: 'Observe that although system constraints might be conceived of as pancultural, ritual concerns are *patently dependent on cultural definition* and can be expected to vary quite markedly from society to society' (Goffman 1981: 17; my emphasis). However, such cultural variance does not mean that we cannot generalise. Instead, Goffman claims to be offering a way of identifying those characteristics of social situations which have particular implications for the management of talk. For instance, restaurants and used car lots offer what Goffman calls different 'strategic environments'. The car salesman, unlike the waiter, will want to establish a selling relationship which allows for an extended period of salesmanship. Consequently, customer enquiries will not tend to produce the kind of truncated responses found in the restuarant.

Again, as Mehan (1979) points out, in classrooms conversational exchange will follow a different logic (usually of the form — teacher: question; pupil: answer; teacher: evaluation). Goffman insists that the constraints in these different settings are ritual and not simply conversational. For instance, an utterance by a pupil is not simply 'a turn at talk' but a display of an obligation 'to participate in this testing process' (ibid.: 54).

The c.a. response to this kind of criticism is not hard to work out. I suppose it would go something like this:

1. Of course, nobody would deny that different settings are related to the character of what is done. Indeed ethnomethodology (and, by implication, c.a.) is centrally concerned with how members display the contextedness of their talk.
2. However, context is primarily important in shaping the *content* of talk.
3. In order to communicate that content, speakers must attend to *formal* (and probably universal) rules of conversational sequencing.*

Nowhere does Goffman accept the implication that c.a.'s 'system constraints' are more fundamental than his 'ritual constraints'. Sometimes, however, he concedes that they work in the same direction. For instance, both provide for the possibility of corrective action when rules are broken. Unlike simple grammars, both are centrally concerned with how 'remedies' are used to lessen the impact of potentially offensive

---

*This is an *invented* response but one which I feel is in accord with the arguments of c.a. See Sacks *et al* (1974: 699; quoted on p: 125 above).

acts — whether an overlapping utterance or an unintended personal sleight.

However, Goffman emphasises that ritual and system constraints often work against each other. For instance, he reports a study of Indians in an Oregon reservation which shows that obligations of modesty often require young women who are asked questions either to remain silent or to offer an utterance that bears no relationship to the question (ibid.: 25–6). Although he does not say so, one assumes that this failure to maintain a QA sequence is not negatively sanctioned by these Indians (on 'silence' as a strategy, see also Basso's paper discussed in Chapter 5, pp. 98–9).

Culturally-identified contexts are also important in understanding how utterances can fail to work. For instance, for 'I do' to work as a consent to marriage, a vast array of legal procedures, as well as institutional and ceremonial arrangements, have to be attended to. As Austin's (1971) work on speech acts reveals, context is determinative of the significance of utterances and, Goffman (1981) implies, that context cannot be reduced to an utterance's positioning relative to others. Moreover, Goffman insists that verbal utterances sometimes tell us only limited things about the character of an interaction. He offers the case of 'perfunctory service contacts' as at a supermarket check-out counter (ibid.: 38). Here no words may be passed between employee and client other than those initiated by the statement of a cash sum to be paid. Yet a series of physical moves by the customer precedes and follows this statement: adopting a position in a queue, placing goods on the counter, placing goods in a bag and, finally, removing the bag.

I would add an example of entirely non-verbal interaction. London Transport trains offer a reduction if one travels after 10 a.m. ('cheap day returns'). The problem that commuters face is when a train leaves soon after 10 o'clock but no cheap ticket will be sold before then. So the aim is to get to the front of the queue. But, given that people are coming all the time to buy 'ordinary' (i.e. non-cheap) tickets, what is the queue? If you position yourself in the queue before 10 o'clock, then you risk coming to the ticket counter before you can obtain a cheap ticket. If this happens, you will have to return to the back of the queue. The interactional solution I and some others adopt is to stand apart from the queue for ordinary tickets but to position myself against the side of the ticket counter and to display that I am attending to the time on the clock and to the movements of the ticket clerk. My aim is to emphasise that I am not 'hanging about', but queuing. When somebody else comes to stand behind me, I know that I have succeeded.

In these examples, talk is non-existent or secondary. As Goffman puts it:

> Quite routinely, the very structure of a social contact can involve physical, as opposed to verbal (or gestured) moves. Here such words as do get spoken are

fitted into a sequence that follows a non-talk design. . . . Words can be fitted to this sequence; but *the sequencing is not conversational.* (ibid.: 38–9; my emphasis)

The implication of a fundamentally behavioural rather than conversational sequencing of talk is that, curiously, we might analyse talk in terms of *interactional* rather than *conversational* units.

Goffman offers us three metaphors for talking about such interactional units:

1. As moves in some language-game: 'an utterance which is a move in one game may also be a move in another. . . . And a move may sometimes coincide with a sentence and sometimes with a turn's talk but need do neither' (ibid.: 24).
2. As interactions involving mentionable events: as interactional units 'something in the order of: mentionable event, mention, comment on mention — giving us a three-part unit, the first part of which is quite likely not to involve speech at all' (ibid.: 48).
3. As an interplay of reference and response: 'What conversation becomes is a sustained strip or track of referencing, each referencing tending to bear, but often deviously, some retrospectively perceivable connection to the immediately prior one' (ibid.: 72).

Two observations are in order about the nature and consequences of Goffman's challenge to c.a. First, Goffman combines great insight with limited systematisation. If c.a. offers us rigour and order, Goffman provides metaphor and compelling example. So, as Strong (1983) has commented in a review of *Forms of Talk*, the value of Goffman's work is as a stimulus to research rather as a set of tabulated 'findings'. Consequently, it is nearly impossible to provide a balance-sheet of the relative merits of Goffman's emphasis on culturally-defined rituals and c.a.'s concern with formal rules of sequencing talk. Some kind of category-error would confound any such assessment.

My second observation is that, as Goffman often emphasises, we need both an understanding of talk and of non-verbal behaviour. C.a.'s implicit recognition of this argument is shown by its early concentration on telephone conversations where (apart from the telephone bell) non-verbal communication is notably absent and so does not 'interfere' with an analysis of purely verbal sequencing rules. More recently, workers in this tradition, like Heath, have begun the difficult task of constructing an apparatus to describe the relationship between speech and body movement. Using the apparatus, Heath (forthcoming) has shown how, in medical consultations, patients may encourage the doctor to re-establish eye-contact or to view a part of their body by means of both hesitations and physical gestures, such as hand movements. While the notation is at the present far less developed than that used in the analysis of talk, Heath's work offers an encouraging indication that the thrust of Goffman's argument is well taken by c.a.

CONCLUSION: DESCRIPTION AS A SOCIALLY-ORGANISED ACTIVITY

> the observations I have so far made . . . give you some sense . . . of the fine power of a culture. It does not, so to speak, merely fill brains in roughly the same way, it fills them so that they are alike in fine detail. (Sacks 1974: 332)

Sacks' 'observations' are based on the beginning of a story found in a children's book. It runs: 'The baby cried. The mommy picked it up.' He notes a number of things about these two sentences. For instance, we hear the 'mommy' as the 'mommy' of the baby, and hear the baby's cries as the 'reason' why the mommy picks him up. Not only do we all hear the story this way, but we hear it as 'a possible description' without having observed the circumstances which it characterises.

This carries two implications. First, it is a tribute to 'the fine power of a culture', as quoted above. Second, it suggests that sociologists should seek to analyse, rather than simply trade off, taken-for-granted practices which they share with laymen — in this case 'doing descriptions'. As Sacks puts it:

> What one ought to seek to build is an apparatus which will provide for how it is that any activities, which members do in such a way as to be recognisable as such to members, are done, and done recognisably. (ibid.)

In this concluding section, I shall briefly outline Sacks' attempt to build such an apparatus for 'description'. The aim will be to emphasise the original broad sweep of c.a.'s concerns (perhaps lost in the 'communication engineering' of the late 1970s), and, through this, to link up this chapter once more with the theme which it shares specifically with Chapter 5 but more generally with the book as a whole — the theme of 'description'.

For reasons of space, I shall telescope Sacks' account into four related points:

1. Categories

One only has to read accounts of the 'same' event in two different newspapers to realise the large number of categories that can be used to describe it. For instance, as feminists have pointed out, women, but not men, tend to be identified by their marital status, number of children, hair colour and even chest measurement. Such identifications, while intelligible, carry massive implications for the sense we attach to people and their behaviour. Compare, for example:

A. 'Shapely, blonde, mother of five', with
B. '32-year-old teacher'.

Both descriptions may 'accurately' describe different aspects of the same person. But each constitutes very definitely how we are to view that person (for instance, in A, as purely a body).

2. Collections

Each identity is heard as a category from some collection of categories (what Sacks calls a membership categorisation device — MCD). For instance, in A and B above, we hear 'mother' as a category from the collection 'family', and 'teacher' as located in a collection of 'occupation'. The implication is that to choose one category from an MCD excludes someone being identified with some other category from the same device. So MCDs are organised around what Saussure calls 'paradigmatic oppositions' (Chapter 3, p. 58). They generally involve polar oppositions so that to call someone a 'mother' excludes her being seen as a 'father'.

3. Consistency

Sacks suggests a 'hearing rule' which structures how we hear descriptions. When a speaker uses two or more categories to describe at least two members of a population and it is possible to hear the categories as belonging to the same collection, we hear them that way. That is why, in the story with which Sacks begins, we hear 'baby' and 'mommy' in relation to the collection 'family'. Furthermore, a related 'consistency rule' (Sacks 1974: 333) suggests that once one category from a given collection has been used to categorise one population member, then other categories from the same collection *may* be used on other members of the population.

The import of the consistency rule may be seen in a simple example. If we use an abusive term about someone else, we know that a term from the same collection can be used on us. Hence one of the reasons we may avoid name-calling is to avoid the development of this kind of slanging-match.

4. Category-bound activities

Many kinds of activities are commonsensically associated with certain membership categories. So, by identifying a person's activity (say, 'crying'), we provide for what their social identity is likely to be (in this case, a 'baby'). Moreover, we can establish negative moral assessments of people by describing their behaviour in terms of performing or avoiding activities inappropriate to their social identity. For instance, it may be acceptable for a parent to 'punish' a child, but it will be unacceptable for a child to 'punish' a parent. Notice that, in both cases, 'punish' serves as a powerful picture of an activity which could be described in innumerable ways. Social life, unlike foreign films, does not come with sub-titles attached. Consequently, how we define an activity is morally constitutive of it. So if, like other sociologists, Sacks is talking here about norms, unlike them (and members) he is not treating norms as descriptions of the *causes* of action. Instead, he is concerned with how 'viewers *use* norms to provide some of the orderliness, and proper orderliness, of the activities they observe' (ibid.: 339; my emphasis).

Three studies have shown the explanatory power of Sacks' apparently formalised MCD apparatus. Sacks' own work on transcripts of tape-recorded conversations between staff and clients at a Suicide Prevention Centre reveals how people constitute being suicidal as having 'no one to turn to' (Sacks 1967). People who said they might commit suicide would typically review various collections like families and friends, claiming that such collections provided proper or appropriate persons to turn to at moments of crisis. Since they had no one available in such collections, they would say they had 'no one to turn to'. Equally, staff would try to elicit simple identifications of the caller which would allow them to suggest who might be an appropriate person to seek help from. So, for instance, if a person was unmarried or had no children, they might ask if a parent was alive.*

This 'search procedure' was based on staff knowledge of pair relationships, like husband–wife, mother–daughter, and so on. Like Atkinson's (1978) work on coroners' courts (discussed in Chapter 2, pp. 32–4), Sacks' study shows how the use of such commonsense knowledge constitutes the sense of 'suicide'.

In very different settings, the constitutive character of descriptions has been revealed by Baruch (1982) and Murphy (forthcoming). Baruch shows how parents of handicapped children, when interviewed, formulate their 'story' largely in terms of what they had done for their child. By emphasising their own interventions and underplaying the independent roles of their own children and of medical staff, they assert their recognition of (and responsibility towards) moral rules of parenting.

Finally, Murphy has examined how such rules are portrayed in the pages of a parents' 'advice' magazine. Comparing recent issues of the magazine with those of the 1940s, she shows how there is today less direction of parents via clear-cut instructions and more provisional 'advice'. However, consonant with the inbuilt authoritarianism of liberal postures, discussed by Foucault (see Chapter 4, pp. 82–91), the areas of surveillance, to which both parents and children are exposed, have steadily expanded.

*My discussion of Sacks' paper is based on the account in Cuff and Payne (1979: 179–81).

These accounts of description, geared to Sacks' seminal paper, remind us that close attention to linguistic forms need not result in an empty formalism. In identifying MCDs, we are very close to sociology's traditional roots in the study of norms and roles. When wedded to a sensitive attention to non-verbal behaviour and to the ritual organisation of a range of interactional settings, c.a. ceases to be a sectarian activity and participates in the central task of describing the moral order.

FURTHER READING

The most thorough presentation of conversational analysis is found in Sacks, Schegloff and Jefferson's (1974) paper. *Sociology* (January 1978) devoted its whole issue to the topic. The most satisfactory textbook presentation of c.a. is in Schwartz and Jacobs (1979).

For sensitive critiques from the point of view of ethnography, see Goffman's (1981) essay on 'Replies and Responses', and Dingwall's (1980) paper on 'orchestrated encounters'.

7 New styles in old clothes: combining quantitative and qualitative methods in the analysis of discourse

In this chapter I want to make some practical suggestions about how quantitative data can be incorporated into qualitative research. These suggestions flow from my own recent research experience in a number of studies discussed below. I shall also discuss some examples of qualitative research by other authors in related areas. I have been careful to choose examples of what I believe to be good qualitative research in order to avoid the charge of having constructed a 'straw man'. None the less, I try to show how the value of this work might have been deepened by the use of some simple counting procedures.

Having briefly indicated my modest aims, it is perhaps worth noting some questions which will be *excluded* from this chapter. I am not concerned here with the *theory* of quantification in terms of concepts of measurement and critiques of the global applicability of quantitative measures and statistical tests (Cicourel 1964). This also means that I shall not consider the admittedly important relation between modes of counting and methods of social control in technologically-advanced societies (Cicourel 1964; Habermas, 1972).

In another sense, also, I am not concerned here with the politics of quantitative data. Undoubtedly, the analysis of official (and other) statistics can offer useful weapons in political debates (Irvine *et al.* (eds) 1979). In this chapter, however, I am simply concerned with how we ground our generalisations — whatever their political import. I shall now clarify the rationale behind this concern.

Since the 1960s, a story has got about that no good sociologist should dirty his hands with numbers. Sometimes this story has been supported by sound critiques of the rationale underlying some quantitative analyses (Blumer 1956; Cicourel 1964). Even here, however, the story has been better on critique than on the development of positive, alternative strategies. So, many thousands of British sociology students have been encouraged to dismiss quantitative research. More seriously, a generation of young researchers have been thrown out into a sceptical world with their heads full of the standard critiques of positivism but often empty of ideas about how to match exciting theories with rigorous research designs. This has been a recipe for woolly thinking. It is no coincidence that the dominant narrative form of British sociology in the 1980s is the essay. And this essay retails either a theoretical synthesis (or critique) or a 'suggestive' study of selected fragments of qualitative data.

Using terms deployed by Halfpenny (1979), two dominant versions of research have been deployed: positivism and interpretivism. As illustrated in Table 7.1 below, these approaches have been defined as polar opposites. In terms of the research output of young researchers, there is no question that the interpretivist paradigm is a clear winner in recent British sociology. Powerful critiques of positivism are mobilised to justify this preference. Instead of attending to the social construction of meaning, positivist research is shown to use a set of *ad hoc* procedures to define, count and analyse its variables (Silverman 1975). Understandably, most recent research has preferred, instead, to describe and illuminate the meaningful social world as prescribed by the interpretivist paradigm. Only the epistemological trap-door of the infinite regress, suggested by the phenomenon of reflexivity, can threaten the unwary traveller on his pre-ordained path towards illumination (Hammersley and Atkinson 1983: pp. 14–23).

Table 7.1: Polar oppositions in sociological research

Approach	Example	Method	Aims
Positivism	Variable analysis (e.g. Durkheim's *Suicide*; Lipset's *Union Democracy*)	Counting	Testing hypotheses; generalising; predicting
Interpretivism	Verstehen sociology; interactionism	Observing	Generating hypotheses; illuminating; describing

The first motive behind this chapter is to undermine the assumption that these two paradigms are incommensurable or, indeed, that they offer any worthwhile description of the major alternative directions of sociological research. This does *not* mean that I shall be arguing that positivism is *superior* to interpretivism: not only would this conflict with my aim of rejecting the simple oppositions between the two traditions, it would also run counter to my earlier critiques of positivism (Silverman 1970) by which I still largely stand. Thus, I do not attempt here to defend quantitative or positivistic research *per se*. I am not concerned with research designs which centre on quantitative methods and/or are indifferent to the interpretivist problem of meaning. Instead (and this is my second aim) I want to try to demonstrate some uses of quantification in research which is qualitative and interpretive in design: this provides the 'new style' to the 'old clothes' that figure in the title of this chapter.

The various forms of ethnography, through which attempts are made to describe social processes, share a single defect. The critical reader is forced to ponder whether the researcher has selected only those fragments of data which support his argument. Where deviant cases are cited and explained (*cf.* Strong 1979; Heath 1981), the reader feels more confident about the analysis. But doubts should still remain about the persuasiveness of claims made on the basis of a few selected examples.

I shall try to show that simple counting techniques can offer a means to survey the whole corpus of data ordinarily lost in intensive, qualitative research. Instead of taking the researcher's word for it, the reader has a chance to gain a sense of the flavour of the data as a whole. In turn, the researcher is able to test and to revise his generalisations, removing nagging doubts about the accuracy of his impressions about his data.

Now, of course, some case like this has often been made out for quantitative research. Then, in practice, the whole argument has been vitiated by the use of crass counting procedures which arbitrarily categorise the data and then try to retrieve meaning by *ex post facto* interpretations of tests of significance. As Baruch (1982), following Blumer (1956), has pointed out, 'one must examine the actual ways actors invoke features of their culture rather than impose them on the data if one is to account for orderly social action' (ms.: 10). The point, then, is to count the countable, preferably in terms of the categories actually used by the participants. Rather than treat the actors' language as a transparent guide to societal realities, one must analyse the realities constituted in their words — both talk and text (*cf.* Silverman and Torode 1980). We can turn Blumer's critique of variable analysis on its head: simple methods of counting can deepen and extend qualitative analysis of linguistically-structured realities.

This kind of exercise in synthesis, related to the practical problems of conducting research, seems doubly appropriate in the mid-1980s. First, all debates between schools of sociology have largely exhausted themselves. Today, they are largely confined to the least adventurous undergraduate courses in sociological theory and to the most boring texts ever eager to parade their new syntheses between the most trendy current figures (Derrida linked to Habermas; Foucault to Gramsci). Second, the economic crisis of western states and a series of right-wing governments, allied to an unsympathetic mass media, has meant that the social sciences need more than ever to convince sceptical laymen of their rigour and applicability to the real world. As Cicourel (1964) noted twenty years ago, in a bureaucratic–technological society, numbers talk. Today, with sociology on trial, we cannot afford to live like hermits, blinded by global, theoretical critiques to the possible analytical and practical uses of quantification.

What follows is organised according to the following rationale:

1. All my examples derive from the area with which I am most familiar — the analysis of the discourses that arise in different institutional settings.
2. Three forms of data relevant to discourse analysis are examined sequentially: ethnographies, conversations and texts.
3. For each kind of datum, a 'good' qualitative study is briefly discussed and the possible use of quantification as an additional research method is considered.
4. Following this review, I discuss the role of simple methods of counting in relation to each kind of datum.

The selection of research studies is idiosyncratic because in topic (4) I refer only to my own work; and principled, because in topic (3) I exclude studies which have been predominantly quantitative or unconcerned with discourse analysis.

ETHNOGRAPHY: CLINIC ROUTINES

In this section, I want to compare two attempts to interpret the social organisation of hospital clinics. I will use Bloor's (1976) study of ear, nose and throat (ENT) clinics and my own (1984) work on oncology clinics. Both studies share an interactionist framework, both are concerned with the same corpus of theory on medical encounters deriving from Freidson's (1971) account of professional dominance. Bloor, however, makes no attempt to count his data. Using some of my own data, I shall attempt to show the uses of simple counting procedures in sustaining claims about actor's behaviour.

Bloor observed nearly 500 consultations at the outpatient clinics of eleven ENT specialists. The patients were all under 15 and were being seen for the first time at this clinic. Like my own study, Bloor was unable to tape-record patient (or parent) exchanges with doctors, and relied on note-taking.

Bloor is concerned with what Freidson has called 'functional autonomy' — independence from lay evaluation and control. He is particularly interested in how such autonomy may be generated in the *process* of professional–client interaction rather than as a *structural* property of the medical profession. In this study, he wants to show how doctors' autonomy may vary according to the character of the setting and the routine work practices different doctors use to manage everyday medical tasks.

Bloor suggests that these routines ensure a high degree of consistency over a large number of consultations carried out by any one doctor. They also serve as a resource for minimising problems in decision-making: 'by following his familiar routines, the specialist sets in train a course of events through which he may unproblematically give assent to one of his stock of familiar forms of therapeutic intervention' (Bloor 1976: 54).

Bloor instances three kinds of clinic routine:

1. 'Informal, pragmatic rules-of-thumb concerning which symptoms and signs the specialist feels to be . . . minimally acceptable for . . . intervention' (decision rules).
2. 'Standard investigatory routines [used] . . . to operationalise . . . decision rules' (search procedures).
3. 'The seating arrangements in the consultation room and access to certain investigatory procedures' (clinic organisation).

Bloor's study is largely concerned with how such routines may serve to deny parents any potential influence over the disposal. He argues that a great deal depends on whether the doctors' decision-rules allocate much importance to the parents' account of the history relative to the examination and the referral letter. He cites an example of a consultation where a parent's account of problems is undercut by the specialist's (Dr F.) appeal to the contrary evidence offered in the referral letter.

Bloor also suggests that the form of search procedures used in the history-taking can affect the potential for parental influence. Here he quotes from a consultation where Dr A. appears to offer a great deal of space for a mother to make her own assessment of the troublesomeness of symptoms. However, where the parental history of sore throats was not corroborated by the examination, Bloor reports that Dr A. would be more likely to cross-examine the mother and to emphasise quantitative information in the history.

Bloor continues in this vein, making a number of neat conceptual distinctions between what he calls 'inhibitory', 'reactive' and 'reconciliatory' routines. He is not afraid to cite deviant cases — for instance, Dr B., who would sometimes leave the final decision to the parents — and to attempt to incorporate them into his account.

Bloor's paper makes a clear contribution to the substantive debate on professional dominance and to the theoretical discussion of the role of routine practices in everyday settings. However, uncertainties remain about the warrant for making his claims about what his data reveal. The extracts from his notes of doctor–parent communication are used only as 'illustrations' and 'examples'. Given the huge amount of data he collected, the amount presented here is very tiny.

Faced with the inevitable extent of selection of data, the reader must have doubts about the representativeness of the extracts presented. These doubts may partially be quelled by the undoubted cogency of Bloor's conceptual apparatus and by the extent to which the reader can mobilise his commonsense knowledge to 'see' in the extracts the processes suggested by the researcher. However, even if the reader is prepared to grant, largely on trust, that the extracts are representative, he must regret the lack of any kind of overall measure of the features of the sample as a whole or of sub-samples relating to the styles of different doctors — styles which Bloor tries to characterise on the basis of one or two brief exchanges. Above all, as with so much purely qualitative research, one is struck by the huge amount of data that are simply lost in the discussion. Although the whole corpus of data undoubtedly influences the researcher's impressions of what is going on, this process of influence is as hidden from the reader as the 'hidden agenda' of the consultation, described by Bloor, may be hidden from patients or parents.

In my study of oncology clinics, I used some simple quantitative measures in order to respond to some of these problems. The aim was to demonstrate that the qualitative analysis was reasonably representative of the data as a whole. Occasionally, however, the figures revealed that the reality was not in line with my overall impressions. Consequently, the analysis was tightened and the characterisations of clinic behaviour were specified more carefully.

Elsewhere (Silverman 1984), I have compared doctor and patient behaviour in three British oncology clinics. A major aim was to compare what, following Strong (1979), I called the 'ceremonial order' observed in the two NHS clinics with a clinic in the private sector. I shared an interest with Bloor in interactionist accounts of the form of medical consultations. My method of analysis was largely qualitative and, like him, I used extracts of what patients and doctors had said as well as offering a brief ethnography of the setting and of certain behavioural data. In addition, however, I constructed a coding form which enabled me to collate a number of crude measures of doctor and patient interactions.

My impression was that the private clinic encouraged a more 'personalised' service and allowed patients to orchestrate their care, control the agenda, and obtain some 'territorial' control of the setting. In my discussion of the data, like Bloor I cite extracts from consultations to support these points, while referring to deviant cases and to the continuum of forms found in the NHS clinics.

The crude quantitative data I had recorded did not allow any real test of the major thrust of this argument. None the less, it did offer a summary measure of the characteristics of the total sample which allowed closer specification of features of private and NHS clinics. In order to illustrate this, I shall briefly look at the data on consultation length, patient participation and widening of the scope of the consultation.

My overall impression was that private consultations lasted considerably longer than those held in the NHS clinics. When examined, the data indeed did show that the former were almost twice as long as the latter (20 minutes as against 11 minutes) and that the difference was statistically highly significant (significant at 0.001; χ^2 = 69, 1 d.f.). However, I recalled that for special reasons, the NHS leukaemia clinic had abnormally short consultations. I felt a fairer comparison of consultations in the two sectors should exclude this clinic and should only compare consultations taken by a single doctor in both sectors. This sub-sample of cases revealed that the difference in length between NHS and private consultations was now reduced to an average of under 3 minutes. This was still statistically significant, although the significance was reduced (significant at 0.02; χ^2 = 6.2). Finally, however, if I compared only *new* patients seen by the same doctor, NHS patients got 4 minutes more on average — 34 minutes as against 30 minutes in the private clinic (difference not significant at 0.10). This last finding was not suspected and had interesting implications for the overall assessment of the individual's costs and benefits from 'going private'. It is possible, for instance, that the tighter scheduling of appointments at the private clinic may limit the amount of time that can be given to new patients.

As a further aid to comparative analysis, I measured patient participation in the form of questions and unelicited statements. Once again, a highly significant difference was found: on this measure, private patients participated much more in the consultation (significant at 0.001, χ^2 = 22.5). However, once more taking only patients seen by the same doctor, the difference between the clinics became very small and was *not* significant (at 0.10). Finally, no significant difference was found in the degree to which non-medical matters (e.g. patient's work or home circumstances) were discussed in the clinics.

These quantitative data were a useful check on over-enthusiastic claims about the degree of difference between the NHS and private clinics. However, it must be remembered that my major concern was with the 'ceremonial order' of the three clinics. I had amassed a considerable number of exchanges in which doctors and patients appeared to behave in the private clinic in a manner deviant from what we know about NHS hospital consultations. The question was: would the quantitative data offer any support to my observations?

The answer was, to some extent, positive. Two quantitative measures were helpful in relation to the ceremonial order. One dealt with the extent to which the doctor fixed treatment or attendance at the patient's convenience. The second measured whether patients or doctor engaged in polite small-talk with one another about their personal or professional lives. (I called this 'social elicitation'.) As Table 7.2 shows, both these measures revealed significant differences, in the expected direction, according to the mode of payment (significance at least 0.05).

Table 7.2: Private and NHS clinics: ceremonial orders (based on Silverman 1984)

	Private clinic (n = 42)	NHS clinics (n = 104)
Treatment or attendance fixed at patients' convenience	15 (36%)	10 (10%)
Social elicitation	25 (60%)	31 (30%)

Now, of course, such data could not offer proof of my claims about the different interactional forms. However, coupled with the qualitative data, they provided strong evidence of the direction of difference, as well as giving me a simple measure of the sample as a whole which contexted the few extracts of talk I was able to use. I do not deny that counting can be as arbitrary as qualitative interpretation of a few fragments of data. However, providing the researcher resists the temptation to try to count everything, and bases his analysis on a sound conceptual basis linked to actors' own methods of ordering the world, then both types of data can inform the analysis of the other.

CONVERSATIONS: THE 'STAGES' OF THE CONSULTATION
Continuing in the same substantive area, I now want to compare two studies which are both broadly concerned with the ordering of the stages of medical consultations. Heath (1981) is interested solely in the opening sequence in doctor–patient interaction. His approach is based on the literature on conversational-sequencing. Like most conversational analysis (c.a.), the concerns are formal — the development of an apparatus to describe the general forms of conversation. Sometimes, as with Moerman (1974), it is claimed that these forms are universal, extending beyond English and American usage. Hence, Heath is not concerned with the substance of the encounter nor with the particular character of the setting in which it takes place.

Although Heath states that he has data on around 4500 consultations, he is content to use extracts from only seven consultations to make his points. Conversely, in a study of paediatric cardiology consultations (Silverman 1981), in addition to qualitative analysis, I used quantitative measures to depict some summary features of an admittedly much smaller sample (34 consultations). The study arose out of entirely substantive concerns — the apparently different form taken by consultations where a Down's Syndrome child was the patient. In turn, this difference was explicated by reference to situation-specific, rather than universal, conversational forms.

Heath suggests that every doctor–patient encounter follows a single sequence. This sequence may contain five possible stages:

1. 'A summons initiated by the doctor where the appropriate next move is the patient's going to the consulting room' (Heath 1981: 75).
2. A greeting sequence typically initiated by the doctor.
3. 'An identity-check sequence, for example
   Dr: Is it Jill?
   Patient: Yes.'
4. The doctor now reads the medical record-cards if he has not read them prior to the patient entering the surgery.
5. The doctor initiates first topic.

Heath points out that patients do not talk about their illnesses prior to the doctor's first topic-initiator. However, such initiators vary in form according to whether this is a new or return appointment. New appointments are made at the patient's volition. Here doctors initiate the first topic through such forms as: 'How can I help you?', or 'What can I do for you?' Heath suggests that these kinds of first topic-initiators:

> display the lack of knowledge the doctor has concerning the patient's reason for the visit. As a generalised offer of help, they serve to provide an interactional domain for the disclosure and elicitation of particular troubles (ibid.: 79).

Conversely, such topic initiators as 'Ah, it's your first visit, isn't it?', or 'How are you, Mister X?' are found in return appointments. They display that the doctor knows certain facts about why the patient is here. 'How are you?' is normally only found in return appointments because, where a doctor could not be assumed to know the reason for a visit, it could be confused with a greeting.

Heath does refer, in passing, to some measures of the sample as a whole. For instance, he notes that, out of a corpus of data of approximately 4000 consultations, there are only three instances of 'How are you?' being used to initiate first topic in a new appointment. He also analyses one of these instances, as a deviant case, and shows how such an enquiry, in a new appointment, does not serve to initiate first topic. The patient's reply ('Fine') is treated as a return greeting and the doctor immediately selects one of the standard forms of first topic initiators ('Well, what can I do for you?').

Heath's paper shows c.a.'s concern with rigour, but illustrates some of the problems in its search for universals. Where the aim is to say something about a single form, like the interview, the propositions that one produces may be so general that their value is doubtful. How newsworthy is it, for instance, to be told that at new appointments doctors display lack of knowledge about the patient's reason for the visit? Moreover, as Dingwall (1980) has suggested, 'the interpretive context of the encounter' surely plays an important part in its social organization. (See Chapter 6, pp. 125–7.)

Because of his search for universal propositions, Heath's analysis lacks sensitivity to how the particulars of the setting (e.g. GP or hospital clinic, kind of illness, age and social background of the participants) influence the actors' interpretive work. In his work there are no measures, however simple, of features relevant to the interpretive context of the encounter other than those relating to stage of treatment.

In my study of a paediatric cardiology clinic I noted that, in the case of children with diagnosed congenital heart disease (CHD), the usual form of the consultation was for the doctor to convince the parents that, despite appearances to the contrary, their child was ill and that active intervention was called for. This was associated with a stress on clinical symptoms and a de-emphasis on the social qualities of the child.

This was quite different from the clinics observed by Strong (1979), which treated multiply handicapped children. There, because little could usually be done, the child was viewed primarily in social terms and a great deal of emphasis was placed on mothers' evaluation of their children's social performance. At this clinic, however, because medical intervention was usually successful, doctors saw no point in dwelling upon the child as a social object and sought to convince parents to view their children as clinical objects.

I at once noted that consultations with Down's Syndrome children provided a deviant case: their consultations took the form noted by Strong rather than the form observed with 'normal' children with CHD. Once again, there were ample transcript data which could be used to offer qualitative support to this inference. However, some simple quantitative measures, related to the relevant interpretive context, proved to be quite revealing.

Like Heath, I was interested in first topic-initiators. However, independent of whether this was a new or return appointment, I noted striking variations in the initial elicitation question. In a random sample of 22 consultations with 'normal' children, the doctor referred to the child's 'wellness' in 13 cases. In a sample of ten Down's consultations, the doctor mentioned 'wellness' in only one case and, even here, in an oblique way: 'From your point of view, a well baby?' (Silverman 1981).

As I argued, this avoidance of 'wellness' creates a space for other criteria to be used in deciding upon an appropriate disposal. To assess a child in terms of 'wellness' implies a medical obligation to try to restore the unwell child to a state of health. By avoiding references to 'wellness', social criteria, such as 'enjoyment of life', can come to play an important part in doctor–parent assessment of the Down's child.

These and other quantitative data produced in the research can play no more than a suggestive role. The sample is too small to make tests of significance worthwhile and the figures merely supplement and strengthen the qualitative analysis. None the less, the variables counted represent rather more than empty boxes derived from theoretically-conceived categories imposed on the data. First, they were based on detailed ethnographic data which suggested what Dingwall, quoting Goffman, refers to as the 'locally realised resources' employed by the participants. Second, I counted in terms of the categories actually used by doctors and patients rather than employing an external grid to map out the situation. Such grids cannot always be avoided — for instance, in the oncology clinics I counted 'questions'. However, a concentration on the situational particulars, as described by the actors, should be accorded a great deal of importance in both qualitative and quantitative work.*

There is no reason, in principle, why c.a. should not use simple counting procedures in order to substantiate its claims. Indeed, we have already seen how Heath does refer to a count he made on his whole sample. However, because of c.a.'s suspicion of ethnographic data which complicate its search for universals, it is likely that such counting will remain on a purely formal level and hence insensitive to the interpretive context of the encounter. This underlines the point I was trying to make earlier. The aim is not to count for counting's sake, but in order to establish a thoughtful dialogue with qualitatively-derived insights about the setting and actors' version of the situation-at-hand.

TEXTS: THE POLITICS OF DISCOURSE

British and American social scientists have never been entirely confident about analysing texts. Perhaps, in (what the French call) the Anglo-Saxon cultures, words seem too ephemeral and insubstantial to be the stuff of scientific analysis. Better, then, to leave textual analysis to literary critics and to concentrate on clearly social phenomena — actions and the structures in which they are implicated.

This uncertain, sometimes cavalier, attitude to language is reflected in the way in which so many sociological texts begin by fairly arbitrary definitions of their terms. The classic model is Durkheim's *Suicide* which

*Heath (personal correspondence) supports this argument with the proviso 'that one can show in empirical detail that participants . . . design and orientate their actions . . . with respect to such particulars.' He adds, quite justifiably, I believe, that 'one of the difficulties with certain forms of ethnographic work . . . is that situational influences are *stipulated* but not infrequently left relatively *unexamined*' (my emphasis).

offers a 'conclusive' definition of the phenomenon in its first few pages and then rushes off to investigate it in these terms. As others have pointed out, this method rules out of court any analysis of the very social processes through which suicide is socially defined — particularly in the context of coroners' own definitional practices.

In most sociology, then, words are important simply as a jumping-off point for the real analysis. Where texts are analysed, they are usually presented as 'official' or 'commonsense' versions of social phenomena, to be undercut by the underlying social phenomena displayed in the sociologist's analysis of social structures. The model is: people *say* X, but we can *show* that Y is the case.

Two exceptions apply to this general rule. First, content analysis is an accepted method of textual investigation, particularly in the field of mass communications. However, although it offers precise counts of word use, its theoretical basis is unclear and its conclusions can often be trite. Second, more recently, ethnomethodology has provided an analytic framework for the analysis of texts. In the work of Garfinkel (1967) and Zimmerman (1974), for instance, attention has been paid to the commonsense practices involved in assembling and interpreting written records. This work has refused to reduce texts to a secondary status and has made an important contribution to our understanding of everyday bureaucratic practices.

Anglo-Saxon culture, in which these two approaches have arisen, makes clear-cut disciplinary boundaries. Perhaps this is why, generally speaking, 'words' are allocated to the humanities and 'structures' to the sciences. French culture, on the contrary, creates unities around 'methods' rather than disciplines. The signal contribution of Saussure was to generate a method which showed that 'structures' and 'words' are inseparable. For Saussure, words and other signs only make sense when treated as part of a system. The system is constituted by differences and relations. Difference arises through structures of opposition (black/white, yes/no) where the choice of one unit necessarily excludes the salience of the other unit in the pair. Relations are seen in the links between a stem word (e.g. 'link') and what may precede (unlink, cuff-link) and follow it (link-up, linked). (For further discussion of Saussure's method, see Chapter 3, pp. 56–8.)

The significance for textual analysis is that Saussure's structuralism shows that a text can be analysed as a system. Just as economics is concerned with a synchronic analysis of the relations between the parts of an economic system, so linguistics undertakes such an analysis of the parts of a textual system. Words are not a preliminary to an investigation of reality, they are a reality in their own right. So the move outside the system (into history or social structures) can be illusory and reductivist.

Initially at least, everything must be analysed at its own level.

Structuralism has produced works of much theoretical elegance in both French and Anglo-Saxon scholarship. Apart from the work of Lévi-Strauss on myth, and Bernstein and Bourdieu on classification, one particularly thinks of Barthes' (1975) classic analysis of a whole short story by Balzac, and Douglas's (1975) treatment of the response of an African tribe to an animal that was anomalous in relation to their system of classification.

I want now to consider the methods by which one study in the structuralist–semiotic tradition addresses its data, and to introduce another study of my own to illustrate how simple counting can substantiate the claims of work in this tradition.

Burton and Carlen (1979) are interested in how official reports function in British politics to legitimate the state in the context of potentially threatening events. They argue that the role of the official version of these events is 'to confront, incorporate and suppress the alternative, unofficial version' (Burton and Carlen 1979: 70). They call this unofficial version 'the Other of the discourse'. The part of their book I want to consider is concerned with the case of a police officer (Detective Sergeant Challenor) who was found to have planted bricks on suspects and to have used violence on them. The James Report which followed these events, they argue, managed the narrative history to show (i) that Challenor was mentally ill at the time, and (ii) that this could not have been known then.

In eight pages, Burton and Carlen attempt to deconstruct the James Report. Quoting brief extracts, they suggest that it cites as the 'Other' a reference by James to the possibility that:

> at West End Central Station . . . an atmosphere had developed whereby police-officers and Detective Sergeant Challenor in particular, could use violence and show disrespect to persons in custody, and could indulge in fabrication of evidence without exciting attention. (ibid.: 71)

Burton and Carlen then argue that the Report immediately renders the Other unspeakable. They quote James' 'conclusion' that there was no such 'atmosphere' at the police station in question.

According to Burton and Carlen, the James Report succeeds by means of five basic textual manoeuvres:

1. It establishes a fairy-tale structure, as depicted in Propp's structural analysis of myths. This provides for a villain (paranoid schizophrenia), a hero (Challenor) and a heroic stage (the police station).
2. It establishes the credibility of the characters as depicted in the text by inviting the reader 'to trust the privileged judgement of those who, because they actually heard and saw the witnesses are best empowered

to judge [their] credibility' (ibid.: 74). Hence a witness favourable to the official version of events is described as 'a most impressive and frank witness', while a suspect who had a brick planted on him is described in derogatory terms.

3. Like the common law judge, it appeals to precedent where useful while, where necessary, it overturns precedent, while at the same time maintaining the principle of precedent intact.

4. It manipulates narrative-time by presenting an episodic history of events that fragments a situation of cumulative bizarre events into a series of separate moments.

5. It appeals to what we all know about how people are likely to behave in particular situations even if we did not witness the actual events. Thus, the authors quote James' thanks at the outset to the inquiry's assessor for his 'experience and understanding of human-nature [upon which] I have made heavy calls' (ibid.: 74).

This summary presentation does not give a true flavour of Burton and Carlen's work, which is marred by too brief a data analysis and an uneconomical use of a surplus of theoretical terms. However, even if their study hardly achieves the elegance of, say, Barthes (1975) or Douglas (1975), it is recognisably in the same structuralist tradition. Although the authors do theorise about the relation between official discourses and the character of the state, the focus of their data analysis is entirely on the realities set into play by the texts themselves.

In such an analysis, however, we have as always to be careful about our warrant for making claims about the data. Burton and Carlen show awareness of one aspect of this problem: mirroring the very practices they describe. Thus they refer, somewhat archly, to their study as an 'unofficial report' and refuse to accept that it is grounded in any correspondence theory of truth.

This settles, by fiat, the problems of infinite regress. However, it fails to answer the charge that, whatever the rival epistemological claims involved, both their analysis *and* the official reports they describe make assertions based on very little data. Both methods seek to persuade the reader that, confronted with any given textual fragment, 'we can see that' a favoured reading applies.

Now of course, at a certain point, As Blum (1974) has suggested, such persuasion is an inescapable part of the scientific enterprise. The question remains whether we can use any more props to our argument than a fragment of data followed by a 'we see that . . .' kind of statement. This question arose when I examined (Silverman 1982) a collection of papers discussing the future of the British Labour Party (Jacques and Mulhern (eds) 1981). Although written before the 1983 election débâcle, many of the contributions provided a good instrument for predicting its outcome in relation to Labour's shrinking social base.

I selected two short papers by little-known trade union leaders which seemed to propose alternative versions of Labour's political past and future. In this discussion, I shall only consider the four-page text by Ken Gill. Gill argues that the post-1950 period has seen a 'picture of advance' for the Labour Party. This advance is indexed by a move towards left-wing policies and left-wing leaders in both unions and the Labour Party.

One immediate critical rejoinder to this argument is that organisational and ideological advances have to be judged in relation to popular support — which, with one or two exceptions, dropped continuously at general elections after 1950. However, this is to remain in a sense *outside* of Gill's text. Like Burton and Carlen's analysis, despite its structuralist pretensions, such arguments tend to use isolated extracts and summaries as a means of deploying critiques or deconstructions. Outside structuralism, contrasts between texts and 'theory', or texts and 'reality', are the very stuff of academic and practical debates. Inevitably, however, they can result in empty victories in mock battles.

Following a structuralist method, my aim was to avoid interpreting Gill's text in terms of alternative versions of reality but, instead, to enter within it. Such *internal* analysis must seek to establish and deconstruct the realities the text itself sets into play. There was no difficulty in the programme. The problem was to find a method which would allow these realities to be described without appealing to the 'we see that . . .' strategy.

In order to get a sense of Gill's paper as a whole, I went through the text listing the subjects or agents mentioned. The agents named fell into four broad categories. References to trade unions and to groups defined by class were counted as instances of economic agents. These were distinguished from references to theorists, to political parties or tendencies. This produced Table 7.3.

Table 7.3: Gill's agents

Agent	Number
Economic	16
Theoretical	5
Political	9
None of the above	1
Total	31

Table 7.3 was used to support the suggestion that Gill's analysis concentrates on economically-defined subjects or subjects defined with reference to other formal institutions. This apparent preference for formal structures was underlined when I counted the 'level' of agent to which Gill refers. Although not all the agents were classifiable in these terms, I discovered a clear preference for agents with an official or high-level position, as shown in Table 7.4.

Table 7.4: Agents' level

Level of agent		Number
Leader or theorist		14
No rank or lower rank		3
Unclear		14
	Total	31

Table 7.3 substantiated the impression that Gill has constructed a narrative which tells its tale from the top down. It is largely a tale of economic subjects, organised by existing institutions and their leaders. Moreover, further analysis revealed that Gill's text concentrates on activities relating to policy-making, or occupying particular political positions. In only five cases did he refer to an agent's action; all these cases related to economic struggles.

These simple tabulations supported my argument that Gill's practice contradicted his theory. While Gill theorises about movements towards socialism and democracy, the structure of his text is consistently élitist. Put another way, the élitist form of his tale runs directly contrary to its democratic message.

Some of this could, of course, be demonstrated by the use of brief extracts from Gill's piece followed by critical exegesis. However, this standard procedure of traditional (political, literary) criticism cannot generate such an analysis so forcefully or economically. Critical exegesis is prone to two damaging limitations: it may appeal to extra-textual realities, while de-emphasising the realities constructed in the text under consideration and/or, like Burton and Carlen, it may base its case on isolated fragments of a text supported by a 'persuasive' argument.

At this point, the reader may ask: doesn't your own method bear a striking resemblance to content analysis? If so, doesn't it risk the charges of triviality and of imposing (extra-textual) realities on the data through its methods of classification? In which case, can't your argument against traditional criticism be turned against yourself?

Now, of course, the tabulations I have just presented do share with content analysis one characteristic: both involve counting instances of terms used in a text. However, unlike some content analysis, the terms counted are *not* determined by an arbitrary or commonsense version of what may be interesting to count in a text. It is not coincidental that I have counted Gill's agents or 'subjects'. The theory of the subject is central to structuralism and semiotics. As Benveniste has demonstrated, the textual construction of subjects points to the implausibility of attempts to reduce texts to extra-textual realities — 'I' is not such a reality because we can all speak as 'I's. The politics of the construction of the subject — such an important theme in recent French and feminist thought — is thus explored here not in order to reduce Gill's text to an arbitrary scheme, but in order to demonstrate, as economically as possible, the productivities at work within it. In western cultures, at least, subjects are intrinsic to narratives: by analysing the construction of subjects, we get to the heart of the work of the text.

CONCLUSION

I have tried to show the uses of simple methods of counting in largely qualitative studies. Two of the studies I have examined use purely descriptive statistics; a third introduces some straightforward correlations. This concentration on description is not coincidental.

The kind of interpretive sociology which I have been discussing is doubly interested in description. First, like all scientific work, it is concerned with the problem of how to generate adequate descriptions of what it observes. Second, however, unlike other kinds of sociology; it is especially interested in how ordinary people observe and describe their world. Many of the procedures I have discussed here aim to offer adequate (sociological) descriptions of (lay) descriptions. Once this is recognised as the central problematic of the interpretive paradigm, then these procedures can be extended to what people say and write in a far broader range of settings.

For instance, Baruch (1982) has analysed interviews with parents of handicapped children in relation to the subjects they mention. Using Sacks' (1974) powerful account of how we describe reality through membership categorisation devices (MCDs), Baruch has counted pairs of agents referred to by parents.

A commonsense assumption might be that, when asked 'to tell the story' about their child's handicap, parents would describe events largely in terms of the child's relation to medical professionals. Instead, Baruch found that in a majority of instances the story was told via the relation between the *parent* and the child. Moreover, he demonstrated how this relationship was formulated in largely a moral fashion. Interviewees appealed to norms of responsibility and caring in order to depict themselves as adequate parents.*

Baruch's work demonstrates how Sacks' elegant schema of relations between MCDs can be applied empirically across a large body of data. By using quantitative techniques in an area opened up by ethnomethodology, Baruch shows, as Sacks had always implied, that the gap between the two sociologies (positivism and interpretivism) is less significant than many people imagine: meaning is intimately linked to morality.

As American interactionists, like Becker and Geer (1960) have recognised, adequate sociological description of social processes needs to look beyond purely qualitative methods. Everything depends, however, on the relation between the quantitative measures being used and the analytic issue being addressed: 'The usefulness of . . . statistics is a function of the theoretical problematic in which they are to be used and on the use to which they are to be put within it' (Hindess 1973: 45).

FURTHER READING

The classic interactionist critique of survey research and its method of counting is Blumer's (1956) paper. The most well-known ethnomethodological critique of the assumptions underlying quantitative method is Cicourel (1964). This book also addresses the politics of quantification, as does Hindess (1973) and Irvine *et al.* (eds) (1979). Cicourel (1968) also reveals the social organisation of counting in everyday settings.

Halfpenny (1979) provides a useful overview of the response to quantification by a number of research traditions in sociology. Although many recent schools tend to reject counting, Becker and Geer (1960) and Hindess (1973) show its applicability to interactionst and Marxist traditions, respectively.

---

*Baruch's work shows that analysis of interview data can regain credibility by avoiding treating accounts as descriptions of actual events, and by focusing instead on how people generate descriptions. As Baruch argues, far from being a dry topic, unrelated to substantive issues, it goes to the heart of questions of morality and social order. This is central to my argument in Chapter 8.

8 A place for interview data

For many years, survey research provided the main source of data for sociology. For instance, Brenner (ed) (1981) reports studies which indicate that, during the 1960s, around 90 per cent of all the papers in the two leading American sociology journals were based on data derived from interviews and questionnaires.

More recently, however, first interactionism then ethnomethodology have begun to question the value of data derived from 'artificial' settings like interviews, which were understood by purely external concepts, and it now became the fashion to concentrate on naturally-occurring settings which were to be observed and/or recorded at first hand.

It should at once be noted that the critique of the value of interview data unknowingly shared an assumption with more traditional approaches. As Hammersley and Atkinson (1983) have pointed out, this kind of naturalism unwittingly agrees with positivism that the best kind of data are somehow 'untouched by human hands' — neutral, unbiased and representative. In some senses, then, naturalists are the inheritors of the positivist programme, using different means to achieve the same unquestioned ends.

In accord with the overall thesis of this book, I shall argue that the opposition between artificial and naturally-occurring data is another methodological red herring. Neither kind of data are intrinsically better than the other; everything depends on the method of analysis.

The implication is that multiple sources of data can often be useful in clarifying research problems. However, I do not follow Denzin (1970) in believing that data gathered in different settings can simply be added up to offer a more complete overall picture of a given phenomenon. Here, as in Chapter 5, I shall emphasise the positivist rationale that underlies some interactionists' fascination with data triangulation.*

*Dingwall (personal correspondence) has suggested that triangulation has some value where, for instance, it reveals the existence of public and private accounts of an agency's work. Here 'interview and field data can be combined . . . to make better sense of the other.' I entirely accept Dingwall's point. His example shows triangulation being used to address the *situated work* of accounts rather than, as in Denzin's case, to do *ironies*.

In brief, the task of this chapter is to outline some of the uses and limits of data gathered from interview settings. Following my discussion of Bhaskar (1979) in Chapter 2, my position will, I hope, be consistently realist. Realism implies that social structures are 'real', in the sense that they are reflected in social relations which may be hidden from (though expressed in) the perceptions of the individual. This means that interview data display cultural realities which are neither biased nor accurate, but simply 'real'. Interview data, from this point of view, are not 'one side of the picture' to be balance by observation of what respondents actually do, or to be compared with what their role partners say. Instead, realism implies that such data reproduce and rearticulate cultural particulars grounded in given patterns of social organisation.

To take a concrete example: when parents of handicapped children are first interviewed, they often offer 'atrocity' stories, usually about the late discovery or inadequate treatment of their child's condition. It is tempting to compare what they say with observations of what has happened and with medical workers' accounts. However, as Baruch (1982) points out, such a comparison is based on the assumption that interview responses are to be valued primarily in terms of their accuracy as objective statements of sets of events. Conversely, we might address the moral forms that give force to 'atrocity' stories, whatever their accuracy. Right or wrong, biased or unbiased, such accounts display vividly cultural particulars about the moral accountability of parenthood.

The significance of such cultural realities implies that we must reject also ethnomethodologists' claims that interviews can only be a topic but never a resource for sociological analysis. Although some ethnomethodologists (e.g. Atkinson 1982) have recently shown an interest in interview data, that interest has been limited to its conversational sequencing relative to natural conversation. This has meant that no self-respecting ethnomethodologist wants to carry out interviews. Instead, (s)he studies other people's interviews as examples of skilful, practical accomplishments. This *formal* concern identifies the structures of communication purely with conversational sequencing. Apart from Sacks' work on 'description', as I pointed out in Chapter 6, it excludes important aspects of the moral order concerned with the structure and content of narratives.

I shall now consider, in turn, positivist, interactionist and ethnomethodological versions of interview data, before outlining a realist alternative. As outlined in Table 8.1, I shall consider each approach in terms of the types of knowledge it believes is provided by interview data, its criterion of validity and, very briefly, the policy implications it attaches to its analysis.

Table 8.1: Approaches to interview data*

	Positivism	Interactionism	Ethnomethodology	Realism
Type of knowledge	Facts about the world.	Interviews as symbolic interaction.	Conversational practices.	Display of realities.
Criterion of validity	Following protocol/ comparability of different interviews.	Intersubjective depth/ 'triangulated' evidence.	Consensus among analysts.	Analytic induction.
Policy implications	Control and manipulation of 'variables'.	Debunking/'mutual translatability'.	Functions of existing conversational practices.	Understanding policy options in the context of constraints.

*In this table, as elsewhere in this chapter, I am indebted to discussions with Barry Glassner and Geoffrey Baruch.

POSITIVISM

Type of knowledge

In standard methodology texts, geared to a statistical logic based principally on survey research, interview data give access to 'facts' about the world. Although these facts include both biographical information and statements about beliefs, all are to be treated as accounts whose sense derives from their correspondence to a factual reality. Where that reality is imperfectly represented by an account, checks and remedies are to be encouraged in order to get a truer or more complete picture of how things stand.

Here are the six kinds of topics to which, according to a standard text, interview questions are addressed. Notice how these writers envisage problems and remedies in relation to each topic:

1. *'Facts'*. These relate primarily to biographical information about the respondent, to statements from informed sources about the structures, policies and actions of organisations, and to descriptions of an event or a community. In this last case, it is possible to weed out 'inaccurate' descriptions by comparing different people's statements:

   > If respondents occupying widely different positions in the community agree on a statement, there is much better ground for accepting it as true than if only one of these respondents makes the statement. On the other hand, contradictions between the reports of apparently reliable informants provide important leads for further investigation. (Selltiz *et al*. 1964: 245)

2. *'Beliefs about facts'*. In questions about beliefs or attitudes, no interpersonal cross-checking of statements is appropriate. However, Selltiz *et al*. point out that it is always important to check first whether the respondent has any beliefs about the topic in question, otherwise, the researcher may put words into his mouth (ibid.: 246).

3. *'Feelings and motives'*. Here, because 'emotional reactions are frequently too complex to report in a single phrase' (ibid.: 248), Selltiz *et al*. recommend the use of open-ended questions, allowing respondents to choose their own terms.

4. *'Standards of action'*. These relate to what people think should or could be done about certain stated situations. Here it helps to link such standards to people's experiences. Where someone has actually faced a situation of the type described, his/her response is likely to be more reliable.

5. *'Present or past behaviour'*. Again, specific questions related to actual rather than hypothetical situations are recommended.

6. *Conscious reasons for 1–5.* Rather than simply ask 'Why?', Selltiz *et al.* recommend that the researcher should examine broad classes of considerations that may have determined this outcome (e.g. 'the history of the act or feeling', or 'the characteristics in a given entity that provoke a given reaction') (ibid.: 253).

In each of these six topics, the task of the interview is to elicit a body of facts 'out there' in the world. For positivists, an observation that interview responses might be an outcome of the interview setting would be heard as a charge against the validity of the technique. To the extent that this possibility arises, checks and remedies are built into the research design. Similarly, for positivists, the language of the interviewee serves primarily as an instrument for the communication of external psychological or sociological facts.

Criterion of validity

The aim of interviews for positivists is to generate data which hold independently of both the research setting and the researcher or interviewer. One way of achieving this is by attempting standardised interviews. Consequently, Selltiz *et al.* are rather suspicious of unstructured interviews. Although they concede that they are more flexible than pre-scheduled interviews and can allow more intensive study of perceptions and feelings, they have inherent problems for positivists: 'The flexibility frequently results in a lack of comparability of one interview with another. Moreover, their analysis is more difficult and time-consuming than that of standardised interviews' (ibid.: 264).

Even more important for validity than the type of interview selected, is the need to follow a standardised protocol. So Selltiz *et al.* offer an Appendix entitled 'The Art of Interviewing' which provides a set of rules and taboos. Interviewers *should* ask each question precisely as it is worded and in the same order that it appears on the schedule. They should *not* show surprise or disapproval of an answer, offer impromptu explanations of questions, suggest possible replies, or skip certain questions. Similarly, Brenner offers a list of 'do's' and 'don'ts' ('basic rules of research interviewing' — Brenner 1981: 129–30), which are defended on terms of the necessity of standardisation:

> 'In order to ensure adequacy of measurement in a data collection programme it is of primary importance to secure, as much as is possible, the equivalence of the stimulus conditions in the interviews. If these are not equivalent, measurement may be biased, and it may be unwarranted to group responses together for the purposes of statistical analyses. (ibid.: 115)

Although Brenner is more sceptical than Selltiz *et al.* about the prospects of obtaining 'literal measurement' in the interview situation (ibid.: 156), the statement quoted indicates that he shares with them the same statistical and behaviouralist (or stimulus-response) logic. Following that logic, he calls for more research on social interaction in interviews as a means 'of improving the quality of research interviews . . . and increasing the degree of social control over the measurement process' (ibid.: 156).

Policy implications
For positivists, interviews provide facts about the world which, if properly collated, can be fed directly back into the world. So, for instance, Selltiz *et al.* report studies which relate participation in groups to the ability of members to elect their leaders. They link such studies to straightforward policy changes encouraging more democratic processes in small groups. Within the widely-held behaviouralist logic, if it can be shown that influence X is associated with a favoured action Y or belief Z, then X is increased as a stimulus to achieve the desired response Y or Z.

For all positivists, whether behaviouralists or not, research-based public policy is about the control and manipulation of well-defined variables. The only limit on such social engineering is the extent to which statistical measures offer the prospect of legitimate generalisations from the data and also the relevant values of the community and the researcher (which define whether Y and Z are valued).

INTERACTIONISM

Type of knowledge

> Interviews must be viewed, then, as social events in which the interviewer (and for that matter the interviewee) is a participant observer. . . . Interview data, like any other, must be interpreted against the background of the context in which they were produced. (Hammersley and Atkinson 1983: 126)

> I wish to treat the interview as an observational encounter. An encounter . . . represents the coming together of two or more persons for the purpose of focused interaction. (Denzin 1970: 133)

For positivists, interviews are essentially about ascertaining facts or beliefs out there in the world. While it is acknowledged that interviewers interact with their subjects, such interaction is strictly defined by the research protocol. Consequently, positivists only become seriously interested in interviewer–interviewee interaction when it can be shown that interviewers have departed from the protocol (Brenner 1981).

Conversely, for interactionists, interviews are essentially about symbolic interaction. Whatever the topic addressed by the questions, they are social events based on mutual participant observation (Hammersley and Atkinson 1983) which produces a 'focused interaction' (Denzin 1970). Consequently, the context of the production of a recognisable interview is intrinsic to understanding any data that are obtained. While positivists aim for a clear-cut distinction between research interviews and other forms of social interaction, interactionists argue that that aim is unobtainable. The distinction between these two positions is summarised in Table 8.2.

Table 8.2:   Two versions of the interview relationship

	Positivism	*Interactionism*
Status of interviewer	Object — following protocol.	Subject — constructing interview context.
Status of interviewee	Object — revealing items relevant to research protocol.	Subject — complying with or resisting this construction.

Criterion of validity

When interactionists assess what makes interview responses valid, they continue to depart from the positivist position. If interviewees are to be viewed as subjects who actively construct the features of their cognitive world, then one should try to obtain intersubjective depth between both sides so that a deep mutual understanding can be achieved.

The practical implication is that most interactionists tend to reject pre-scheduled standardised interviews and to prefer open-ended interviews. Denzin offers three reasons for this preference:

1. It allows respondents to use their 'unique ways of defining the world' (Denzin 1970: 125).
2. It assumes that no fixed sequence of questions is suitable to all respondents.
3. It allows respondents to 'raise important issues not contained in the schedule' (ibid.).

As Hammersley and Atkinson (1983: 110–11) point out, however, it is somewhat naive to assume that open-ended or non-directive interviewing is not in itself a form of social control which shapes what people say. For instance, where the researcher maintains a minimal presence, asking few questions, this can create an interpretive problem for the interviewee about what is relevant. I would also add that this preference for a particular form of interview is defined in terms of avoiding bias which is entirely appropriate to a positivist approach. Indeed, if one examines closely how interactionists provide for the validity of interview data, strongly positivist assumptions are revealed which considerably undercut the simple polarity proposed in Table 8.2.

Denzin, for instance, lists a number of 'problems' which can 'distort' interviewees' responses (Denzin 1970: 133–8):

(a) Respondents possessing different interactional roles from the interviewer.

(b) The problem of 'self-presentation' especially in the early stages of the interview.

(c) The problems of 'volatile', 'fleeting' relationships to which respondents have little commitment and so 'can fabricate tales of self that belie the actual facts' (ibid.: 135).

(d) The difficulty of penetrating private worlds of experience.

(e) The relative status of interviewer and interviewee.

(f) The 'context' of the interview (e.g. home, work, hospital).

Denzin writes about all these problems as 'sources of invalidity' (ibid.: 136). As I argued in Chapter 5, there is an inconsistency in his position which, no doubt, reflects strains within interactionism itself. For to see encounters as potentially invalid is to impose a positivist framework upon an interactionist perspective. Either interviews are situated encounters where what is said makes sense only in context, or they are simply research instruments designed to get at facts which are context-free. Positivists are entirely consistent in maintaining the latter position. Denzin, however, seems to occupy both positions, arguing in theory for the former position but often, in practice, rejecting it. Consequently, he can, at one and the same time, discuss interviews as observational encounters and recommend data triangulation as means of attaining greater validity.

There is present here a dilemma between choosing to focus on the *content* of what people are saying as a neutral report on the world (the positivist position) or treating interviews as situated ceremonial orders where the focus is on the *force* of what people are doing and saying (what I take to be the interactionist theory). The dilemma is well stated by West (1979): 'Essentially, the problem revolves around the distinction between the content of accounts, which at face value might be used to support various propositions, and what people are 'doing' with their talk' (West 1979: 719). Unfortunately, like Denzin, West seems to want to have it both ways. For he goes on:

> perhaps both [content and 'doing'] can be employed to advantage; the former by invoking some notion of validity or plausibility established by Denzin's principle of 'triangulation', the latter by recognising the situated nature of accounts and

treating them as procedures, resources or methods by which people 'do' interpretative work within particular contexts. (ibid.)

In a footnote at the end of this piece, West appeals to ethnomethodology as an
example of this latter concern. I shall shortly turn to this approach. First,
however, I want to examine briefly the policy implications of interactionist
treatments of interviews.

Policy implications
There is a strongly relativist streak in interactionism. This arises because of
its refusal to accept the objective status of social reality as defined by
positivist sociologists. If social situations are real only because they are so
interpreted by participants, then it becomes difficult to maintain any firmly-
based ethical line about social institutions. Faced with this difficulty, interactionists have argued for two kinds of policy implications that are consistent with an overall relativist position. First, they have suggested that a
focus on the contingency of definitions of reality can provide some much
needed debunking of absolutist claims about society. Thus, in the work of
Hughes (1956) and Berger (1966), accounts of social interaction are used to
deflate the pretensions of participants. This debunking motif is criticised in
Chapter 9, pp. 187–8.

If this suggestion emphasises the distancing of the sociologist from his
subjects, a second policy direction is much more concerned with aiding
people through active intervention in social settings. Here the aim is to help
people to understand better 'how the other half lives' (and feels), by increasing mutual knowledge between them. With its emphasis on understanding
definitions of the situation, interactionism is well placed in this respect.

In his postscript to *Knowledge and Human Interests* (1972), Habermas
reveals what is involved in this kind of policy concern. Although his reference point is the German Idealist tradition (particularly Dilthey), there is a
concern with 'meaning-creation' which is common to nineteenth-century
German thought and twentieth-century American interactionist work. The
shared hermeneutic ambition locates understanding in the process of mediation between the meaning structures of observer and observed. The aim is
greater understanding between different systems of thought, i.e. mutual
translatability. This expresses what Habermas calls 'the knowledge-
constitutive interest' of hermeneutics. In turn, it is to be distinguished from
the interests of positivist approaches in predicting behaviour in order to
control it better.

Conceived in policy terms, it is clear that Habermas intends to under-line
the relative benevolence of hermeneutics. Unlike the paternalism or, at
worst, the despotism of the positivist interest, an interest in greater understanding appeals to liberal sentiments. However, Habermas now unveils a

third interest which reveals the limits of such sentiments. His emancipatory interest is concerned with analysing the structures which shape and limit human practice and understanding. Rather than creating better understanding of meanings, it seeks to show how meanings are often imposed. Its aim is, therefore, not better communication within existing structures but emancipation from those structures which, in Habermas's view, 'deform' or 'distort' communication. It must remain questionable, however, whether such a noble aim is necessarily reflected in the political applications of social science. The reader should be reminded of the apparently inescapable connection between forms of knowledge and modes of social control revealed in Foucault's work (see Chapter 4, pp. 82–91).

Interactionism does share with Habermas an optimistic version of knowledge as enlightenment. Ethnomethodology, the next approach I shall discuss, has, as will shortly be argued, a much more conservative view of the social function of knowledge.

ETHNOMETHODOLOGY

Type of knowledge

Garfinkel (1967) introduced the distinction between resource and topic in order to show the background knowledge used by sociologists in describing and explaining social phenomena. We all make the social world our topic. However, some of us use our everyday knowledge as a tacit resource in generating findings. In this case, we are constructive sociologists (i.e. constructing sense through unexplored methods). Alternatively, we might examine the reflexive relation between lay and professional accounting procedures and between all accounts and the social world. Here, we engage in ethnomethodology. In Zimmerman and Pollner's (1971) terms, our concern is no longer with social facts but with the factual character of social processes.

Interviewing is a social process which is obviously open to such an epistemological shift. When ethnomethodologists consider interviews, the type of knowledge they seek is always located in the context of the factual production of the interview itself. For them, interview data report not on an *external* reality displayed in respondents' utterances but on the *internal* reality constructed as both parties contrive to produce the appearances of a recognisable interview.

The earliest attempt to set out this version of interview data was made by Cicourel (1964). Constrained by the power of the then dominant empiricist version of research method, Cicourel was forced to set out his approach within the framework of a traditional methodology textbook. The result is a many-layered narrative whose moral implies a radical epistemological break, yet is stated within the confines of a survey of the uses and limitations of conventional research techniques. For Cicourel, previous advice about good interview technique offers a revealing insight into our dependence on everyday knowledge of social structures when conducting and interpreting research interviews. As he writes:

> The subtleties which methodologists introduce to the novice interviewer can be read as properties to be found in the everyday interaction between members of a society. Thus the principles of 'good and bad interviewing' can be read as basic features of social interaction which the social scientist presumably is seeking to study. (Cicourel 1964: 68)

For Cicourel, the remedies recommended by methodologists derive from the very knowledge of the social world which should be made problematic. Moreover, the 'errors' they detect are not really obstacles to social research but rather exhibit basic properties of social interaction. We must learn, he suggests, to 'conceive of the error as evidence not only of poor reliability but also of "normal" interpersonal relations' (ibid.: 74).

Cicourel parallels Garfinkel's (1967) awe at the 'amazing, practical accomplishment' of research findings which, inevitably, are reflexively linked to everyday procedures for 'looking' and 'finding'. Ironically, he is full of praise for methodology texts like Hyman *et al.* (1954), which is dubbed 'excellent' on two occasions (Cicourel 1964: 85, 93). The irony arises because he wants to utilise their desired success in achieving a degree of invariance not as a resource but as a topic:

> In spite of the problem of interviewer error, 'somehow' different interviewers with different approaches produce(d) similar responses from different subjects. The question then becomes one of determining what was invariant or, more precisely, how were invariant meanings communicated despite such variations. (ibid.: 75)

For Cicourel, there is no distinction between the practical skills of methodologists, researchers and interviewers. All are uniformly concerned with what he calls 'the synchronisation of meaning'. All use 'rules of evidence' deriving from a single conceptual scheme based on assumed common relevances, stocks of knowledge, typifications, recipes, rules for managing one's presence before others, and so on. These shared 'commonsense devices for making sense of the environment' (ibid.: 100) are presupposed in conducting or analysing interviews.

While Cicourel throughout refers to Alfred Schutz's work on the 'natural attitude' as the point of departure for any analysis of the interview, later ethnomethodological studies have narrowed the analytic viewpoint. Sacks' precise analyses of the sequencing of conversation have replaced Schutz's general statements about 'interpretive procedures' as the major resource for the analysis of interaction.

Although most work here has been concerned with 'mundane conversation', we can extrapolate some features of the analysis relevant to our concern with interview data. First, interviews give access to knowledge of internal conversational practices. Second, these practices work through placing utterances in sequences of actions. As Atkinson and Heritage put it, 'For conversational analysts, therefore, it is sequences and turns-within-sequences, rather than isolated utterances or sentences, which are the primary units of analysis' (Atkinson and Heritage 1982: 3).

A basic sequence of actions in a recognisable interview is a series of questions and answers (*cf.* Silverman 1973). After a question, as Sacks puts it, 'the other party properly speaks, and properly offers an answer to the question and says no more than that' (Sacks 1972: 230). However, after the answer has been given, the questioner can speak again and *can* choose to ask a further question. This chaining rule can provide 'for the occurrence of an indefinitely long conversation of the form Q–A–Q–A–Q–A . . .' (ibid.).

Although question–answer sequences do arise in mundane conversation, they seem to provide a defining characteristic of interview talk. The chaining rule gives a great deal of space to the interviewer to shape the flow of topics, while interviewees depend upon being granted a right to ask questions themselves (Silverman 1973).

Hughes has noted this asymmetry of interactional rights, based on a question/answer format. In medical consultations:

> The asking of a question in itself constrains the patient to give an answer on the same topic. Having heard the answer to the question as the end of the patient's utterance, the doctor is free to interrupt and the turn to initiate continually comes back to him. To introduce a new point he simply moves on to the next question without necessary recourse to certain practices common in everyday conversations. (Hughes 1982: 369)

Hughes' work suggests that treating interviews as displays of conversational practices, unexpectedly, may feed into studies of power and authority. However, as Garfinkel (1967) himself has noted, ethnomethodological studies derive strictly from a Durkheimian/Parsonian social order perspective. Within such a perspective, even Hughes denies that power lies at the heart of the medical interview. Instead, he proposes that, where difficulties arise, it is simply because of misunderstandings based upon different bases of knowledge. None the less, within this kind of functionalist approach, question/answer chains are to be seen as: 'an effective means of producing orderly sequences of talk and an appearance of mutual understanding in circumstances where the competence or knowledge of one of the participants is problematic' (ibid.: 367). I shall shortly comment on the policy implications of this kind of treatment of interview data.

Criterion of validity

The discussion above has highlighted ethnomethodologists' conviction that sociological analysis necessarily uses everyday (members') knowledge as a resource. The question that then arises is the kind of distinction to be drawn between everyday and sociological analyses of social phenomena. As Turner puts it:

> It is increasingly recognised as an issue for sociology that the equipment that enables the 'ordinary' member of society to make his daily way through the world is the equipment available for those who would wish to do a 'science' of that world. (Turner 1974: 197)

That this is a problem for ethnomethodologists themselves (as apart from their critics) is revealed in Atkinson and Heritage's (1982) critique of 'analytic traditions in which "native intuitions" . . . are treated as an adequate analytic base' (1982: Preface). The solution seems to consist, first, in recognising one's dependence on members' knowledge and then, second, in making it problematic in a way that would never arise for members. This two-stage model is well stated by Turner:

> The sociologist inevitably trades on his members' knowledge in recognising the activities that parties to an interaction are engaged in . . . [(s)he] must then pose as problematic how utterances come off as recognisable unit activities. (Turner 1974: 204–5)

Turner appears to imply a model of the ethnomethodologist working as a single figure, unravelling his/her internal understandings. The more common model, however, is of *group* activity. So Atkinson and Heritage (ibid.) refer to 'group data analysis sessions' at which 'the production and use of transcripts are essentially *research activities*' (original emphasis).

Assembling and analysing transcripts through such group work defines the criterion of validity being used. Consensus among analysts establishes, first, that the data are genuine (and not, for instance, mistranscribed). Second, such consensus is the basis for claiming (through comparison with other data) that what has been observed is an instance of a particular kind.

Ethnomethodologists, then, operate, like Kuhnian scientists, with a community version of reality and truth. Clearly, this does *not* mean that everyday knowledge is identified with truth. As in Schutz's model, such knowledge only offers a first-order body of data which must then be reassessed through second-order community standards. Thus it is an ethnomethodologist and not Durkheim who has written: 'Folk beliefs have honourable status but they are not the same intellectual object as a scientific analysis' (Moerman 1974: 55).

Policy implications

We may distinguish here the *use* of *research* interviews from the *study* of interviews in *everyday* life. In neither kind of setting do ethnomethodologists see very many policy implications but the response is rather different to each.

Ethnomethodologists all insist that interactional data collected from naturally-occurring settings are what they prefer to work with. Like laboratory studies and observational field notes, research interviews mean that 'the observer must necessarily manipulate, direct or otherwise intervene in the subject's behaviour' (Atkinson and Heritage 1982: 1). Given their insistence on the rich particulars of everyday behaviour and their sophisticated methods of transcription of data, conversational analysts see no need to create 'artificial' research settings. As such, they go beyond Cicourel's tentative suggestion that the time is not ripe for research interviews since we lack a 'precise theory [of] . . . the kinds of interpretive "rules" employed for managing one's presence before others' (Cicourel 1964: 87). However, as we have seen, ethnomethodologists and conversational analysts are prepared to *study* interviews (i.e. to use them as a topic, if not a resource). None the less, it has already been implied that their functionalist model provides very little space for developing positive policy implications.

As we have seen, Hughes' treatment of the consultation as an interview does lead him to recognise the patient's 'limit[ed] . . . opportunities to offer elaboration or introduce new points' (Hughes 1982: 374). Nevertheless, he concludes that 'an organisation of talk that permits the production of ordered sequences of topically relevant talk offers obvious mutual advantages' (ibid.). Similarly, Atkinson rejects critiques of 'formal' inter actions (including interviews) as

> likely to be stronger on recommendations for their elimination or modification than on the identification of basic organisational problems (such as accomplishing and sustaining shared attentiveness, topical relevance, turn-taking, etc.) that may none the less have to be resolved somehow or other. (Atkinson 1982: 114–15).

Although Atkinson goes on to note that current procedures are not necessarily 'the only or most efficient ones imaginable' (ibid.: 115), his functionalist perspective is likely to be most significant as a constraint on innovation rather than an encouragement to it. While I would accept the power of functionalism, I also agree with Weber that it should be used as no more than an 'initial orientation'. It remains to be seen whether the sociological imagination can detect more positive implications from interview studies.

REALISM

Type of knowledge

We have seen how the three approaches that have been considered differ in the status they accord interview material. One important dimension is whether interviews are treated as straightforward reports on another reality or whether they merely report upon, or express, their own structures. The former externalist position is shared by those I have called positivists. The latter internalist position is maintained by ethnomethodologists. Interactionists probably are closer to the former position, while recognising that the complexity of the interview situation is not fully grasped by positivist notions of bias or error.

According to externalists, interviews can, in principle, be treated as reports on external realities. The only condition is that strict protocols are observed. For internalists, interviews do present interesting data. But these data express interpretive procedures or conversational practices present in what both interviewer and interviewee are *doing* through their talk and non-verbal actions.

The question remains whether any bridging position is possible between these two apparently incompatible perspectives. In this section, I shall argue that interviews do indeed display realities which extend beyond the reality of conversational practices, so that when interviews take place, we witness both artful and possibly *universal* conversational practices *and* the display of cultural particulars expressing variable social practices. Put another way, the internalist concern with form and universality and the externalist commitment to content and variability are complementary rather than contradictory.

The easiest way I can demonstrate this complementarity is through a brief review of the status of interviews within interactionism. As already noted, there is a tension in interactionism between internalist and externalist versions of interview data. Put in simpler terms, interactionists are not too sure whether interviews are purely 'symbolic interaction' or express underlying external realities.

This tension is seen at its clearest in discussion about whether interview data can be biased. Within positivist work, there is a clear assumption that bias is a problem both because of bad interviewers *and* bad interviewees. Thus we hear about the inability of 10 per cent of the adult population to fill out 'even simple questionnaires' (Selltiz *et al.* 1964: 241), and about the untrustworthiness of some respondents and their unfortunate lack of comprehension of social scientific language (Brenner (ed.) 1981: 116–17). These fears of bias are reflected in interactionist concerns about how informants may distort social reality (Hammersley and Atkinson 1983: 105–7) or conceal what the interviewer most wants to know (Denzin 1970: 130). Both positivists and interactionists find a common concern, then, in the various ways in which interviewees are not fully moral or not intellectually up to scratch.

However, there is another more helpful tendency in interactionism. This suggests that we need not hear interview responses simply as true or false *reports* on reality. Instead, we can treat such responses as *displays* of perspectives and moral forms. This need to preserve and understand the reality of the interview account is central to the argument of interactionists like Hammersley and Atkinson about the importance of accounts 'as evidence of the perspectives of particular groups' (Hammersley and Atkinson 1983: 106). However, it also arises in some otherwise positivist arguments, as in Brown and Sime's claim that 'An account is neither naive nor an apology for behaviour, but must be taken as an informed statement by the person whose experiences are under investigation' (Brown and Sime 1981: 160). Finally, such a position is intrinsic to Garfinkel's (1967) argument that accounts are part of the world they describe.

How can we mobilise these points of agreement to formulate a position which will incorporate the valuable sides of both internalist and externalist arguments? In order to explain the position suggested here, I shall separate analytically two linked arguments, namely that interviews display cultural particulars, and these particulars vary in relation to different social practices and arrangements.

Ironically, an early paper by Sacks (1974) will provide an illustration of the first argument.* In analysing a children's story, Sacks does, of course, follow ethnomethodologists' concern with form rather than content (with what Garfinkel terms 'the formal structure of practical actions'). However, in a section of the paper which has been relatively neglected by conversational analysts, he makes it clear that it is not only in the sequencing of conversation that powerful social forms operate. In particular, he examines the way descriptions and norms are applied and invoked in constructing intelligible narratives.

Now there is little point, for our present purposes, in presenting Sacks' conclusions here. We need only observe that the apparatus that he develops directs attention to quite traditional sociological concepts like norms and roles. Although his concern is naturally with the formal procedures through which hearers and viewers may *use* norms to generate descriptions, he does not question that members' accounts are replete with descriptions based on appeals to norms and roles.

The implications are clear-cut. First, in studying accounts, we are studying displays of cultural particulars as well as displays of members'

---

*This paper was discussed in different terms in Chapter 6, pp. 134–7.

artful practices in assembling these particulars. Second, there is no necessary contradiction in seeking to study *both* particulars *and* practices. Sacks himself, for instance, seeks to establish the norms at work in children's stories in order to give an account of the artful practices through which they are assembled. It is equally possible, as Baruch (1982) has shown, to study the cultural norms at work within a narrative and to understand how their power derives from *both* their cultural base *and* their use in relation to a set of formal rules with an apparently inexorable logic. As Sacks acknowledges, the *content* of his formal membership categorisation devices is cultural through and through, arising, for instance, in how the collection 'family' is put together in a particular society. However, as he points out, once a category from one collection is used there are powerful pressures to draw on the same collection in subsequent descriptions. This can have unintended consequences — slanging-matches for instance, can get locked into a pattern of mutual insult once the first insulting term is used.

Sacks' work reveals that, for analytic purposes and in real life, form and content depend upon each other. It underlines my first argument: interviews (like other narratives) display cultural particulars — which are all the more powerful, given the connections which members make between them.

The term 'cultural particulars' seems, however, to head in two different directions. 'Culture' emphasises a factual, objective structure; 'particulars' seems to relate to contingent, subjective versions of reality. We now, therefore, need to develop our sense of the way in which particulars reveal social structures.

A fine illustration of the approach I recommend is offered in Douglas (1975).* In her study of an African tribe, the Lele, she notes the limits of two common ways of studying other cultures: cultural imperialism, which assumes that it is self-evident that our own practices are rational; and relativism. Both are deficient because they offer no basis for comparing causal systems, including our own. The way forward that Douglas suggests is explicitly Durkheimian. She argues that the properties of classification systems derive from (and are properties of) the social structures in which they are embedded. In particular, society and nature are reciprocally constituted. There is a moral order with rules about what is morally right, necessary and self-evident. This order depicts nature in a way which supports and reinforces the social order.

It follows that, as researchers, we need to see each cognitive universe as a whole, as a finite range of various patternings or combinations of

---

*Douglas's elegant study is discussed elsewhere in this book. Because of its multiple research implications, I make no apology for returning to it here.

elements. In turn, these combinations are reciprocally related to social practices — classification systems derive from and are enacted within practical actions. For instance, the Lele's celebration of the scaly anteater (the pangolin), an anomalous entity which would be taboo in many cultures, exhibits their practices of exchange with other tribes (and, hence, their preparedness to cut across classification systems).

It is clear that Douglas's method is not only Durkheimian but structuralist. First, it shows the inseparability of cognitive systems and social structures. Second, it proceeds by establishing the cultural elements and their rules of combination — in line with Saussure's dictum that elements have no 'essential' meaning but their sense arises in their relation to and difference from other elements.

The leap from an ethnography of a tribe to the analysis of interview data is not as great as it looks. Using a structuralist method, the analyst should seek to establish the cognitive universe or cosmology being displayed; no additional pieces of information are needed, only the elements present and the way they combine. Following Durkheim, the researcher can then seek to relate such cosmologies to the body of practices in which they are embedded (from another tradition, we might say that the need is to relate language-games to the forms of life in which they have their home). At both stages, interview data are being treated as nothing less (but also as nothing more) than *displays of reality*.

Criterion of validity

Realists would tend to agree with ethnomethodologists that knowledge of social reality is inevitably an 'insider's' knowledge. Put more concretely, to understand what is displayed in interview accounts we are forced to mobilise our commonsense knowledge. For instance, in understanding a description by locating the collection to which a membership categorisation device refers, we depend upon 'what everyone knows' about social organisation (e.g. that 'mommy' and 'baby' refer to the collection 'family'). However, this dependence on common sense need not mean that common sense is sufficient to provide the validity of a sociological account. If this were so, then sociological knowledge would stand on very shaky ground. Consequently, ethnomethodologists, as we have already seen, appeal to the rigorous character of group data analysis sessions as a baseline for their claims to discover regularities.

Like ethnomethodologists, realists recognise that sociologists' analytic purposes may differ from the pragmatic concerns of members. However, it would be a mistake to suggest that any one criterion of validity — other than rigour — underlies the treatment of interview data recommended here. So, for instance, as has already been suggested in Chapter 5, testing propositions by means of analytic induction can be a useful method in the analysis of qualitative data. However, where data can be sensibly quantified, simple counting methods and statistical tests are appropriate. (The rationale behind the *selective* use of quantification is discussed in Chapter 7.)

Policy implications

Let me begin by reviewing the policy implications of the three perspectives considered earlier. Ethnomethodology's practical functionalism means that it is more concerned to show the limits of reform than to suggest what Garfinkel dismissively calls 'remedies'. Its aim is to reveal the 'amazing practical accomplishment' of social order and its posture is one of awe rather than critique. While the other perspectives have an interest in social reform, I have shown, using Habermas, the limits of their aims.

Expressed in crude political terms, ethnomethodology is conservative, interactionism is liberal, while positivism is authoritarian. Habermas, on the other hand, offers a critical interest whose emancipatory concerns are clearly radical. However, as others have noted, Habermas rarely moves off a purely theoretical plane, while the psychoanalytic elements in his theory have curiously élitist elements, involving subjects in understanding their 'false consciousness'.

What, then, are the alternative policy implications of the realist approach to interview data that I have developed here? First, I agree with the ethnomethodological critique of using interview data as a basis for directly evaluating non-interview settings. For instance, Waitzkin (1979) is surely mistaken to treat an interview response from patients (that they want a large amount of information) as providing a poor evaluation of medical consultations (which give less information). As Stimson and Webb (1975) have noted, patients, when interviewed, are likely to tell stories which cast them in a favourable light and hence have an unknown relation to what they expected or did in the situations they describe.

However, to accept that interview tales cannot be blindly applied regardless of context does not mean that they have no practical relevance. Consider the argument, deployed earlier, that interviews display cultural particulars which are articulated in morally powerful ways. Returning to a medical setting, now envisage the lack of space often provided for patients to do this kind of moral work. In a 'typical' medical consultation, for instance, descriptions are often based on clinical collections with little relevance to the membership categorisation devices familiar to the patient (put crudely, for the hospital doctor descriptions will be done in terms of organs and pathology rather than, say, in terms of family connections). Through what Sacks calls 'consistency' and 'economy' rules, devices, once used, will tend to structure all the descriptions that follow.

Let us assume, as Baruch's (1982) work implies, that this constitutes a problem for patients and, more especially, parents of young patients. One policy implication that might be drawn would, however, misunderstand the relation between narrative and context. To suggest that the clinic should be reorganised and/or doctors trained to communicate better overlooks the fact (and this is Atkinson's (1982) point) that the *present* organisation of the clinic serves functions that may be important — for instance, in allowing sufficient time for the examination of the patient and of the available data. Training doctors to communicate better, while perhaps desirable, may also overlook the link between particular communication patterns, social structures and the tasks to be performed in them (i.e. different modes of communication are appropriate in different contexts).

This suggests a form of policy intervention related to the structural constraints posed by different interactional settings. In a recent study (Baruch 1982), an additional paediatric clinic was created after the parents had time to collect their thoughts, following a necessary but medically-structured first outpatient consultation. At this second clinic, the doctor was of junior rank and the child was not examined. In the first clinic, the need for speedy diagnosis and parental shock and unfamiliarity with the medical agenda determined a medically-structured encounter. In the second clinic, without these structural constraints, parents were able to ask questions more freely and to engage in a display of parental responsibility. In this way, what had been learned from an interview study about parents' moral frameworks was put to good use by creating a new situation which lacked the constraints of existing forms. Moreover, the researchers were content merely to change the interactional constraints; no directions were given to the participants about how to act in the new clinic. Such a non-authoritarian version of social policy has several advantages:

1. It does not depend on the training of communication skills often with an unknown relation to the context in which such skills are to be applied.
2. It allows participants to innovate in ways unforeseen by researchers.
3. Innovations are likely to continue after researchers leave the setting because the participants themselves continue to fashion their practices to their own needs.

CONCLUSION: INTERVIEWS AND THE DISPLAY OF MORAL ADEQUACY

This chapter has addressed the polarity between artificial and naturally-occurring data that has arisen in sociological research. Unlike most of the other oppositions which I have been discussing, this one has a relatively modern origin — namely, in what Hammersley and Atkinson (1983) call the naturalist perspective. Naturalism desires to get at data 'untouched by human hands'. This is reflected in its preference for observation. Conversely, I have argued that all data display cultural realities which are neither biased nor accurate but simply real. In saying this, I do not mean to imply that bias and accuracy are not problems, but that they may arise only in the *analysis* of data not in the form or content of data (except in so far as participants are troubled by bias or accuracy).

In terms of interview data, I have argued that the way forward is to concentrate upon the moral and cultural forms that they display. This requires a focus on how they function as displays of moral adequacy. As Cuff (1980) has noted, when accounts are about a social unit of which the teller is a member, they talk about 'unit events' in which the teller is inextricably implicated. When such events are heard as 'troubles', members know that they are likely to be heard as one-sided or partisan unless their accounts consider their own involvement and responsibility. Hence, people often present and then exclude what Cuff calls 'determinate alternative possible accounts' of their behaviour.*

Interviews share with any account this involvement in moral realities. They offer a rich source of data which provide access to how people account for both their troubles and good fortune.

Such observations are hardly surprising since the evidence for it is immediately before our eyes in our everyday experience. Only by following misleading correspondence theories of truth could it have ever occurred to researchers to treat interview statements as accurate or distorted reports of reality. Ironically, however, when such distortion is diagnosed, it is treated as an indication of a moral shortcoming on the part of the respondent (i.e. as 'concealment', 'lack of intelligence', etc.). We are led ineluctably to the Durkheimian conclusion that moral forms suffuse the social world.

FURTHER READING

Positivist versions of the interview are represented by Selltiz *et al.* (1964) and Brenner (1981). Denzin (1970, Chapter 6), gives an interactionist account. A more recent treatment from the same position is found in Hammersley and Atkinson (1983, Chapter 5).

Cicourel's (1964) text gives an early ethnomethodological version of interview data. A later version from the point of view of conversational analysis is offered by Atkinson (1982). Although the realist position on

---

*For a much fuller discussion of Cuff's work and its application to the analysis of interview data, see Baruch (1982).

interview data has, as far as I know, received no detailed exposition, Voysey (1975) and Baruch (1982) give highly relevant case-studies, reporting research on the families of handicapped children. In each case, the families' accounts are treated in a manner which is in line with that proposed here.

9 Practical interventions: what can social science contribute?

> The question is not whether we should take sides, since we inevitably will, but rather whose side are we on? (Becker 1967: 239)

Not all sociologists would agree with Becker's call for moral or political partisanship. Perhaps responding to state apparatuses which are at best suspicious of the purposes of social science, many would go on the defensive. They might find it easier or more acceptable to argue that their concern is simply with the establishment of facts through the judicious testing of competing hypotheses and theories. Their only slogan, they would say, is the pursuit of knowledge. They would claim to reject political partisanship, at least in their academic work; they are only, they would say, partisans for truth.

I am not, for the moment, concerned to make a detailed assessment of either Becker's statement or the defensive response to it which I have just depicted. Although if forced to choose between them, I should opt for Becker's position, I believe both contain dangerous simplifications. As I shall later show, the partisans for truth are mistaken about the purity of knowledge, while Becker's rhetoric of 'sides' is often associated with a style of research which is unable to discover anything because of its prior commitment to a revealed truth (the plight of the underdog, the inevitable course of human history, etc.). Curiously, both positions can be élitist, establishing themselves apart from and above the people they study.

For the moment, however, I want to stress a more positive feature of both arguments. Both recognise that no simply neutral or value-free position is possible in social science (or, indeed, elsewhere). The partisans for truth just as much as the partisans of the 'underdog' are committed to an absolute value for which there can be no purely factual foundation. As Weber pointed out in the early years of this century, all research is contaminated to some extent by the values of the researcher. Only through those values do certain problems get identified and studied in particular ways. Even the commitment to scientific (or rigorous) method is itself, as Weber emphasises, a value. Finally, the conclusions and implications to be drawn from a study are, Weber stresses, largely grounded in the moral and political beliefs of the researcher.

More than twenty years ago, Gouldner (1962) pointed out how Weber had been grossly misinterpreted by positivist sociologists. Because Weber had suggested that purely scientific standards could govern the *study* of a sociological problem, they had used him as the standard-bearer for a value-free sociology. They had conveniently forgotten that Weber had argued that the initial choice and conceptualisation of a problem, as well as the subsequent attempt to seek practical implications from its study, were highly 'value-relevant' (to use Weber's term).

The 'minotaur' of a value-free sociology which positivists had conjured up from misreading Weber is effectively destroyed by Gouldner. As Denzin (1970) shows, the myth of value-freedom is shattered not only by the researcher's own commitments but by the social and political environment in which research is carried out. Grant-giving bodies will seek to channel research in particular directions: there is no. *neutral* money whether one is speaking about the well-meaning 'initiatives' of research councils or the more sinister funding schemes of the tobacco industry or the war-machine (Horowitz 1965). Moreover, organisations that are studied are likely to want some kind of return in terms of 'facts' (assumed to be theory-free and always quantifiable) as well as support for their current political strategy. Finally, as Dingwall (personal correspondence) has pointed out, governments may sponsor 'window-dressing' research to buy time and to legitimate inaction; while, as Denzin points out, the researcher may desire nothing more than a publishable paper, this pressure-group activity is bound to have an impact on the work.

Given the constraints under which research takes place, how may the researcher respond? To answer this question, I want to characterise three different research roles which have been prescribed or adopted. These are presented in summary form in Table 9.1.

The rest of this chapter will be devoted to a brief exposition and critique of these three versions of the researcher's role. This will be followed by an attempt to develop an adequate answer to a better question: not 'whose side are we on?' but 'what can social science contribute?' (Becker 1967a: 23).

VERSIONS OF THE SOCIOLOGIST'S ROLE

Scholar

In his two famous lectures 'Science as a Vocation' and 'Politics as a Vocation' (Weber 1946), given in 1917, Weber enunciated basic liberal principles to a student audience. Despite the patriotic fervour of the First World War, he insisted on the primacy of the individual's own conscience

Table 9.1: *Whose side are we on? Three answers*

Role	Politics	Commitment	Example
Scholar	Liberal	Knowledge for knowledge's sake—protected by scholar's conscience.	Weber, Denzin
State counsellor	Bureaucratic	Social engineering or enlightenment for policy-makers.	Popper, Bulmer
Partisan	Marxist or conservative	Knowledge to support both a political theory and a political practice	Marx, Habermas, political research centres (e.g. Hoover Institute, Adam Smith Institute)

as a basis for action. Taking the classic Kantian position, Weber argued that values could not be derived from facts. However, this was not because values were less important than facts (as logical positivists were soon to argue). Rather, precisely because 'ultimate evaluations' (or value choices) were so important, they were not to be reduced to purely factual judgements. The facts could only tell you about the likely consequences of given actions but they could not tell you which action to choose.

For Weber, the very commitment to science was an example of an ultimate evaluation, exemplifying a personal belief in standards of logic and rationality and in the value of factual knowledge. Ironically echoing certain aspects of the 'Protestant Ethic' whose historical emergence he himself had traced, Weber appealed to the scholar's conscience as the sole basis for conferring meaning and significance upon events.

Weber's appeal to Protestantism's and Liberalism's 'free individual' is fully shared, 50 years on, by Norman Denzin. Denzin (1970) rejects any fixed moral standards as the basis for research. He will not accept, for instance, that sociologists cannot conceal themselves or use disguised research techniques. Nor is he prepared to recognise that research must necessarily contribute to society's own self-understanding. Both standards are, for him, examples of 'ethical absolutism' which fail to respect the scholar's appeal to his own conscience in the varying contexts of research. Denzin's stand is distinctively liberal and individualist: 'One mandate governs sociological activity — the absolute freedom to pursue one's activities as one sees fit' (Denzin 1970: 332). What 'one sees [as] fit' will take into account that no method of sociological research is intrinsically any more unethical than any other. Citing Goffman, Denzin argues that, since the researcher always wears some mask, covert observation is merely one mask among others.

The same appeal to individual judgement is made over the issue of confidentiality. When it comes to decisions about what to publish: 'these decisions must rest with his conscience for he more than any other person has the intimate knowledge of the consequences of his actions. Abstract ethical rules cannot solve the issues that daily arise in sociological research' (ibid.: 337).

Denzin does suggest that the pursuit of research in terms of one's own standards should have certain safeguards. For instance, subjects should be told of the researcher's own value judgements and biases, and should be warned about the kinds of interpretation the research may generate within the community. But he is insistent that the ultimate arbiter of proper conduct remains the conscience of the individual sociologist.

Weber and Denzin's liberal position seems rather unrealistic. Curiously, as sociologists they fail to see the power of social organisation as it shapes the practice of research. For while Denzin acknowledges the role of pressure-groups, he remains silent about the privileged authority of the 'scientist' in society and about the deployment of scientific theories by agents of social control as mobilising forms of power/knowledge. *

There is also an élitist element concealed in liberalism's appeal to the individual's own ethical judgements. This is demonstrated most clearly in Habermas's (1972) critique of what he sees as the irrational elements in Weber's ethical theory. Weber, says Habermas, elevates above all else the figure of the heroic individual making a choice which cannot be grounded in facts or in fixed moral standards. This 'decisionist' ethics is, he claims, irrational since it allows no possibility of dialogue with others. Ultimately, Habermas argues, it came to be adopted by the Nazis in their rhetoric of 'heroism' and 'will'.

Even if one is unhappy about such an attempt to derive Nazism from liberalism, Habermas's critique remains fairly powerful. How successful a rebuttal of a colleague's critique of, say, the political implications of your research is it to say that you are simply following your own conscience? Moreover, does it encourage a dialogue when, in response to a query from someone you are studying, you argue that you are proceeding 'as you see fit' (Denzin)?

State counsellor

Even liberal individualists may occasionally move away from their 'hands off' attitude towards others. Denzin, for instance, considers the value of the information that sociologists may offer to participants:

> The investigator may open new avenues of action and perception among those studied. Organisational leaders may be ignorant of the dysfunctional aspects of certain programs, and an exposure to the sociologist's findings may correct their misconceptions. (ibid.: 338)

*See Foucault's discussion of the prison and of the social construction of sexuality in Chapter 4, pp. 82–91.

Notice how Denzin uses 'organisational leaders' as his example of 'those studied'. Just as many sociologists automatically side with the underdog, so also there is a considerable weight of sociological work which identifies with the problems and interests of the 'leaders' or 'top dogs'. We saw an early example of this in the Hawthorne studies (Chapter 4, pp. 72–4). A contemporary example is provided by Bulmer (1982). Despite having a general title *The Uses of Social Research*, his book turns out to be solely a discussion of how social research may be used by 'policy-makers'. It will thus serve as an example of what I have called in Table 9.1 bureaucratic politics where the researcher adopts the role of state counsellor.

It is at once clear, however, that Bulmer's bureaucrat-cum-researcher is intended to work at arm's length from the administration, offering no simple solutions and preferring to provide knowledge rather than to recommend policies. This is Bulmer's 'enlightenment model' of social research. It is based on a rejection of two other versions of the uses of research — 'empiricism' and the 'engineering model'.

I have set out below Bulmer's depictions of each of the three models:

(1) Empiricism
This assumes that facts somehow speak for themselves. It reflects the administrative view that research is a neutral tool for the collection of facts for the use of policy-makers. Failing to take account of the post-Weberian consensus that facts can only be recognised in terms of theoretically-derived categories, its 'bucket theory of mind' (Popper) is, Bulmer suggests, wholly inadequate. This is not merely a methodological quibble as Bulmer demonstrates, empiricism fails because it offers no way of '[bringing] to bear the *insights* of social science — rather than merely the *factual* products of social research' (Bulmer 1982: 42).

(2) The engineering model
This seems to be based on Popper's (1972) own version of the contribution of research to 'piecemeal social engineering'. Derived from Popper's rejection of attempts at revolutionary social changes, the engineering model takes off from the definition, presumably by the bureaucracy, of a social problem. It then proceeds, in Bulmer's version, through a sequence of four stages: (i) the identification of the knowledge that is required; (ii) the acquisition of social research data; (iii) the interpretation of the data in the light of the problem; and (iv) a change in the policy.

Bulmer implies that the proponents of the engineering model are politically naive. Bureaucrats often know precisely what policy changes they wish to make and commission research in such a way that the end-product is likely to legitimate their thinking. He also points out that, in large organisations, it is often action rather than research that is needed.

Moreover, where problems need to be analysed, the application of common sense is often quite sufficient.

(3) The enlightenment model

This is Bulmer's preferred model. Citing Janowitz (1972), Bulmer sees the function of applied research as the provision of knowledge of alternative possibilities. Its role is to enlighten bureaucrats, and not to recommend policies or to choose between administrative options. This means that it *rejects* a number of research aims (Bulmer 1982: 153–4) including: (i) the provision of authoritative facts (because facts are only authoritative in the context of theories); (ii) Supplying political ammunition (because this is based, Bulmer points out, on the 'sterile' assumption that there are 'left-wing' facts as opposed to 'right-wing' facts); (iii) doing tactical research, as in government think-tanks (because this reduces the social scientist to a mere technician); and (iv) Evaluating policies (because this is based on the rejected engineering model of applied social research).

Instead, Bulmer *proposes* two research aims which are consistent with his enlightenment model: (i) interaction — offering mutual contact between researchers and policy-makers; and (ii) conceptualisation — creation of new problems for policy-makers to think about through the development of new concepts.

The weaknesses of Bulmer's enlightenment model are already implied by my labelling his approach the 'state counsellor'. I would argue that it offers an attractive version of how researchers who are already employed as functionaries of the state can preserve a degree of professional freedom. Pursuing 'enlightenment', they are relatively freer to define problems in terms of their own interests rather than to have them imposed on them by their political bosses (as empiricism or the engineering model implies). However, this 'professional' freedom is, to some extent, a fraud, for in Bulmer's discussion the enlightenment model never brings into question the role of research as the supplier of concepts and information to the powers-that-be. Precisely because it represents applied research as the hand-maiden of the state, 'enlightenment' offers a purely bureaucratic version of politics: as such, it totally fails to address the political and moral issues of research which is at anything other than arm's length from the state.*

A case in point is the famous Project Camelot (Horowitz 1965). This was a research project funded in 1963 by the Pentagon with a budget of 6 million dollars. Its purported aim was to gather data on the causes of

---

*Stewart Clegg (personal correspondence) suggests that this underplays the need to call upon the organisational capacities of the state in order to produce real changes. His point reveals the dilemma that worthy ends may depend upon elitist means.

revolutions in the Third World. However, when it became clear that such research was to be used as a basis for counter-insurgency techniques, it created a storm of protest and the project was withdrawn.

Horowitz points out that many social scientists had been prepared to overlook the source of the money when offered such big research funding. Presumably, they might have defended themselves as seeking merely to spread 'enlightenment' rather than to engage in political or social engineering. However, this in no way settles the moral issue over whether social scientists should have this kind of relationship to such a government agency. Conceived in terms of counter-insurgency, Bulmer's preferred research roles of interaction and conceptualisation take on an altogether more sinister undertone.

Partisan

If the state counsellor is co-opted by administrative interests and the scholar deludes himself that he can stand apart from a socially-organised world, then the partisan's role would seem to be altogether more defensible. Unlike the scholar, the partisan does not shy away from his accountability to the world. Unlike the state counsellor, however, (s)he holds the ruling bureaucracy at arm's length. Instead, the partisan seeks to provide the theoretical and factual resources for a political struggle aimed at transforming the assumptions through which both political and administrative games are played. None the less, I believe that there are serious problems with the role of researcher as partisan. I shall try to demonstrate this briefly using examples from Marxist social science. I must stress, however, that this is not intended as a critique of Marxism in general, but merely of particular mechanistic and élitist tendencies in certain Marxist thought. Indeed, I turn to Marx's work as a non-élitist alternative at the end of this chapter.

Again, partisanship clearly arises on the Right as well as on the Left. Therefore, I might just have well used examples of *conservative* applied research which, although operating with a professedly anti-élitist ideology, uses an equally mechanistic account of how society operates (the 'hidden hand' of the market).

Mechanistic Marxists explain social institutions and beliefs as a simple outcome of underlying economic relations and contradictions. Their model is one of superstructural appearances and sub-structural realities. We have already encountered such mechanistic interpretations in the discussion of the social origins of Fascism in Chapter 3, pp. 52–6.

The problem that such interpretations create for research is quite simple: how can research ever discover anything new when everything can already be deduced from known economic laws? Research is thus reduced to Kuhn's (1970) 'normal science' — tracing out the details of an already known, indubitable theory.

To take what may appear to be a contrary example. Althusser's (1971) account of ideology differs from many mechanist Marxists in treating ideology as a material reality in its own right. None the less, his proposal that ideology is always part of an ideological state apparatus which interpellates (or constitutes) individuals as subjects in a single way (as big and small, as bottom dogs in relation to top dogs), is clearly mechanistic. Consequently, Althusser directs research away from depicting the multiplicity of subject-relations that are certainly discoverable in the real world.*

A second problem with the partisanship of mechanistic Marxism is that it encourages an élitist relation with subjects not unlike that engendered by adopting the role of the scholar. The theorist is assumed to know best, and ordinary people are depicted as unwitting tools of the system awaiting education by the theorist.

Marx himself appears to have been ambivalent about this issue. On the one hand, he uses the eminently élitist notion of false consciousness — implying that, if someone sees the world in ways other than the theory prescribes, this means that he, but not the theory, is mistaken. On the other hand, in his *Theses on Feuerbach*, he ridicules the élitism present in liberal theories about improvement in conditions through education. Here he asks the very pertinent (and anti-élitist) question: 'who educates the educator?'

In contemporary Marxism, a number of élitist strains are present. For instance, it is possible that Habermas's (1972) notion of an 'emancipatory' interest, geared to the revelation of 'systematically-distorted communication' may reduce the subject to a mere patient (see Chapter 7, p. 164).

Having introduced this medical model, I want briefly to turn to an example of a recent research study of doctor–patient interaction which, I believe, exemplifies the problems that arise when the researcher takes on the role of partisan. The paper to which I am referring is Howard Waitzkin, 'Medicine, Superstructure and Micropolitics' (1979).†

Waitzkin has the laudable aim of relating 'the everyday micro-level interaction of individuals' to 'macro-level structures of domination' (Waitzkin 1979: 601). Unfortunately, as Rayner and Stimson (1979) point out, he uses a mechanistic version of Marxism based on notions of the material base and the superstructure, which reduce medicine simply to an ideological state apparatus of the capitalist state.

Knowing what he is going to find, Waitzkin treats his data largely as illustrative of a preconceived theory. Using the categories of 'relations of

---

*For a further discussion of Althusser's theory of the subject in relation to individualist accounts of society, see Chapter 2, pp. 36–7.
†Useful critiques of this paper which are much more detailed than that found here are made by Rayner, Stimson and Strong (1979).

production', 'class relationships' and 'medical control of everyday life' (this last category involving, surely, a bit of an *ad hoc* addition to Marxist theory), he cites examples of data which he believes are favourable to his interpretations. I shall only use here his discussion of 'relations of production'.

Waitzkin offers three very brief examples of theoretical analysis under this head, and each is followed by a short data extract:

(i) 'Doctor–patient interaction parallels the situation in the workplace, where information is concentrated in the hands of the few' (ibid.: 604). Waitzkin cites his quantitative data which indicate that, in the average consultation lasting 20 minutes, doctors spend only just over 1 minute 'transmitting information'. This seems relevant to his theoretical claim, although one should be wary of the assumption that the transmission of information by the doctor is the purpose of the consultation. Curiously, Waitzkin gives no indication of patients' participation. Moreover, his finding that doctors generally underestimate patients' desire for information may be a research-generated artefact — if I am given a questionnaire asking me how much information I want, I may exaggerate in order to appear a responsible citizen who seeks to be well-informed. In practice, I may be satisfied with rapid diagnosis and effective treatment.

(ii) The doctor, Waitzkin claims, 'is in a position to enforce industrial or home discipline through ideological messages about the work ethic' (ibid.: 604–5). To support this assertion he simply quotes from a consultation where, in the context of asking about the patient's 'energy' and hearing that the patient feels 'tired', the doctor asks whether he is 'able . . . to work a regular day?' When the patient confirms this, the doctor says, 'Wonderful'. At the very least, Waitzkin is making very limited data do a great deal of analytic 'work'. Without any evidence to the contrary, the reader might prefer to read the doctor's question about the patient's employment as simply establishing the status of the latter's comment about feeling 'tired'.

(iii) 'Objectification in doctor–patient interaction . . . using machine-like references for parts of the body . . . parallels the use of the wage-earner or home maintainer as machine-like human capital' (ibid.: 605). Here Waitzkin cites an account by a doctor of the workings of the pituitary gland. But there are two problems here. First, he does not explain how it is possible to explain the workings of bodily organs without using some machine-like metaphor. Second, consistent with his failure to attend to what patients are doing, he makes nothing of the fact that, according to his own transcript, the doctor's explanation stems from an interruption by the patient of the doctor's diagnosis statement. If doctors were really so much in control as Waitzkin implies then such interruptions would be unthinkable.

Waitzkin's paper illustrates some of the more unfortunate consequences of the researcher adopting the role of the partisan. In the same way as the Bible advises 'look and ye shall find', so the partisan looks and inevitably finds examples which can be used to support his theory. Two things never seem to strike him:

(i) that what he finds is true but not necessarily caused by the factors in his theory (for instance, Strong (1979) suggests that the use of the machine analogy may be a feature of medical consultations in all industrialised social systems); and

(ii) that contrary evidence should be hunted down and followed up (for instance, Waitzkin notes — but makes nothing of — his own apparently contrary findings that women patients receive more information, while 'doctors from working-class backgrounds tend to communicate *less* information than doctors from upper-class backgrounds') (ibid.: 604).

Just as the partisan does not seek to be surprised by his data, (s)he tends to be élitist in regard to political change. Not surprisingly, Waitzkin seeks to encourage 'patient education' to invite the questioning of professional advice (ibid.: 608). At the same time, as we have seen, he makes nothing of patients' self-generated attempts to challenge professional dominance. Marx's question 'who educates the educator?' seems entirely apposite.

SELF-RIGHTEOUSNESS AND SOCIOLOGICAL IMPERIALISM

Having taken up Becker's question 'whose side are we on?' and depicted three roles adopted by sociologists (scholar, state counsellor and partisan), I have found major problems in how these roles have been exercised. We would thus seem to be back at square one. Shortly, I shall try to be more positive and indicate the scope for what I believe to be a fruitful relation between sociology and society. However, before doing so, I want to continue a little further on this pessimistic tack, for if we can understand better the social and moral roots of sociology's failure to find a defensible role for itself, we shall be in a better position to come up with an acceptable alternative.

A common theme in my depiction of how sociologists have practised their chosen role is the element of self-righteousness that seems to have been present. The scholar pretends to be apart from the world and claims special rights for his conscience. The state counsellor makes no bones about his worldly involvement, but seeks to escape definitions of himself as a mere technician. Finally, the partisan makes claims to know how things really are while all too often ignoring what people are actually saying and doing.

If there is anything in the charge of self-righteousness, then it would indeed put sociology in a curious situation. After all, as Berger and Kellner (1981: 12) have argued, sociologists depict themselves in terms of their special ability to unmask delusions. Yet, if sociologists are themselves possessed of delusions of grandeur, expressed in a self-righteous style, then the boot is on the other foot with a vengeance. Perhaps, as Strong implies, sociologists should have conducted a sociology of knowledge-style investigation into their own unmasking, debunking, sceptical motif. For:

> Scepticism has considerable dramatic rewards. In writing in this fashion, sociologists both formulate themselves as members of some insightful and incorruptible élite and, at the same time, gain considerable pleasure by the exposure and thus potential overthrow of those whom they dislike. (Strong 1979: 201)

To illustrate Strong's important argument, I shall summarise part of his thesis about sociology's treatment of medicine. He seeks to show that the charge of medical imperialism ('the increasing and illegitimate medicalisation of the social world' — ibid.: 199) looks pretty rich when it comes from a 'fellow profession within bourgeois society' with its own 'imperial ambitions' (ibid.). His central argument is, then, that:

> A sociological critique of medicine, however radical, cannot be disinterested for, whatever its intentions, it also serves to advance sociologists' own cause. Thus, ambition may lead sociology to distort the nature of medical imperialism and exaggerate its threat: to overlook the limits to medical expansion that currently exist within our society and, finally, to neglect the potential danger posed by its own imperialism and that of its allies. (ibid.: 199)

Before taking up Strong's central argument about 'sociological imperialism', I want briefly to present what he says about the limits to 'medical imperialism'. This is shown in summary form in Table 9.2. Strong concludes that while the thesis of 'medical imperialism' remains unproven, there still remain considerable grounds for concern about the social role of medicine. In particular, the increased use of psychoactive drugs, the claim that new biological technologies (e.g. relating to reproduction) are 'medical' even though they may not involve disease, and the exclusion of certain categories of patient from bourgeois legal freedoms (e.g. 'children, mental patients, prisoners and, to a much lesser extent, women' (ibid.: 212)).

Table 9.2: The sociological critique of medical imperialism and Strong's rebuttal

The sociological critique	Sociology's 'distortions'	Limits to medical imperialism
1. The medical monopoly of service provision.	The lack of comparative material on areas where medicalisation is generally acceptable and successful.	State financial constraints on medical expansion (e.g. care of old people now being transferred in Britain from hospitals to the community).
2. Medical control of the nature of that service and of the criteria for judging medical work.	The lack of historical data: the appeal to a 'golden age' prior to medicine.	The centrality of 'biological' matters to medicine's conception of its task — the downgrading of psychiatric issues as irrelevant or even 'dirty' work.
3. Medical attempts to expand their empire — the medicalisation of existing problems, the creation of new problems.	Medicine's mixed and often negative response to areas that might be colonised (e.g. alcoholism).	The lack of legal constraints upon patient behaviour.
4. Medical emphasis upon the individual — failure to examine the role of social processes in illness behaviour.	Varying levels of state control over medical expenditures (e.g. compare UK and USA).	
5. The addiction of patients to medicalised products — the further stimulation of medical expansion.	Are patients addicted? The limited number of GP visits in the British Health Service (on average between 2 and 4½ per patient per annum).	

Strong's arguments go some of the way to substantiate my concerns about the self-righteousness of some sociologists. For, as he shows, the bases and consequences of sociology's critique of medicine are largely self-serving.

For Strong, sociology has used a basic strategy of any professional group as a means to attack another:

> Given the relatively open trade in ideas, every profession is free to compete with every other to provide formulations and solutions for contemporary social issues. 'Discovering' social problems and, more especially, casting them in such terms that one has exclusive rights to them, is the basic strategy of every bourgeois profession. (ibid.: 202)

In pursuit of its vested, professional interest, sociology has shown an ability to define its product in a flexible, acceptable way: 'According to the times, it can threaten capitalists either with consumers or with workers and in both cases offers its services as interpreter, mediator, and ultimately, perhaps, planner' (ibid.: 203). This means that sociology can conceal its professional interest behind quite genuine convictions about the emancipatory role of social science. As Strong dryly notes about two critics of medicine: 'As well as calling for the rights of the people to be recognised, they also call for a massive increase in the research budget devoted to sociology' (ibid.: 204). Finally, 'a fully social model of health' (ibid.: 212) might, Strong reminds us involve far more massive intervention for changing people's behaviour than anything required by organic medicine. As Foucault (1977, 1979) has shown, defining everyday matters as 'social' has been a major route through which public institutions come to survey and monitor every aspect of our lives.

THE PROSPECTS FOR INTERVENTION

'What can social science contribute? (Becker 1967a: 23).

Having set out the case against many of sociology's attempts to enter the political and moral arena, I now want to be more positive and to indicate some ways in which the discipline may make a useful contribution to society. Just as I began this chapter with a question of Becker's, I start in the same way here. Notice, however, how his earlier polemical statement about 'sides' gives way here to a more limited question about 'contribution'. This signals that, from now on, I too shall drop the polemics and adopt a more practical frame of reference.

A useful way to start will be to list Becker's own suggestions about the possible contributions to the study of social problems that the social sciences can make. Namely (ibid.: 23–8),

(i) 'Sorting out the differing definitions of the problem' — establishing the assumptions used by different parties and the degree of irreconcilable conflict involved.

(ii) 'Clarifying assumptions and checking them against the facts' — for instance, in the current panic about mugging in British cities it is not generally recognised that nearly all the victims of muggings are young people. Consequently, many old age pensioners live in terror, afraid to walk the streets.

(iii) 'Discovering strategic points of intervention' — by using comparative work to reveal the social consequences of different policies — for instance, the consequences of decriminalising addiction in the UK.

(iv) 'Suggesting alternative moralities' — avoiding defining social problems in purely administrative terms; for instance, as Roth has pointed out, the problem may not be why TB patients leave hospital against advice but why any stay.

I believe that all of Becker's suggestions make useful starting-points for discussing the role of sociology in society. I shall, therefore, now briefly illustrate an example of how they may be given some substance by referring to a recent study of state intervention in the field of childcare (Dingwall *et al.* 1983). However, I believe that Becker does not sufficiently follow through the anti-élitist sentiments revealed by his opposition to purely administrative moralities. Consequently, in a concluding section, I shall discuss what I shall call 'non-authoritarian' interventions in social policy.

Following Becker's list in order, what are the differing definitions of the problem of 'child abuse'? Dingwall and Eekelaar (1963) claim that 'A curious alliance of left and right libertarians is proclaiming that intervention has increased, is increasing and ought to be diminished.' Those on the Right appeal to the sacredness and inviability of family life in order to attack state intervention (e.g. Mount 1982). Left-wing critics, like Donzelot (1980), suggest that agencies of the state explain poverty as moral failure, while trying to spread norms of moral respectability. The consequence is the intrusive surveillance of families for moral failure, such as child abuse.

What degree of conflict is there between these assumptions? Allowing for different degrees of emphasis, surprisingly little, argues Dingwall. Both left- and right-wing critics overplay the right of the family to privacy versus the right of children to be protected. Consequently, both fail to recognise that the proper end of protecting children against abuse may require state intervention:

> we must be prepared to will the means [to this end], which are organisations with the powers effectively to detect, investigate and sanction parental misconduct. Those who profess the ends while denouncing the means only invite accusations of naivete, at best, or hypocrisy, at worst. (Dingwall and Eekelaar 1983)*

---

*This argument does not, however, address the problems of using 'professionals' to investigate 'laymen' — a problem central to this chapter.

Again, following Becker, what happens when we check the assumption of steadily increasing intervention against the facts? Looking first at the statistics, Dingwall and Eekelaar show that, in England, the increase in the numbers of children in care in recent years has been minimal. As regards new admissions to care through parental abuse and neglect, these actually have fallen in the last available statistics.

Dingwall et al.'s (1983) study suggests the reasons for this very limited state intervention: cultural norms and structural constraints. Three cultural norms serve to minimise the extent to which agencies seek care orders:

(i) 'The rule of optimism' implies that the moral probity of adults must be assumed unless there is crushing contrary evidence.

(ii) Professionals concerned with child abuse, like others trained in the social sciences, tend to be cultural relativists. They therefore assume that most patterns of child rearing may be justifiable as a cultural statement.

(iii) Common sense assumes a hypothesis of 'natural love' between parents and children. Professionals in the field therefore recognise that a charge of abuse amounts to an allegation that the parents concerned do not share a common humanity. Consequently, such charges are minimised.

The major structural constraint upon intervention is that effective action depends upon a combination of agencies with distinct patterns of accountability and methods of relating to clients. The most intrusive surveyors of family life, health visitors, have the fewest resources to enforce compliance. Social workers often have high turnover making continuity of surveillance difficult and find it difficult to appeal to coercive measures when parents are apparently open, friendly and compliant. Finally, local authority lawyers tend to treat child care work as having low status and family solicitors are torn between representing the parents and the child.

These cultural and structural constraints mean that state intervention in this area ultimately depends upon the presence of either of two relatively rare factors: (i) a lack of parental compliance, involving attempts to conceal information and/or to prevent inspection of the home; and (ii) the emergence of usually 'private' family conduct into the 'public' sphere (via, for instance, the involvement of social control agencies, such as the police).

The 'facts' revealed by Dingwall et al. highlight the fragile assumptions upon which the debate about state intervention in family life is based. This suggests that Becker's third proposed area of impact for social research — discovering strategic points of intervention through comparative studies — requires a great deal of work in order to identify informal practices as well as formal structures. Dingwall et al. stress that the whole issue has been clouded by unexamined sociological and political assumptions.

Sociologists tend to assume that cultural relativism is 'good', while social control and informal practices are 'bad'. However, this research shows how cultural relativism may expose children to abuse, while informal practices may be based on sound commonsense principles. Even the concept of social control fails to do justice to the complex motives and institutional structures of professional agencies. Furthermore, the assumption of the Left that state surveillance should be limited may today suit very well the politics of the Right. After all, conservative governments have every interest in cutting financial support for caring agencies and, given the technological revolution, the state no longer has such a need to intervene in family life to promote a well-disciplined, 'moral', labour force.

Dingwall *et al.* conclude that the present system of child protection in England could be improved in detail. For instance, they demonstrate the predictable ability of middle-class parents to 'work the system' in their favour, and the absurd situation where only the child but not the parents has a right to legal representation in child care hearings. However, shorn of misleading and contradictory assumptions, 'there is no real evidence that [the present system] . . . has got the balance [between child protection and family primacy] seriously wrong, except by the standards of ideological purists' (Dingwall and Eekelaar 1983). In a real sense, then, Dingwall *et al.* succeed in Becker's prescribed task of 'suggesting alternative moralities'. Their research indicates that the problem is *not* why the state intervenes so much in family life, but why it intervenes so little.

NON-AUTHORITARIAN INTERVENTIONS

Dingwall's research and Strong's polemic usefully cut away some of the pretensions of sociologists and of professionals who accept fashionable but problematic sociological notions like cultural relativism. In my own research on clinics, I too have argued that social and psychological 'experts' can be just as constraining for patients as experts on the body (i.e. doctors). So, in hare-lip/cleft-palate clinics, I have suggested that teenage patients should *not* be subject to interrogation, however well-meaning, by psychologists or social workers (Silverman 1983). How such adolescents feel about their looks can properly remain a private matter. The professional's only interest should be in hearing whether a cosmetic operation is wanted. Here, the state and its agencies should function to facilitate desired action *not* to construct patients' 'states of mind'.

However, although the *sentiments* of this kind of research are non-authoritarian, its practice still looks like that of the expert who preaches to the layman. The same could be said about Becker's four suggested 'contributions' of social science, all of which pose the expert in the active role and make the layman passive.

At the end of Chapter 1, I quoted a statement which goes to the heart of the matter. Because it identifies the problem so well, I make no apology for repeating it here. The problem with the 'authority' claimed by experts is that:

(1) it treats research as static information, a 'thing' to be transferred between people like a package;

(2) it separates researchers from the larger community by treating the community as a passive audience, whose role is to accept the findings of the research;

(3) the researcher assumes a privileged position *vis-à-vis* the larger community because of the presumed superiority of knowledge gathered by scientific methods. (Mehan 1979: 204)

This problem is easily stated and less easily solved. Mehan himself suggests correctly, I believe, that the solution lies in a continuing dialogue between researcher and participants. Such a dialogue can provide 'ways of looking critically at social circumstances' (ibid.: 205) and encourage people to work out the actions or changes that are likely to be most effective.

This kind of reasoning lay behind the provision of an additional pre-inpatient clinic as a result of research (Baruch 1981; Silverman 1981) at a paediatric cardiology unit. As I mentioned in Chapter 8, doctors were not told how to behave at this clinic, nor were parents instructed about what they might ask or do. The research team, in consultation with medical staff and parents, had simply provided an open space in relatively neutral territory. Consequently, without many of the usual constraints, both sides used this space to innovate in ways we could not have foreseen. Although one should not be too dewy-eyed about the social and political consequences of 'open spaces' (consider, for instance, Basil Bernstein's (1974) telling analysis of the prospects for teacher manipulation in the 'open classroom'), here, at least, was an attempt to allow participants to have a more active role in innovation.

The worry about authoritarian forms of social intervention is, of course, nothing new. Marx's depiction of the élitism of would-be 'educators' was, after all, written in 1846. However, Marx did not simply state the problem, he also offered one ingenious alternative, as recently noted by Bodemann (1978).

Marx's 'Workers' Enquiry' (*Enquête Ouvrière*),* unlike other contemporary surveys which were based on the responses of bureaucrats or other 'honourable citizens', was addressed to workers themselves. Marx argued that only the workers could 'describe with full knowledge the evils which they endure; only they and not providential saviours can energetically

*English translation in Bottomore and Rubel (eds) (1956: 203–12).

apply remedies to the social ills which they suffer' (Marx, quoted by Bodemann 1978: 407). Using a conventional research method, the questionnaire, as a 'didactic and political' instrument (ibid.: 408), Marx asked questions which were meant to generate further questions in the minds of the workers surveyed. For instance, workers were invited to think about the nature of the labour contract, as this question shows: 'In the event of the contract being broken, what penalty is imposed on a) the worker b) the employer if it is his fault?' (ibid.: 409). Even technical questions of economics (and, by implication, of surplus value) could, Marx believed, be re-invented by workers themselves, as a response to items like the following: 'Indicate changes in *the price of the commodities* which you produce or the services which you provide and indicate for comparison whether your wage *has changed at the same time*, or whether it has remained the same' (ibid.; original emphasis).

Used like this, much-criticised research instruments, like the questionnaire, *can* be used to generate a dialogue rather than to provide experts with packaged information. Once again, as structuralists teach us, elements (like questionnaires) have no meaning or value in themselves. Only when articulated with other elements do they acquire a positive or negative value.

Marx's inventive 'enquiry' is an appropriate point to end a book which has sought consistently to argue against polarised systems of thought and, by implication, for self-education through lateral thinking. The 'enquiry' shows how political partisanship need not degenerate into élitism (Marx's 'providential saviour'). It also underlines that research need not degenerate into either a bureaucratised product, carried out by rote, or a haphazard collection of anecdotes. There is no call for defeatism: research may be difficult and demanding but it *can* be done well and it *is* worth doing.

FURTHER READING

Weber's essay 'Science as a Vocation' (Weber 1958) is the classic statement of the relation between fact, value and policy in the social sciences. For a critique of Weber's positivist supporters, see Gouldner (1962). A recent neo-Marxist attempt to redefine research in terms of its 'human interest' is provided in the final part of Habermas (1972). Becker's famous article 'Whose Side Are We On?' is the most satisfactory treatment of policy issues from an interactionist position (Becker 1967). A discussion of the relation between social science and state policy is provided in Bulmer's short book, *The Uses of Social Research* (1982). Horowitz's

(1965) essay 'The Life and Death of Project Camelot' gives a fascinating case-study of one way in which this relation may develop, while Strong's (1979) paper 'Sociological Imperialism and the Profession of Medicine' is essential reading for those inclined to take at face-value some of the pretensions of social scientists. Finally, Foucault's writings, discussed at length in Chapter 4, are clearly relevant to any discussion of how the concept of the 'social' is put into practice.

References

Adelman, C. (ed.) (1981) *Uttering, Muttering: Collecting, Using and Reporting Talk for Social and Educational Research*, London: Grant McIntyre.

Althusser, L. (1971) 'Ideology and ideological state apparatuses', in *Lenin and Philosophy and Other Essays*, London: NLB.

Atkinson, J.M. (1978) *Discovering Suicide*, London: Macmillan.

Atkinson, J.M. (1982) 'Understanding formality: the categorization and production of "formal interaction" ', *British Journal of Sociology*, 33, 1, 86-117.

Atkinson, J.M. and Drew, P. (1979) *Order in Court*, London: Macmillan.

Atkinson, J.M. and Heritage, J.C. (eds) (1982) *Structures of Social Action: Studies in Conversation Analysis*, Cambridge: Cambridge University Press.

Atkinson, P. (1981) 'Inspecting classroom talk', in Adelman, C. (ed.) (1981), *op. cit.* 98-113.

Austin, J.L. (1971) *How To Do Things with Words*, Oxford: Oxford University Press.

Barthes, R. (1967) *Elements of Semiology*, London: Jonathan Cape.

Barthes, R. (1975) *S/Z*, London: Jonathan Cape.

Baruch, G. (1981) 'Moral tales: parents' stories of encounters with the health profession', *Sociology of Health and Illness*, 3, 3, 275-96.

Baruch, G. (1982) *Moral tales: Interviewing Parents of Congenitally-Ill Children*, unpublished PhD thesis, University of London.

Bauman, Z. (1982) *Memories of Class*, London: Routledge & Kegan Paul.

Becker, H.S. (1953) 'Becoming a marihuana user', *American Journal of Sociology*, 59, 235-42.

Becker, H.S. (1967) 'Whose side are we on?', *Social Problems*, 14, 239-48.

Becker, H.S. (ed.) (1967a) *Introduction to Social Problems: A Modern Approach*, New York: John Wiley, 1-31.

Becker, H.S. and Geer, B. (1960) 'Participant observation: The analysis of qualitative field data', in Adams, R. and Preiss, J. (eds), *Human Organization Research: Field Relations and Techniques*, Homewood, Ill.: Dorsey.

Becker, H.S., Geer, B., Hughes, E. and Strauss, A. (1961) *Boys in White*, Chicago, Chicago University Press.

Benveniste, E. (1971) *Problems in General Linguistics*, Miami: Miami University Press.

Berger, P. (1966) *Invitation to Sociology*, Harmondsworth: Penguin.

Berger, P. and Kellner, H. (1981) *Sociology Re-Interpreted*, Harmondsworth: Penguin.

Bernstein, B. (1974), 'Sociology and the sociology of education', in Rex, J. (ed), *Approaches to Sociology*, London: Routledge.

Bhaskar, R. (1975) *A Realist Theory of Science*, Leeds: Leeds Books.

Bhaskar, R. (1979) *The Possibility of Naturalism*, Brighton: Harvester.

Birdwhistell, E.L. (1970) *Kinesics and Context*, Pennsylvania University Press.

Bittner, E. (1965) 'The concept of organization, *Sociological Research*, 31, 240-55.

Blau, P. and Schoenherr, R. (1971) *The Structure of Organizations*, New York: Basic Books.

Blau, R. and Scott, R. (1963) *Formal Organizations*, London: Routledge.

Blauner, R. (1964) *Alienation and Freedom*, Chicago: Chicago University Press.

Bloor, M. (1976) 'Professional autonomy and client exclusion: a study in ENT clinics', in

Wadsworth, M. and Robinson, D. (eds), *Understanding Everyday Medical Life*, London: Martin Robertson.

Bloor, M. (1983) 'Notes on member validation', in Emerson, R.M. (ed.), *Contemporary Field Research: A Collection of Readings*, Boston: Little, Brown, 156–72.

Blum, A. (1974) *Theorizing*, London: Routledge.

Blumer, H. (1956) 'Sociological analysis and the "variable" ', *American Sociological Research*, 21, 633–60.

Bodemann, Y.M. (1978) 'A problem of sociological praxis: The case for interventive observation in field work', *Theory and Society*, 5, 387–420.

Bottomore, T.B. and Rubel, M. (eds) (1956) *Karl Marx: Selected writings in sociology and social philosophy*, New York: McGraw-Hill.

Brenner, M. (ed.) (1981) *Social Method and Social Life*, London: Academic Press.

Brown, J. and Sime, J. (1981) 'A methodology for accounts', in Brenner, M. (ed.), *op. cit.*

Bulmer, M. (1979) 'Concepts in the analysis of qualitative data', *Sociological Review*, 27, 4, 651–77.

Bulmer, M. (1982) *The Uses of Social Research*, London: Allen & Unwin.

Burton F. and Carlen, P. (1979) *Official Discourse*, London: Routledge & Kegan Paul.

Cicourel, A.' . (1964) *Method and Measurement in Sociology*, New York: Free Press.

Cicourel, A.V. (1968) *The Social Organization of Juvenile Justice*, New York: John Wiley.

Cicourel, A.V. (1973) *Cognitive Sociology*, Harmondsworth: Penguin.

Clegg, S. and Dunkerley, D. (1980) *Organization, Class and Control*, London: Routledge & Kegan Paul.

Cuff, E.C. (1980) 'Some issues in studying the problem of versions in everyday situations', Department of Sociology, Manchester University Occasional Papers No. 3.

Cuff. E.C. and Payne, G.C.F. (eds) (1979) *Perspectives in Sociology*, London: Allen & Unwin.

Culler, J. (1976) *Saussure*, London: Fontana.

Dalton, M. (1959) *Men Who Manage*. New York: John Wiley.

Denzin, N.K. (1970) *The Research Act in Sociology*, London: Butterworth.

Dingwall, R. (1980) 'Orchestrated encounters: an essay in the comparative analysis of speech-exchange systems', *Sociology of Health and Illness*, 2, 2, 151–73.

Dingwall, R. (1981) 'The ethnomethodological movement', in Payne, G., Dingwall, R., Payne, J. and Carter, M. (eds), *Sociology and Social Research*, London: Croom Helm, 124–38.

Dingwall, R. and Eekelaar, J. (1983) 'Private lives, public protection and a sense of freedom', *Guardian: Society Tomorrow*, December.

Dingwall, R. and Murray, T. (1983) 'Categorization in accident departments: "good" patients, "bad" patients and "children" ', *Sociology of Health and Illness*, 5, 2, 127–48.

Dingwall, R., Eekelaar, J. and Murray, T. (1983) *The Protection of Children*, Oxford: Basil Blackwell.

Donzelot, J. (1979) *The Policing of Families*, London: Hutchinson.

Douglas, J.D. (1967) *The Social Meanings of Suicide*, Princeton, N.J.: Princeton University Press.

Douglas, M. (1975) 'Self-evidence', in *Implicit Meanings*, London: Routledge.

Dreyfus, H. and Rabinow (1982) *Michel Foucault: Beyond Structuralism and Hermeneutics*, London: Harvester.

Durkheim, E. (1974) *Sociology and Philosophy*, New York: Free Press.

Foucault, M. (1970) *The Order of Things*, London: Tavistock.

Foucault, M. (1977) *Discipline and Punish*, Harmondsworth: Penguin.

Foucault, M. (1979) *The History of Sexuality: Volume I*, Harmondsworth: Penguin.

Foucault, M. (1980) *Power/Knowledge*, ed. Gordon, C., New York: Pantheon.

Friedson, E. (1971) *Profession of Medicine*, New York: Dodd Mead.

Garfinkel, H. (1967) *Studies in Ethnomethodology*, Englewood Cliffs, N.J.: Prentice-Hall.

Giglioli, P.-P. (ed.) (1972) *Language and Social Context*, Harmondsworth: Penguin.

Glaser, B. and Strauss, A. (1967) *The Discovery of Grounded Theory*, Chicago: Aldine.

Goffman, E. (1968) *Asylums*, Harmondsworth: Penguin.

Goffman, E. (1981) 'Replies and responses', in *Forms of Talk*, Oxford: Basil Blackwell.
Gouldner, A. (1954) *Patterns of Industrial Bureaucracy*, Glencoe, Ill.: Free Press.
Gouldner, A. (1962) 'Anti-minotaur: The myth of a value-free sociology', *Social Problems*, 9, 199–213.
Greimas, A.J. (1966) *Semantique Structurale*, Paris: Larousse.
Gumperz, J. and Hymes, D. (eds) (1972) *Directions in Socio-Linguistics*, New York: Holt, Rinehart & Winston.
Habermas, J. (1972) *Knowledge and Human Interests*, London: Heinemann Educational Books, 301–17.
Halfpenny, P. (1979) 'The analysis of qualitative data', *Sociological Review*, 27, 4, 799–825.
Hammersley, M. and Atkinson, P. (1983) *Ethnography: Principles in Practice*, London: Tavistock.
Hawkes, T. (1977) *Structuralism and Semiotics*, London: Methuen.
Heath, C. (1981) 'The opening sequence in doctor–patient interaction', in Atkinson, P. and Heath, C. (eds), *Medical Work: Realities and Routines*, Farnborough: Gower.
Heath, C. (1983) 'Computer-aided diagnosis in the consultation', *Sociology of Health and Illness*, 5, 3, 332–44.
Heath, C. (forthcoming) 'International participation: the coordination of gesture, speech and gaze, in Leonardie, P. and D'Orzy, V. (eds), *The Proceedings of the International Symposium on Analysing Discourse and National Rhetoric.*
Hindess, B. (1973) *The Use of Official Statistics in Sociology*, London: Macmillan.
Horowitz, I.L. (1965) 'The life and death of Project Camelot', *Transaction*, 3, 3–7; 44–7.
Hughes, D. (1982) 'Control in the medical consultation: Organizing talk in a situation where co-participants have differential competence', *Sociology*, 16, 3, 359–76.
Hughes, E. (1956) *Men and Their Work*, Glencoe, Ill.: Free Press.
Hyman, H. *et al.* (1954) *Interviewing in Social Research*, Chicago, Chicago University Press.
Hymes, D. (1972) 'Models of the interaction of language and social life', in Gumperz, J. and Hughes, D. (eds), *op. cit.*, 35–71.
Irvine, J. *et al.* (eds) (1979) *Demystifying Social Statistics*, London: Pluto.
Jacques, M. and Mulhern, F. (eds) (1981) *The Forward March of Labour Halted*, London: Verso.
Janowitz, M. (1972) *Sociological Models and Social Policy*, Morristown, N.J.: General Learning Systems.
Jeffery, R. (1979) 'Normal rubbish: deviant patients in casualty departments', *Sociology of Health and Illness*, 1, 1, 90–107.
Johnson, F.G. and Kaplan, C.D. (1980) 'Talk-in-the-work: Aspects of social organization of work in a computer center', *Journal of Pragmatics*, 4, 351–65.
Keat, R. and Urry, J. (1975) *Social Theory as Science*, London: Routledge.
Kuhn, T.S. (1970) *The Structure of Scientific Revolutions*, 2nd edn, Chicago: Chicago University Press.
Laclau, E. (1977) *Politics and Ideology in Marxist Theory: Capitalism, Fascism, Populism*, London: NLB.
Laclau, E. (1981) 'Politics as the construction of the unthinkable', unpublished paper, translated by Silverman, D., mimeo: Department of Sociology, Goldsmiths' College.
Landsberger, H. (1958) *Hawthorne Revisited*, New York: Cornell University Press.
Lindesmith, A.R. (1947) *Opiate Addiction*, Bloomington, Ind.: Principia Press.
Lindesmith, A.R. (1952) 'Comment on W.S. Robinson's "The Logical Structure of Analytic Induction" ', *American Sociological Review*, 17, 492–93.
Lipset, S.M., Trow, M. and Coleman, J. (1962) *Union Democracy*, Garden City, N.Y.: Anchor Books, Doubleday.
Macfarlane, A. (1978) *The Origins of English Individualism*, Oxford: Basil Blackwell.
MacPherson, C.B. (1962) *The Political Theory of Possessive Individualism*, Oxford: Oxford University Press.
Marx, K. (1973) *Grundrisse: Foundations of the Critique of Political Economy*, translated with a foreword by Nicolaus, M., Harmondsworth: Penguin.

Mehan, H. (1979) *Learning Lessons: Social Organization in the Classroom*, Cambridge, Mass.: Harvard University Press.

Mehan, H. and Wood, H. (1975) *The Reality of Ethnomethodology*, New York: Wiley Interscience.

Merton, R.K. (1957) 'On theories of the middle range', in *Social Theory and Social Structure*, Glencoe, Ill.: Free Press.

Michels, R. (1962) *Political Parties*, New York, Collier Books.

Mills, C.W. (1953) *The Sociological Imagination*, London: Harvester.

Mitchell, C. (1983) 'The logic of the analysis of social situations and cases', *Sociological Review*.

Moerman, M. (1974) 'Accomplishing ethnicity', in Turner, R. (ed.), *Ethnomethodology*, Harmondsworth: Penguin.

Moerman, M. and Sacks, H. (1971) 'On understanding in conversation', paper presented at 70th Annual Meeting, American Anthropological Association, New York City.

Moloney, M. (1983) 'Reading political texts: A study of the relations between discourses', unpublished paper, Department of Sociology, Goldsmiths' College.

Moser, C. (1958) *Survey Methods in Social Investigation*, London: Heinemann Educational Books.

Mount, F. (1982) *The Subversive Family*, London: Jonathan Cape.

Murphy, A. (forthcoming) 'The cleft-palate teenager: child, familial, and medical versions of appearance', PhD in progress, Department of Sociology, Goldsmiths' College.

Norris, C. (1982) *Deconstruction: Theory and Practice*, London: Methuen.

O'Neill, J. (1975) *Making Sense Together*, London: Heinemann Educational Books.

Parsons, T. (1949) *The Structure of Social Action*, Glencoe, Ill.: Free Press.

Popper, K. (1972) *The Logic of Scientific Discovery*, London: Hutchinson.

Poulantzas, N. (1974) *Fascism and Dictatorship*, London: NLB.

Propp, V.I. (1968) *Morphology of the Folktale*, 2nd revised edn, ed. Wagner, L.A., Austin and London: Texas University Press.

Rayner, G. and Stimson, G. (1979) 'Medicine, superstructure and micropolitcs — a response', *Sociology of Science and Medicine*, 13A, 611–12.

Robinson, W.S. (1951) 'The logical structure of analytic induction', *American Sociological Review*, 16, 812–18.

Roethlisberger, F.J. and Dickson, W.J. (1939) *Management and The Worker*, Cambridge, Mass.: Harvard University Press.

Roth, J. (1963) *Timetables*, New York: Bobbs-Merrill.

Sacks, H. (1967) *Search for Help: No one to Turn to*, unpublished dissertation: University of California.

Sacks, H. (1974) 'On the analysability of stories by children', in Turner, R. (ed.), *Ethnomethodology*, Harmondsworth: Pengiun.

Sacks, H., Schegloff, E.A. and Jefferson, G. (1974) 'A simplest systematics for the organization of turn-taking for conversation', *Language*, 50, 696–735.

Saussure, F. (1974) *Course in General Linguistics*, London: Fontana.

Schegloff, E.A. (1972) 'Sequencing in conversational openings', in Gumperz, J. and Hymes, D. (eds), *op. cit.*, 346–80.

Schegloff, E.A. and Sacks, H. (1974) 'Opening up closings', in Turner, R. (ed.), *op. cit.*

Schutz, A. (1964) *Collected Papers*, ed. Natanson, M., The Hague: Nijhoff.

Schwartz, H. and Jacobs, J. (1979) *Quantitative Sociology: A Method to the Madness*, New York: Free Press.

Selltiz, C., Jahoda, M., Deutsch, M. and Cook, S.W. (1964) *Research Methods in Social Relations*, revised in one volume, New York: Holt, Rinehart & Winston.

Silverman, D. (1970) *The Theory of Organizations: A Sociological Framework*, London: Heinemann Educational Books.

Silverman, D. (1973) 'Interview talk: Bringing off a research instrument', *Sociology*, 7, 1, 32–48.

Silverman, D. (1975) 'Accounts of organizations: Organizational "structures" and the accounting process', in McKinlay, J.B. (ed.), *Processing People*, New York: Holt, Rinehart & Winston.

Silverman, D. (1981) 'The child as a social object: Down's syndrome children in a paediatric cardiology clinic', *Sociology of Health and Illness*, 3, 3, 254-74.

Silverman, D. (1982) 'Labour's marches: The discursive politics of a current debate', mimeo: Department of Sociology, Goldsmiths' College.

Silverman, D. (1983) 'The clinical subject: Adolescents in a cleft-palate clinic', *Sociology of Health and Illness*, 5, 3, 253-74.

Silverman, D. (1984) 'Going private: Ceremonial forms in a private oncology clinic', *Sociology* vol. 18, No. 2, 191-202.

Silverman, D. and Jones, J. (1975) *Organizational Work*, London: Collier-Macmillan.

Silverman, D. and Torode, B. (1980) *The Material Word: Some Theories of Language and its Limits*, London: Routledge.

Stimson, G.V. and Webb, B. (1975) *Going to See the Doctor*, London: Routledge.

Strauss, A.L. (1978) 'A social world perspective', in Denzin, N.K. (ed.), *Studios in Symbolic Interaction*, Vol. 1, Greenwich, Conn.: JAI Press.

Strauss, A.L., Schatzman, L., Bucher, R., Ehrlich, D. and Sobshin, M. (1964) *Psychiatric Ideologies and Institutions*, New York: Free Press.

Strong, P.M. (1979) 'Sociological imperialism and the profession of medicine', *Sociology of Science and Medicine*, Vol. 13A, 199-215.

Strong, P.M. (1983) 'Review essay: The importance of being Erving: Erving Goffman, 1922-1982', *Sociology of Health and Illness*, 5, 3, 345-55.

Strong, P.M. and Dingwall, R. (1983) 'The interactional study of organizations: a critique and reformulation', mimeo: Wolfson College, Oxford.

Stubbs, M. (1981) 'Scratching the surface', in Adelman, C. (ed.), *op. cit.*

Sudnow, D. (1968) 'Normal crimes', in Rubington, E. and Weinberg, M. (eds), *Deviance: The Interactionist Perspective*, New York: Macmillan.

Turner, R. (ed.) (1974) *Ethnomethodology*, Harmondsworth: Penguin.

Voysey, M. (1975) *A Constant Burden*, London: Routledge.

Waitzkin, H. (1979) 'Medicine, superstructure and micropolitics', *Sociology of Science and Medicine*, 13A, 601-9.

Weber, M. (1946) 'Science as a vocation', in Gerth, H. and Mills, C.W. (eds), *From Max Weber*, New York: Oxford University Press.

Weber, M. (1949) *Methodology of the Social Sciences*, New York: Free Press.

West, P. (1979) 'An investigation into the social construction and consequences of the label epilepsy', *Sociological Review*, 27, 4, 719-41.

Wittgenstein, L. (1968) *Philosophical Investigations*, Oxford: Basil Blackwell.

Wittgenstein, L. (1980) *Culture and Value*, translated by Peter Winch, Oxford: Basil Blackwell.

Wrong, D. (1967) 'The oversocialised conception of man', in Demerath, N.J. and Peterson, R.A. (eds), *System, Change and Conflict*, New York: Free Press.

Zimmerman, D. (1974) 'On the practicalities of rule-use', in Turner, R. (ed.), *op. cit.*

Zimmerman, D. and Pollner, M. (1971) 'On the everyday world as a phenomenon', in Douglas, J. (ed.), *Understanding Everyday Life*, London: Routledge.

Zimmerman, D. and West, C. (1975) 'Sex roles, interruptions and silences in conversations', in Thorne, B. and Henley, N. (eds), *Language and Sex Differences and Dominance*, Rowley, Mass.: Newbury House.

Znaniecki, F. (1934) *The Method of Sociology*, New York: Farrar and Rhinehart.

Name Index

Acourt, P., xii
Adelman, C., 69
Althusser, L., 36-7, 39, 56, 59, 84, 185-6
Arendt, H., 52-3
Atkinson, J.M., 16, 32-5, 46, 75, 121, 124, 127-9, 157, 167-9, 175-6
Atkinson, P., 50-1, 69, 97, 112, 115-7, 139, 156, 161-2, 170-1, 176
Austin, J., 133

Barthes, R., 58, 60, 69, 150-1
Baruch, G., xii, 16, 18, 21, 121, 136, 140, 154-5, 157-8, 172, 175, 177, 194
Basso, K., 97-9, 108, 133
Bauman, Z., 92
Becker, H., 18, 24, 101-3, 112, 155, 178, 187, 190-3, 195
Berger, P., 164, 188
Benveniste, E., 37, 59, 154
Bernstein, B., 150
Bhaskar, R., 29-30, 33-6, 39, 42-3, 48, 70, 77-8, 157
Birdwhistell, E., 9
Bittner, E., 80, 127
Blau, R., 79-80
Blauner, R., 76-7
Bloor, M., 23, 43-5, 116, 141-3
Blum, A., 151
Blumer, H., 138, 140, 155
Bodemann, Y., 194-5
Bottomore, T., 194
Bourdieu, P., 150
Brenner, M., ix, 156, 160-1, 170, 176
Brown, J. 171
Bulmer, M., 112, 180, 182-4, 195
Burton, F., 150-3, 155

Carlen, P., 150-3, 155
Cicourel, A., x, 81, 109, 117, 155, 165-6, 169, 176
Clegg, S., xii, 75, 183
Cuff, E., 48, 96, 106, 123, 176
Culler, J., 58, 60, 69

Dalton, M., 19, 104
Denzin, N., x, 21, 101-7, 109, 112-3, 116, 156, 161-3, 176, 179-81
Derrida, J., 140
Dickson, W., 72, 74
Dingwall, R., xii, 16, 24, 75, 81, 97, 105, 107-9, 112, 114-5, 117, 120, 125-7, 129-30, 137, 156, 179, 191-3
Donzelot, J., 92, 191
Douglas, J., 32-4, 104
Douglas, M., xi, 13-17, 70, 78-9, 151, 112-3
Drew, P., 121, 128
Dreyfus, H., 48
Durkheim, E., xii, 6, 10, 30-4, 40, 42, 61, 71, 75-7, 83, 107, 118, 148, 168, 173

Eekelaar, J., 117, 191, 193

Fisher, S., xiii
Foucault, M., xi-xii, 30, 39, 47-9, 70-1, 82, 92, 136, 140, 165, 181, 190, 196
Frake, C., 99-101, 108
Freidson, E., 141
Freud, S., 76, 86

Garfinkel, H., 20-1, 51, 80-1, 95, 106, 118, 120, 149, 166-7, 171
Geer, B., 24, 155
Giglioli, P., 97-9
Glaser, B., x, 3, 8, 24, 104, 113
Glassner, B., xiii, 158
Goffman, E., 102, 121, 127, 130-4, 137
Goodenough, C., 97, 108
Gouldner, A., 10-11, 179, 195
Gramsci, A., 64, 80, 140
Greimas, A., 59-60
Gumperz, J., 98-101, 117

Habermas, J., 36, 138, 140, 164-5, 174, 180-1, 185, 195
Halfpenny, P., 95, 97, 105, 139, 155
Hammersley, M., 97, 112, 115-7, 139,

Subject Index